Making Gray Gold

Women in Culture and Society
A Series Edited by Catharine R. Stimpson

Making Gray Gold

Narratives of
Nursing Home Care

Timothy Diamond

The
University of Chicago
Press
Chicago and London

THE UNIVERSITY OF CHICAGO PRESS, CHICAGO 60637
THE UNIVERSITY OF CHICAGO PRESS, LTD., LONDON
© 1992 by The University of Chicago
All rights reserved. Published 1992
Paperback edition 1995
Printed in the United States of America
01 00 99 98 97 96 95   5 4 3 2

ISBN (cloth): 0-226-14473-9
ISBN (paper): 0-226-14474-7

Library of Congress Cataloging-in-Publication Data

Diamond, Timothy.
    Making gray gold : narratives of nursing home care / Timothy
Diamond.
        p.   cm.—(Women in culture and society)
    Includes bibliographical references (p.   ) and index.
    ISBN 0-226-14473-9
    1. Nursing homes—United States.   2. Nurses' aides.   I. Title.
II. Series.
RA997.D49   1992
362.1'6'0973—dc20   91-45755
                                                                CIP

⊗The paper used in this publication meets the minimum requirements
of the American National Standard for Information Sciences—
Permanence of Paper for Printed Library Materials, ANSI Z39.48-1984.

For nursing assistants and
the women and men they
care for

Contents

Foreword

Making Gray Gold: Narratives of Nursing Home Care is a cry for change in the huge machine that is the American health care system, particularly in its nursing homes. I wish that every bureaucrat who regulates the industry, doctor who has patients in a home, politician who talks about health care, investor who holds stock in a health care corporation, and health-care researcher would read Timothy Diamond's ethnographic study of the nursing assistants in these homes. He speaks clearly, strongly, bravely, compassionately. My surmise is that the assistants, their patients, and their patients' families would welcome this book.

In Winter, 1981, Diamond was a sociologist studying health care organizations. By accident, he befriended two African-American women who were employed as nursing assistants across the street from a coffee shop all three patronized. To his regret, he had to stop talking to the women, except for rare moments, because they were forbidden to leave their place of employment during lunch periods or breaks.

The curiosity about their work that these women had engendered remained. Diamond enrolled in a vocational school, became certified as a nursing assistant, and went to work, with some ethical qualms, in several homes. As a participant-observer, he did not discover a melodramatic snake-pit of violence and corruption. Residents have birthday parties. Nice people do volunteer work. Doctors ask kindly questions when they check patients and their charts on a monthly visit. Rather than hell, Diamond finds a bureaucratic purgatory run for profit. The graying of America, the demographic fact that its population is aging, has brought gold to some.

Three sectors now collaborate to maintain this purgatory. The first is corporate America, which has built up the health industry. Here, caretaking is a business. The staff of nursing homes is a labor cost, judged by criteria of productivity and efficiency. The second sector is medical America, which, in Diamond's homes, reduces a person to a body, the body of an aging man or woman into a sick body, and the complexities of experience to a chart. The third sector is the government. Through its administration of Social Security, Medicare, and Medicaid, federal and state governments transfer monies to the health care industry. Moreover, public agencies certify nursing homes and approve the schools that train their workers.

Diamond is often scathing about the routines each sector imposes on caretaking, routines so hierarchical, insensitive, and remote from actual human needs that they often make good care impossible. A nurse can dole out an array of prescribed medicines but not an aspirin for a headache. A woman dying of cancer cannot get moisturizing lotion for her itching skin. Nursing assistants must give showers to the patients on a fixed schedule whether the water is hot, warm, or cold. Diamond is also acutely sensitive to language, the impersonal and often demeaning professional jargon of each sector. One teacher in his vocational school, who veers towards self-parody, instructs his students to say "tactile communication" instead of touching. "Lesbian behaviors" is sternly noted on the chart of a 69-year old woman who tries to go to another floor of her nursing home, in order to cuddle with her 89-year-old mother, also in residence. Blending together, in an ugly polysyllabic harmony, these languages screen and deny the visceral, existential realities of everyday.

Diamond is realistic about the difficulties of patient care—the smells of urine and cleaning fluids, the nausea of cleaning up excrement-filled diapers and beds, the multicultural misunderstandings, the separate worlds of the senile. Nevertheless, he is sympathetic to the residents of nursing homes. Largely though not exclusively white women, they find themselves in a downwardly mobile system that transmogrifies them into passive, dependent, isolated paupers. Women who were successful teachers now find themselves treated like little children. Women who were active homemakers and cooks are now recipients of unappetizing if nutritionally correct meals. Carefully, Diamond exposes the intricate webs of relationships residents create with each other and their small, often subtle acts of self-assertion and resistance. A woman tries, surreptitiously, to tip a nursing assistant 15¢ for getting a 50¢ cup of coffee.

Sympathetic though he is to the residents, Diamond's heroines are the nursing assistants themselves. Their labor is both back-breaking physically and emotionally heart-breaking. To it, they often bring "mother's wit," a combination of caretaking skills they have learned with their own families, common sense, and attention to the needs of another dependent human being. Much of the work they do is invisible, unrecorded on official charts. Assured that they are professionals on the front lines of health care, they are nevertheless desperately underpaid. Diamond's first paycheck, after deductions, was $104.50 per week. In order to survive, many must hold two full-time jobs. Not surprisingly, this labor force, the foundation on which a nursing home rests, comes from groups vulnerable because of race, class, and gender. They are, in brief, largely poor women of color, either from the United States or the Third

World. What, an administrator asked Diamond, was a white man doing working for wages like this?

In a grand sociological tradition, Diamond has recommendations for reform. Some of them are pragmatic. He suggests, for example, that unions may be necessary if nursing assistants are to have enough strength to challenge the conditions of their toil. He believes nursing homes ought to listen to their residents and let them share in the shaping of their nights and days. Other recommendations are more radical. For they ask us to transform the moral, social, and economic arrangements that permit some of us to profit from caretaking while the actual caretakers, the menders and tenders of the weak, walk the poverty line.

Recently, one of my elderly aunts died in a nursing home. She had not yet spent down all her savings and could still afford an attractive home with a staff that did not seem frazzled and driven. Her room was pleasant. She had devoted family members who were comfortable with the medical system and could negotiate within it. Although I lived too far away to visit often, I saw her pass from using a walker, to being pushed in a wheelchair, to being bed-ridden. I believe she died without much pain. Reading *Making Gray Gold*, I realized again how comparatively fortunate she was, and her family was. Inseparable from this perception of family luck were anger (because Diamond's profoundly careless purgatories exist), and fear (because I, my family, or my friends might end up in one of them). What if I, at my aunt's age, were to be in a different and more difficult place? What if I were to be strapped in a chair and made to watch TV? Will Timothy Diamond's book, my anger and fear, and the anger and fear of others be strong enough medicine to prevent such decay?

Catharine R. Stimpson

Acknowledgments

This project has taken nearly ten years. So many people have helped me over that time that the book seems more like a collective than an individual effort. All through it, and long before, my family was there with support and with lessons about caretaking. First thanks, therefore, go to my mother, Anne, sisters Mary and Anne, and brother Bob. I have been blessed, too, with having great teachers who introduced me to sociology, feminist studies, and critical thinking—in particular Norm Choate, Derek Gill, Laurel Richardson, and T. R. Young.

After being invited to undertake the research at Northwestern University's Program on Women by its director, Bari Watkins, I met a host of fine scholars who helped keep the work going. Among them were Marj DeVault, Mary Kate Driscoll, Elizabeth Elliott, Susan Hirsch, Lisa Jones, Robin Leidner, Judith Levy, David Maines, Kathy Phillips, Beth Renninger, and especially the program's founder, Arlene Kaplan Daniels, who supported the work at every stage.

In 1983, when Dorothy E. Smith was in residence at Northwestern, I was privileged to have the advice and friendship of this monumental thinker without whom this book could not have been conceived or executed. In a sense the work could be dedicated to her since it is an attempt to apply the sociological method she has outlined.

During the fieldwork I received a fellowship from the Midwest Council for Social Research in Aging. This organization helped me not only to survive but to thrive on the encouragement of its faculty, fellows, and associates, particularly director Warren Peterson, as well as Barbara Brents, Robert Habenstein, Rob John, Helena Lopata, Hal Orbach, and most notably Stan Ingman, who introduced me to the Council and stood by the research in subsequent years.

After that fellowship I received a grant from the Retirement Research Foundation, thanks to the recommendations of Brian Hofland and Bernice Neugarten. Later on, I was invited as a junior scholar to the Rutgers University/Douglass College Laurie Chair in Women's Studies. There I was able to formulate a prospectus for the book under the tutelage of another generous mentor and friend, Alison Jaggar, along with the members of the seminar she coordinated. There, too, I met Catharine R. Stimpson, who offered the book a place in her Women in Culture and Society series, then waited patiently during the several years it took to complete it.

During those years I called on friends for all kinds of support: intellectual, emotional and financial. My deep thanks to Jim Ashby, Sheila Collins, Maureen Connolly, Judith Cook, Fred Elkin, Helen Helwig, Linda Myrick, Lucille Salerno, Angelika Siewert and her family, Lisa Vaughan and especially, Diane Vaughan.

As drafts of the book came together, many people contributed suggestions. Valued readings were made by many already mentioned, and by Gail Arriola, Catherine Boutte, Marie Campbell, Cowan Collins, Rosanna Esparza, Martha Hipskind, Debra Schultz, Susan Steiner, Suzanne Vaughan, and Kath Weston.

Toward the end, while I was teaching at California State University, Los Angeles, I was encouraged by the sociology faculty, and by chairperson Del Kelly and Dean Donald

Dewey, who granted me an academic leave to finish the writing. In Los Angeles I had the opportunity to consult with fellow ethnographers Bill Darrough, Bob Emerson, Linda Shaw, Carol Warren, and especially Emily Abel, who provided the University of Chicago Press with an official and most helpful review of the manuscript.

At the University of Chicago Press senior editor Karen Wilson was warmly supportive, even during the long lulls when it seemed I would never finish. When at last I did, Wilma Ebbitt offered splendid copyediting that clarified the writing and referencing.

Through it all there were those dearest friends without whose critique, confidence and care I never could have finished. Mary Beth Hawkinson, Paul Luken, Adele Mueller, and Judy Wittner were with me every step of the way. Lynn Olson was there steadily with kindness, insight, and love. Judi DiIorio showed through her research that I really could do a participant observation study, and her very special friendship sustained me daily through the whole decade.

These brief expressions of gratitude are linked closely to the final pages of the book. I have enjoyed the rare privilege of having friends whose own research has provided the background for this work. Three-fourths of the people I acknowledge here reappear as references at the end, so I have the pleasure of thanking them again and documenting what I mean by this project being a collective effort.

Finally, I am indebted to the many residents and staffs of the nursing homes where I worked for sharing parts of their lives with me, especially the two nursing assistants who prompted me to undertake the project and who now, in the opening paragraphs, begin the book.

Introduction

It was 9:30 on a Sunday morning in the winter of 1981 when I first heard nursing assistants talk about their jobs. Ina Williams and Aileen Crawford worked in a nursing home across the street from a coffee shop where I spent leisurely weekend mornings.[1] We had seen each other several times in Donna's Café and now were about to have the first of many conversations. While I was enjoying my coffee and newspaper, I joked to Donna that because of some part-time tutoring of students, I was forced to be up and on the move at this early hour.

"It's tough to have to set the alarm on Sundays," I griped.

"Tough?" Donna whipped back, hands on her hips. "Why don't you try getting up at 6:30 to open this place?"

"Tough?" interrupted Aileen from a corner booth, as she and Ina shared a laugh. "Why don't you both try 4:30 like we do six days a week?"

At the time, I looked at them with some skepticism, sure that they were exaggerating. As the months passed, however, and as Ina, Aileen, and I talked at length about our work, it became clear that they were not joking about their early rising. They were two African-American women who had to travel a long way on public transportation before reporting to work at 7:00 A.M. Though they were not kidding about rising at 4:30, they did joke about many things related to the nursing home and their work. As they did, I became curious and asked them to tell me more.

"Nursing assistant," said Ina, "is a new name for nurses' aides, even though we still say 'aides' a lot. In nursing homes we do most of the work—I mean we're the ones with the people." At this point she stroked one hand over the other, suggesting the hands-on nature of her job.

They were curious about my work as well, and they found it odd that I knew so little about theirs.

"You're supposed to know what we do," they teased. "You're the professor."

They were teasing a sociologist, one who had studied health care organizations for almost ten years. When we were getting to know each other I was teaching a course in medical sociology at a nearby university. Statistics indicate that nursing assistants are the largest single category of health care workers and one of the fastest growing occupations in general.[2] What the work actually involves, however, is mentioned in only a handful of books and articles.[3] I had carried an image of these workers, almost all of whom are women, doggedly performing simple, menial tasks.

But when Ina and Aileen came to the coffee shop on those morning breaks, they expressed strong feelings about their work. One day Aileen sat quietly gazing out the window with a sad expression. Eventually she shared her sorrow with us. "One of my ladies died during the night," she said. "I was with her for almost two years. I'm gonna miss that old goat." Another day Ina made a biting quip about the low wage scale: "For what we get, it ain't hardly worth our time to come out here."

Often they got Donna and me laughing over some of the antics in the home, like the couple who ran away and got married at eighty-two, or the ninety-six-year old woman who wore black and gray wigs on different days to confuse the new staff. Almost every time we talked they contra-dicted my image of their work as dull, unskilled labor.

These conversations turned out to be only an introduc-tion to the study reported in this book. We went on talking and laughing during their breaks for several months, and I even asked them if I could start taking notes on their sto-ries. The notion of looking more closely at the nature of their work was dawning on me as a research opportunity. At first I thought of doing some interviews with them and some of their co-workers. Ina and Aileen thought this a bit strange, but they also liked the idea. Then one day they abruptly stopped coming to the coffee shop. It was weeks before Donna and I learned that staff at the nursing home would no longer be allowed to leave the building during breaks or lunch. Since Ina and Aileen lived too far away for them to drop in at the shop before or after work, we seldom met. Still, partly as a result of this forced breach in our developing friendship, my curiosity about their work and nursing home life increased.

From previous studies of health care organizations, I had come to the same conclusion as Robert Butler, then director of the National Institute on Aging, who said in an interview, "We know precious little about what goes on inside nursing homes".[4] That seemed to be true of the pro-fessional literature, yet almost everyone I knew had some personal story to tell about nursing homes, and I began to wonder what they looked like from the inside. Ina and Aileen were no longer available to tell me.

Over the next several months, while I was deciding to undertake research and figuring out what method to pur-sue, I formulated the basic theoretical questions that fed this developing interest. There were nursing homes scat-tered throughout the United States, growing rapidly as health care institutions[5]. Most had pleasant-sounding names referring to a valley or a view, a rest or a happy mood, like Sunset Manor or Pine View Hills or Merry Rest. What was Ina and Aileen's work like that it could give rise to such strong positive and negative reactions? What kind of rules operated there so that our conversations could now be canceled so abruptly? What was life like inside, day in and day out? Who lived in nursing homes, and what did they do there?

These questions crystallized under one overarching research issue, which provides the title of the book. One of my students brought to my attention an article about nursing homes that had appeared in a financial journal. Strongly recommending investment in this growing industry, the author concluded that "the graying of America . . . is a guaranteed opportunity for someone. How the nursing home industry can exploit it is the real question." The title of the article was "Gray Gold." [6]

The author of the article assumed that nursing homes constitute an industry and went on to discuss how they could prosper as such. But nursing homes, like hospitals and other health care organizations, have not always been considered businesses, nor are they now in many societies outside the United States. A sociological approach which does not assume that care for older, frail people is naturally a business might ask how nursing homes have become an industry and how it is that their current expansion comes to be defined in those terms. The terms of exchange that make up an industry—productivity, efficiency, labor, management, ownership, stocks, profits, products—have not always characterized caretaking; they are relatively recent, historically. Moreover, caretaking does not seem to be much like building a car or selling merchandise, ~~nor does it easily conform to the logic of~~ ~~commodity production.~~

So I began to wonder how nursing homes operate as industrial enterprises. How does the work of caretaking become defined and get reproduced day in and day out as a business? What is the process by which goods and services are bought and sold in this context? How, in other words, does the everyday world of Ina and Aileen and their co-workers, and that of the people they tend, get turned into a system in which gray can be written about in financial journals as producing gold, a classic metaphor for money? What is the process of making gray gold?

If this substantive issue explains the title, the subtitle refers to the method I pursued in answering these questions. I wanted to collect stories and to experience situations like those Ina and Aileen had begun to describe. I decided that if they could not come outside to talk about their work, I would go inside to experience the work myself. I became a nursing assistant.

First I went to school for six months in 1982, two evenings a week and all day Saturdays, to obtain the certificate the state required. Then, after weeks of searching for jobs, I worked in three different nursing homes in Chicago for periods of three to four months each. These homes were situated in widely different neighborhoods of the city. In one of them residents paid for their own care, often with initial help from Medicare. In the other two, most of the residents were supported by Medicaid. Between jobs and for several years thereafter, I assembled and analyzed field notes, read the relevant literature, and wrote this book. In the course of writing, I visited many homes across the United States to validate my observations and to update them in instances where regulatory changes had been instituted.

In part, this book is a collective story told by the residents and the nursing assistants I came to know. It is also an analysis of administrative language as contained in formal documents. I weave the two threads together and intersperse my own interpretation of how they are connected. These, then, are my narratives from inside nursing homes.

The motivation to undertake this kind of work flowed from three sources. I had studied the tradition of participant observation in sociology and wanted to contribute to it.[7] Robert Butler's observation that "we know precious little about what goes on inside nursing homes" served as an invitation to a sociologist interested in health care. More important, I was also studying feminist literature and methods. It seemed that, as a white man who wanted to work in this field, it might be valuable for me to experience some of the work that is done largely by women. These influences coalesced in the writings of sociologist Dorothy Smith. Smith suggests a method of practical research that begins in the ordinary everyday world of work that women do. From that standpoint, she argues, much can be learned about how organizations and societies operate. Unfortunately, that standpoint is rendered invisible by the way most administrative and professional documents and texts are constructed. This study follows Smith in exploring the disjunctions between everyday life and administrative accounts of it.[8]

In working through this method I adopted some unconventional approaches, both in collecting data and writing up my findings. While I was getting to know nursing assistants and residents and experiencing aspects of their daily routines, I would surreptitiously take notes on scraps of paper, in the bathroom or otherwise out of sight, jotting down what someone had said or done. Off duty I assembled the notes and began to search for patterns in them. The basic data are these observations and conversations, the actual words of people reproduced to the best of my ability from the field notes. In trying to preserve the context in which things were said and done, I employ a novel-like format so that the reading might move along as in a story. Increasingly, as the chapters proceed, I intersperse sociological commentary with the conversation. The literature and theory that inform these reflections are cited as endnotes rather than as part of the discussion, so as not to interrupt the flow of the narrative. In pursuit of the same objective, I often choose not to pause to indicate which nursing home each speaker was in, but rather to organize comments made in different settings around the key themes they illuminate.[9]

Throughout the investigating and the writing, I maintained formal ties with Northwestern University. I was associated there with the Program on Women in an unpaid capacity as research associate. This affiliation made me eligible for fellowships from organizations that supported research in the fields of aging and women's studies, primarily the Midwest Council for Social Research in Aging. I had to subsist exclusively on nursing assistants' wages for only part of this period. For the rest, grants provided stipends. The fellowships also enabled me to visit workers and residents in many nursing homes in the United States after the fieldwork was completed and to meet briefly some in Canada, England, France, and Switzerland.

The most important connection that these university links provided was the ongoing reassurance from colleagues that what I was doing was ethically and legally valid. For, as I discovered in the course of the project, some people thought otherwise. Some friends and associates to whom I proposed my plan dismissed it outright, declaring it was not feasible: "They'll never let you in, that's all there is to it." Similarly, during and after the fieldwork the first question many people asked was "Did you tell them?" "They" and "them" referred to the administrators and owners, and implicit in these comments was the belief that these were the people who determined who was to enter homes and in what capacity.

I had initially hoped to disclose at every phase of the project my dual objective of working as a nursing assistant and writing about these experiences. In some instances it was possible to disclose this dual purpose, in others it was not. I told many nursing assistants and people who lived in the homes that I was both working and investigating. I told some of my nursing supervisors and some administrators. It was not possible to tell everyone and proceed with the project. Rather than answering here the question "Did you tell them?" with a categorical yes or no, I will refer to it as the analysis unfolds. But the short answer is that as the study proceeded it was forced increasingly to become a piece of undercover research.

The question of disclosure came up with a definite jolt a few moments into my first job interview. It was a state law that all nursing assistant applicants had to attend an approved training program and become certified in order to work in a nursing home. I had not known about this requirement prior to arranging an interview at the home where Ina and Aileen worked. The administrator of the home had agreed to see me on their recommendation. The interview lasted less than one minute.

Before I had a chance to explain my dual objective of work and research, the administrator glared at me across his desk, and probed suspiciously, "Now why would a

white guy want to work for these kinds of wages?"
Shocked by his bluntness, I stumbled for words, but he
was not interested in a response. He continued without
pause, "Besides, I couldn't hire you if I wanted to. You're
not certified." That, he quickly concluded, was the end of
our interview, and he showed me to the door.

Shortly thereafter, I came to note the end of that interview as the beginning of the project. Within days I was off
to sign up for school to obtain a certificate and learn how
to become a nursing assistant.

Part One
Mining the Raw Materials

In the first three chapters I introduce some social and economic characteristics of nursing assistants and nursing home residents. Chapter One describes the training program for becoming a certified nursing assistant and identifies the gender, race, and class dynamics that provide undercurrent themes in later chapters. Chapter Two gives information about nursing assistants' wages and their consequences; it also addresses the international character of the labor force. Chapter Three shifts the focus to nursing home residents and to an economic journey that they experience and speak about.

1

"Welcome to the Firing
Line of Health Care"

The owner of the vocational school stood tall in his three-piece suit on that first night of class, greeting the new recruits to the nursing world with military imagery: "Welcome to the firing line of health care!"

Thirty-six students sat in front of him, all in clean white uniforms, their newly purchased textbooks on the desks, listening intently. We were joining what the owner, the texts, and the teachers continually referred to as the health care team. The school, they said, would teach us our place in that team. "Firing line" in the military means the front lines of battle; here it meant caring for patients. One of the teachers later described the work much as Ina Williams had done in the coffee shop. "Registered nurses," the teacher instructed, "do the paper work nowadays. Your job, at least if you work in a nursing home, as you probably will, will be to deliver the primary care."

The owner, Mr. Cohn, continued his lecture: "You used to be called nurses' aides. In here it's nursing assistants. Things are getting more professional throughout the health care industry. I helped them draft the law. Now nobody works in an extended care facility without a certificate from a course approved by the state Board of Health. There's been a lot of trouble in nursing homes, and some of it is because staff has not been properly trained. We're here to correct that. When you're finished with this course I expect to be able to bounce a quarter on the beds you've made."

Before Mr. Cohn had called the class to attention, the students had milled around, introducing themselves and chatting. It became clear that for most of us being in this particular class was the product of a search for the program that could best fit into our work schedules and budgets. It had meant interviewing at some of the six programs that were available in Chicago. Privately owned schools advertised in the daily papers and beckoned prospective candidates to become health care professionals. Each of the three schools where I interviewed assured me admission, provided I could pay the tuition. At the time, the early 1980s, the fee was $695. This cost did not include the required textbook, uniform, shoes, watch, and thermometer, which added another $200 to the start-up costs. The school I selected had night classes and Saturday clinical training, which was convenient for those who had daytime jobs.

Ms. North, who conducted the interviews, oriented each of us to the program. "Although our school is not responsible for finding you a job," she began, "there are plenty of nursing home jobs out there, and none of you should have any trouble." She went on to describe the state requirement of one hundred hours of theory in the classroom and thirty-six hours of clinical experience.

It was a rushed interview because the waiting room was filled, largely with women of color in their twenties and thirties, and Ms. North seemed anxious to enroll her next candidate. "Do you have any questions?" she asked while closing my file.

I had many questions, but time for just one. "I'm a little uncomfortable being the only man and one of the few white people signing up. Will I be out of place?"

"Not at all," she insisted, "there's need for men in this

field." As she talked she walked toward the door and opened it for me, with a quick "Good luck."

On that first night of class Mr. Cohn continued his welcoming remarks with the assurance that this course was no laughing matter, that the days were gone when nursing assistants were considered unprofessional, and that if we did not pass the tests we would fail the course. Glancing around the room, I could feel the typical jitters of a first class session, but in some ways this was more acute than any I had known, for the whole classroom environment was alien to many. To enroll, it was not necessary to have graduated from high school, and later it became clear that some of the students had not. Some were foreign-born, as was evident from their speech. The people in the classroom were mostly black, though not all American; some were Spanish-speaking, and a few were of Asian origin. It was a class of women, except for three men: one eighteen and white, one mid-thirties and black, the other mid-thirties and white—me. Most students were working at another job during the day, pursuing at night this second career with its virtual guarantee of a job.

"We like to think we're the best in the market," Mr. Cohn noted in concluding his welcoming lecture. "The allied health industry, as we call it in the school business, is the third largest industry in the country, worth over $225 billion. Now, before I dismiss you for tonight, are there any questions?"

Tense silence reigned for a long ten seconds. It was broken by the African-American woman who had seemed least intimidated by his presentation. She asked point-blank, "Are we going to have to deal with dead people?"

Mr. Cohn's military bearing crumpled somewhat, but while the class shared a muted release of laughter, he had time to think of an answer. After clearing his throat, he said, "The job of nursing assistant pushes personal care to the limit. Our teachers are all highly trained registered nurses. You can go into that with them." With that he told us to read the first chapter of the text and dismissed the class.

The textbook, *Being a Nursing Assistant,* introduced us to the work in a different tone, less military and business-like. The dominant motif of the first section was health care professionalism. Like other manuals in the field, almost all of which are written by nurses with graduate degrees, it began with a cordial greeting: "Welcome to being a nursing assistant . . . a very special job, one you can take much pride in. You will be helping people and making your community a better place to live." [1]

After introducing some of the tasks and procedures that nursing assistants perform, the chapter outlined some basic personal qualities required on the job, especially dependability, accuracy, confidentiality, and good personal hygiene. It concluded with a section called "climbing the career ladder." A pyramid graph showed a bar for each step, with nursing assistants at the bottom. Students were advised to work as nursing assistants for a while, then go on to study to become licensed practical nurses (LPNs). After another year of work, they could begin schooling in a registered nurse program to obtain a diploma. Then, after a year of work as RNs, they might enroll in college for a B.S. in nursing, beyond that work for an M.A., and eventually return to graduate school in pursuit of a doctorate.

To suggest that this career ladder was beyond the reach of most of the students in that classroom would be an understatement of great magnitude. Many expressed a combination of pride and anxiety at having achieved their present enrollment. This career ladder would extend from these first days of nursing assistant class through as many as seventeen years, considerably longer than the training required of most physicians.

"What this work is going to take is a lot of mother's wit"

The tensions generated by the introductory lecture and these ideas of career professionalism were reflected in our conversations as we waited for the second class to get under way. Yet within the next half hour they seemed to dissolve. Mrs. Bonderoid, our teacher, saw to that. A registered nurse and nurse practitioner, an African-American woman of about fifty, she must have understood a lot about classroom jitters and about who was sitting in front of her as well. "What this work is going to take," she instructed, "is a lot of mother's wit." "Mother's wit," she said, not "mother wit," which connotes native intelligence irrespective of gender. She was talking about maternal feelings and skills.

The room was nearly filled with mothers, as I later learned, but even the others could tell that some notion had just been introduced that relaxed the tension. The subject matter had been put into a framework more familiar than military metaphors or the promise of professionalism. Able now to inquire about the work from their own base of experience, several students came alive with questions. Beverly Miller, for example, asked again, "Do we have to deal with dead people?"

On this night the answer was different. After a moment of reflection, Mrs. Bonderoid leaned over her podium to get closer to the class and spoke softly and slowly, "You have to look into a patient's eyes as much as you can, and learn to get the signals from there. You have to make that contact, especially when they're dying. It makes it easier for you that way, and sometimes for them, too. And whatever you're thinking at the time, say something to them, always keeping in mind that hearing is the last to go. If you've cared for them and they die, they're not just another dead person, they're still your patient."

"Mother's wit," she repeated several times during those first weeks of class, "use it and you'll stay out of trouble." Naturally I failed to share the precise feeling it induced in the mothers in the room, yet her phrase stayed with me all the time I was working in the homes. "A certain kind of just being there," was how Mrs. Bonderoid once defined it.[2]

She herself practiced mother's wit in the classroom to ease the fears fostered by the threat of tests and failure. Still, the threat hovered over the class from first day to last. She was responsible for teaching a curriculum that had been set by the state, as we had been told in our welcoming lecture, and it was more rigorous than some of us had expected.

The theory primarily concerned biology and anatomy. As in any high school or college biology course, we were responsible for memorizing the rudiments of human anatomy and physiology: cells and tissues first, then the skeletal, muscular, gastrointestinal, nervous, excretory, reproductive, respiratory, circulatory, endocrine, and skin systems, their functions and principal organs. This comprised the core of what was meant by theory in the class; biology was the dominant theory in nursing assistants' education. The textbook made the point succinctly: "All cells, tissues, organs, and systems operate together to form a human being."[3]

The Latin- and Greek-derived polysyllabic words proved challenging, even frightening, to many students, just as they do in high school and college biology classes.

Yet Mrs. Bonderoid managed to calm most of our fears by reviewing former test questions, and she kept interest high by frequent references to what we were all abundantly eager to experience—contact with patients.

If Mrs. Bonderoid was successful in easing these fears inside the classroom, she had a more difficult time reconciling us to the circumstances that greeted us on beginning our clinical training at the nursing home.[4] Half the class, eighteen students, stood in a circle on that first morning, trying to ward off the smells that rose up to greet us: the cleaning chemicals, the stale urine, the lingering odor of leftover powdered eggs. The first hour we spent half-listening to instructions, half-exchanging pleasantries with the residents who came up to greet us in the hall. One woman in a wheelchair was especially curious and convivial. She appeared to be in her nineties, and though her speech was slurred, she spoke continually, supplementing Mrs. Bonderoid's instructions with her insider's knowledge. "Wait till you see my floor," she chuckled. "You'll get some surprises."

We were assigned to various wards and proceeded with a typical day's work, at the side of a nursing assistant on her job. My assigned instructor, Erma Douglas, pulled at my sleeve as she headed down the hall. "Let's go, fella," she said with a smile. "Today you're the nursing assistant's nursing assistant." On the floor we were assigned to, there were four paid nursing assistants at work, one registered nurse, and one licensed practical nurse. The latter two sat at the nurses' station filling out charts and coordinating our work, and twice during the day they dispensed medications. Forty-seven women and eleven men lived on the floor, in two- and three-person rooms.

Our tasks sounded fairly simple on a first scan through the assignment sheet: assist patients with toileting, make

beds, give showers, make notations in the charts for each
of these tasks, and prepare to serve lunch. Yet it turned out
to be a long, sometimes frightening morning for most of
us. We wanted to greet our patients with a smile and a note
of good cheer, but since they were strangers, some inartic-
ulate or only partially coherent, many suffering from physically unattractive maladies, it was clear that this was
going to take some practice. With some, toileting had to
be done while they remained in bed, which meant starting
by cleaning someone who had already defecated, perhaps
hours earlier. I ran to Mrs. Douglas in fear, hoping she
knew some tricks that would make it easier.

"Start with George first. He'll help you," she advised.
"Just go in there and pretend he's your father. After a
while, when you get to know these folks, you'll find out
whose shit stinks and whose don't."

It was some time before I understood what she meant
by this graphic phrase, but it became immediately clear
that she was right about George Lewis. He helped me
through his cleaning, especially with his jokes about being
an expert at how it's done. But, when it came time to wheel
him to the shower, his mood changed abruptly. It was the
middle of winter and the water was not warm. He
screamed and struggled with me all through the shower.
After going through this sequence with four more people,
I was physically and emotionally exhausted, but there was
no time for reflection. The charts had to be filled in to
certify that these five had been toileted and showered, and
before that was half done the lunch trays were arriving.

Back in class the following week, students peppered
Mrs. Bonderoid with questions about the work, the
people, and the place. Because she had a strict course curriculum that needed addressing, she had to quiet the questions as best as she could. Mostly the students wanted to

know how better to perform the tasks that had been so unnerving and how to start conversations with patients. They wanted to know, too, why conditions at the place were as they were, especially why the water was cold. She was prepared to talk about the tasks and how to start conversations, but the conditions of the place, she said, were beyond her control. "You'll work in better places." The subject matter at hand was human physiology, the material for the next examination.

During the classes and the clinical experience, I began taking notes on everything I could, mostly on little squares of paper that fit into my back pocket. I tried to do it unobtrusively—often in the bathroom—but my somewhat frenzied scribbling soon led to the inevitable question.

"What are you doing, Tim, writing a book?" Joanna Santos was the first to ask.

Caught off guard, I responded with a sheepish yes. Shortly thereafter, I decided to tell my classmates, with whom I was becoming increasingly friendly, about my project. It was time, I thought, for a forthright disclosure.[5] So I practiced a little speech and seized a moment before one of the classes to tell everyone that I was a teacher and a scholar and that I hoped to write a book about the work we were doing and about nursing homes.

The rejection I feared did not occur. Instead, most took the disclosure quite casually, saying, "Hey, good luck, Tim" or "Yeah, Tim, keep it up." I was on the financial fringes myself at the time, as they could no doubt see. Perhaps for this reason, or for others, most did not take my announcement with the seriousness that I expected. A friend pointed out that they probably saw me much as they saw Charles Baker, the other mid-thirties man in the class. Charles was an African-American jazz musician who wrote music and, as he said, always carried a tune in his head. They may well have seen both of us as launching a second, safer career, while keeping the first in mind. Whatever they thought, there was enough acceptance so that I could continue taking notes and even be interrupted periodically by students saying, "Hey, don't forget to put this in your book."

As the classes continued, students had more to be concerned about than that one of their members was taking notes. They had notes of their own to take and memorize, and the class was becoming more difficult. The initial awe and excitement of the course gave way to some disgruntlement.

"Why do we have to learn all this biology and take these tests? What's this got to do with the job?" asked Martha Vogel, mother of three, formerly a home health aide.

Charles tossed in an answer to Martha's question before the teacher spoke, one that, while not calming the complaints, cut through them by getting everyone to laugh. "Hey, relax, will yuh?" he said. "What do you expect? This is America. You don't want everybody to know biology, do you? How could anybody get ahead?"

Most students picked up on his irony with its inversion of America as the land of opportunity. But for some this class was one of their early experiences in the United States and was a learning experience about the whole culture. It was, among other things, an exercise in learning its racial divisions. Comments by Vivienne Barnes and Diana Obbu introduced some of the racial dimensions of the work.

Vivienne was Jamaican and had been a nursing assistant in her country for six years. Her first work experience in the States was as a home health aide in a wealthy suburb. One evening, as she, Diana, and I were riding home on the bus, she told a story about the woman for whom she had worked. "You talk so well," Vivienne mimicked, feigning the woman's upper-class accent, "and your nose isn't flat like the others ." Vivienne continued, squinting her eyes in chagrin: "Then a few days later she said, 'You're so cute, I just love you. Oh, by the way, would you scrub my kitchen floor?' "

"That was it!" Vivienne told us, with a flash of her hand. "That's all she had to say. I quit the next day. I knew that for her I was no nurses' aide, I was a black woman."[6]

With Vivienne's comic telling of the tale we all laughed together for an instant—that is, until I interrupted the joviality with a dash of white American ignorance. Like the wealthy suburbanite, I was impressed with Vivienne's perfect diction, her British-sounding speech. It seemed that Diana spoke similarly, so with my newfound wisdom that not all black women sounded alike, I turned to her and asked, "Are you from Jamaica, too?"

"No," she said with only a faint hint of insult. "I'm from Ghana." I had missed the mark by a mere five thousand miles, not to mention the vast cultural differences between the countries. As I tried to recover, she put us all at ease with a remark about how funny white people look when they blush.

I was to meet black women and men from many different societies, and some talked about each other as much in terms of differences as similarities. Both Vivienne and Diana were surprised to discover how poorly American black people were treated. And when I mentioned to Diana something about an American student whom I had called black, she paused, puzzled, and asked, "Oh, do you mean that light-skinned girl?" Over time it seemed less and less likely that there existed any such generic social category as "black."

At the same time, the category was continually being reinvented even within our small circle. Once one of the school supervisors made an announcement to stem the growing tide of criticism about conditions at the nursing home, like the cold water showers and the screams that kept haunting us.

"Your job," admonished the supervisor, "is to deal with the patient; it is not your place to criticize the institution."

Hearing this lecture, Vivienne turned to me and whispered with a wry smile, "Hey, Tim, what do you think? Are they teaching us to be nurses' aides or black women?" She was remembering her experience in the suburbs.

Mrs. Bonderoid had a way of quieting criticism, even racial conflict, by keeping us focused on patient care. As she was taking us through several wards during one of the clinical training sessions, she cautioned us: "Patients have to be one size and one color. Even if they tell you that they want a white nurse instead of a black one, you have to swallow your pride and keep going."

During the clinical sessions she was carefully introducing us to some people with conditions that were initially frightening. Gently folding down the blankets of a woman who appeared to us to be unconscious, she kept on talking to her. Then she turned to us, whispering, "Always assume the patient is conscious." While we tried to bear the lesson in mind, it was difficult not to gasp as we gazed upon the sores that had developed up and down this woman's backside. Mrs. Bonderoid continued, "They call it septicemia, we call them bedsores. One of the most important things you have to do in your work is to keep turning patients and massaging their skin with creams and oils and anything you can think of to prevent these as much as possible." In the midst of this kind of intensive training, student interest remained high, and many would come to class bubbling over with questions.

"Why Don't You Go Back and Do Some Psycho-social Stuff."

Suddenly, one night about midterm in the seventeen-week course, we were met with a surprise when we came to class. Mrs. Bonderoid was gone. She had been fired. We were given no explanation. Though we inquired, we never learned much, beyond rumors that she did not get along with the administration and did not agree with their philosophy. She was replaced by another registered nurse and nurse practitioner, but they had nothing else in common. Our new teacher was a white man.

Clutching a monogrammed briefcase, Mr. Store strode into class and within three minutes set the tone of the teaching style that was to follow. "I have very high standards as a teacher. I've always been a teacher. I mean I've never just practiced nursing. It doesn't matter what you've learned before. In my class we're going to learn how to deal with the whole person: how to take vital signs, how to assess a patient physically, how to read those charts, and how to go in there with some communication skills." Students sat up straight, silent, slightly stunned as he continued. "You're going to learn how to be a professional now and to be proud of your work, even if it's just making a bed. Soon we're going to start reviewing the body's systems. We'll have a test every week, so let's get studying."

It was probably the tests more than anything else that kept the class on edge for the rest of the term. English was a second language for many of the students, and the tests were almost all the written standardized, fill-in-the-blank variety. "Don't forget," Mr. Store would warn us, "your scores go directly to the state!"

The tests focused on biology, anatomy, physiology, nutrition, Latin abbreviations, measurement of fluid intake and output, and the measurement and recording of vital signs (temperature, blood pressure, pulse, and respiration). Mr. Store had some control over what the tests would emphasize and how they were scored, but the content was dictated primarily by the state Board of Health. For the remainder of the term one could hear continual complaints from the students.

"I studied all weekend," Lydia Gonzales, from Mexico, moaned.

"Why can't they make this stuff easy to read?" asked Diana.

"What's all this got to do with nursing homes?" challenged Beverly.

At first I took the tests somewhat lightly, having studied high school and college biology. The casual approach ended abruptly. After a test on the nervous and skeletal systems, for which I had not studied enough, Lydia confided in me, "I know I failed that one, because I couldn't understand the words. And I felt sorry for you, too, watching you sweat during the test." We both failed it.

Mr. Store took over both the classroom and the clinical instruction, and in the latter domain his philosophy was also a radical departure from that of his predecessor. "When you get out on that floor I want to hear some technical terms, some professionalism, like 'ectomy' and 'ostomy.' Don't say a patient is 'mean,' say he's 'acting inappropriately.' Don't say 'touching,' say 'tactile communication.'"

On this theme of communication he offered another piece of advice that provided plenty of material for behind-the-scene comments by students. Toward the end of a clinical session the trainees returned to Mr. Store in his nurses' station. All the assigned tasks having been accomplished, we asked what to do next. After some reflection, he instructed, "Umm . . . why don't you go back and do some psycho-social stuff."

Upon hearing this term for the first time, Beverly Miller asked with thinly veiled sarcasm, "Do you mean talk to them? What do you think we've been doing all day?"

"Never mind, just go do it some more," he retorted quickly. Back we went to the rooms to talk, but now we were engaged in a distinctly professional act, with its own special name. Mr. Store, meanwhile, recorded in his chart that his students had gone to practice communication skills.

After that day, dissension in the class increased. As the clinicals became more frequent, students wanted more and more to know how to treat their particular patients; but within this medical model, basic nursing questions often went unanswered. Cynthia Gibbons asked on at least three different occasions, "What do we do first to start bed care?" She was searching, as we all still were, for ways to cope with the mutual embarrassment of finding excrement in a patient's bed. Remembering my difficulties with George as he lay in his bed, I too considered it a crucial question.

"Well, first get them out of that, then offer them a bed-pan, then move on to a bed bath and teeth care," came the reply. Mr. Store seemed not to understand exactly what Cynthia wanted to know. The question was, How does one "get them out of that"? His answer required that the question be asked again, and yet again. Finally it was abandoned, and we moved on to the more pressing issues of abstract biology.

For his part, Mr. Store asked, "What do you do with

soiled linen?" Students made three tries: "Wash it?" "Clean it?" "Scrub it?" All three answers were wrong. Mr. Store was looking for "Throw it away."

"Why don't you wash it?" asked Vivienne, a six-year veteran of this type of work.

He snapped back quickly, " 'Throw it away' means wash it."

Within his frame of reference, "throw it away" meant that the linen was picked up and thrown into the utility room or down the laundry chute. But nursing assistants had to enter into this process of cleaning up well before they threw sheets down a chute. We had already spent some time in the utility room, scrubbing sheets before they were fit to be sent to the laundry, before they were even clean enough to be called dirty. At the point of removing dirty linen from a bed, some professional health care workers are finished with it, but not nursing assistants and certainly not laundrywomen. They pick up the soiled linen and take it to the next stage of changing dirty into clean. "Throw it away" erased those steps, making them into invisible labor. This instruction was the first of many aspects of the work which, even as they were being taught, remained unnamed.[7]

"Mr. Store," Diana argued, "we don't need to know the six tissue types or all these Latin words, we need to know how to clean someone!"

On this fundamental issue, Mr. Store could only be vague, as though he were proceeding from a different set of assumptions than the questioners. He presupposed the activities of cleaning, but was not able to explain them in terms of what the work actually involved.[8] He and Vivienne got into a heated exchange at one point. She felt insulted when he referred to home health care, the work she had done for six years, as babysitting.

"No, Mr. Store," she objected vehemently, "you don't understand. When you are in someone's home you've got to take care of them in lots of ways. Sometimes you're up with them all night after a full day's work."

On the issue of cleaning people, Mr. Store seemed to know less about its actual practice than did nursing assistant Erma Douglas. She knew the people personally: George, she knew, would help the new recruits. Her lessons proceeded from that specific knowledge, unlike the abstractions that Mr. Store was offering. Even her general principles had more to do with mother's wit than science. "I never wash the head when it's cold, and most times don't put soap on the face at all—it always gets in their eyes or mouth." She stared at me after this instruction, surprised that I did not already know this. "You ain't had no babies, have you?"

"No," I responded.

"I didn't think so," she continued, looking away, shaking her head.

The inconsistencies between these ideas in the classroom and the actual working conditions, at least Mr. Store's and Erma's different entrées to them, reached points of open, cynical humor during the several classes in which we were drilled on the biological systems of the body. Some racial divisions had already surfaced, with some of the angrier American black and foreign-born students calling Mr. Store "that white boy" and some of the white students reacting defensively. Yet even the white students had to recognize by now that, although we were being taught by professional nurses, we were not being taught to be professional nurses; we were being prepared for a different and lower stratum, in which most of our colleagues were nonwhite.

Mr. Store began one class with the question, "What is

the function of the skin?" With racial issues simmering be-
neath the surface, the question met with subdued snicker-
ing, but the lesson continued without pause. "The function
of the skin is to protect and regulate body temperature."
Mr. Store was conscientious and concerned that we would
pass the tests designed by the state Board of Health. He
had time to discuss only what the skin does for the body,
not what it does for society or for the divisions of labor in
this emerging health care industry.

When it came to the reproductive system, incompatibil-
ities between the clinical situations and the scientific biology of the classroom reached the point of absurd humor
and practical contradiction. At the clinical training Janet
Morris, a student in her mid-twenties, was assigned to
tend to Arthur Scott, about fifty, a military veteran bedridden with a leg problem and nervous disorder, but with
all his other faculties fully intact, including sexual.

Janet and I had become friends. She conferred with me
and another student about a dilemma she had encountered
on several occasions after feeding Arthur his lunch. Janet
had quickly became fond of Arthur, empathizing with him
as he lay there in the bed day in and day out, and Arthur
became attracted to Janet. One day as Janet began to tend
to him, he became sexually excited and asked Janet to help
relieve his tension. Janet chose not to, instinctively made a
joke of it, and immediately carried on with the next phase
of her work. But the issue caused her concern, as it must
many nursing students beginning their training. When she
consulted us, she indicated that she had paused to consider
his request. She had, she thought, been faced with a dilemma, a choice between unsatisfactory alternatives.

Two days later Mr. Store asked a question, reading it
from the prescribed curriculum list of answers that we
were supposed to memorize about the biological system.

"What is the function of the penis?" he asked with an unflinching air of scientific detachment. Janet, the other student, and I exchanged quick glances and suppressed a giggle, knowing by then that this was not an environment in which Janet's dilemma could be brought up for reasoned discussion. "The function of the penis," he proceeded, "is to urinate." After this answer he moved on to other questions on the list, stopping to make sure that the students were writing the correct answers in their notes. This biological fact did appear on a test, so from that point of view Mr. Store was fulfilling his duty. Meanwhile, this nursing-as-biology lesson did little for Janet's dilemma and nothing for Arthur's.

"C'mon, Now, When Did You Come Closest to Losing It?"

These incidents are not meant to establish disillusionment as the exclusive or overriding sentiment as the class went on. Indeed, every week uniforms were spotless and texts memorized; and eagerness to get on to employment prevailed right to the end. Even the rumors that nursing homes paid little more than minimum wage did not dampen students' developing interest. In addition, to give credit to Mr. Store and the text, we were learning nursing skills, and most of us spoke proudly about being able to practice this new knowledge.

Moreover, as the weeks went on, the sophistication of the questions increased dramatically, especially when we got to know some people who lived in the clinical training home. The subject matter became ever more fascinating, and inquiries about the causes and trajectories of these peoples' disorders intensified. But interest in returning each Saturday to our full day of clinical training waned somewhat, tempered by our desires to move on to paid

employment. The two groups of eighteen students who attended these all-day clinic sessions complained regularly
that the home was receiving many hours of free labor.

"Why does this place always smell cleaner when we
leave?" was a recurrent quip by Doreen Foster as we
walked out the door. When we learned that this home that
had so shocked us was owned by a multinational hotel
chain, patience wore extremely thin. "If I'd known that,"
confessed Doreen, "I sure wouldn't have worked so hard
for free." Still, optimism prevailed, supported by our
teachers' assurances that we would work in better places.

Toward the end, like students in most professions, talk
and study centered on the final examination, the rite of
passage that would determine whether we were ready to
enter what Mr. Store would occasionally refer to as the
real world. The Clinical Skills Proficiency Test was a six-
part exam, two of the parts involving demonstration by
the student: giving a bedpan, making beds, taking vital
signs and other measurements, and demonstrating proper
procedures for lifting people. The other sections were written tests on recording vital signs, measuring intake and
output of fluids, taking urine and stool specimens, and po-
sitioning patients. Our scores on the clinical exam were
combined with those from the theory part, the anatomy,
physiology, and biology, to determine pass or fail. In the
end, grades did not turn out to be the threat many feared.
All but one person who completed the course passed it.

On passing the test we were considered ready for the
work force. There can be no doubt that confidence, skills,
and courage had increased during the weeks of training,
but much that we would need later was never mentioned.
After the early conversations with Mrs. Bonderoid, the
subject of death did not come up anywhere in the text,
lectures, or tests. Nor, amid copious material about cells,

tissues, and systems, was the question of the causes or consequences of cancer ever raised. We didn't even speculate
why the text pictured patients in hospital beds with call
buttons, whereas in our nursing home most people were
dressed and sat in the day room or walked around the
ward.

"We are cells, and cells are us," Mr. Store was fond of
reminding us, echoing the assertion in the text that "cells,
tissues, organs and systems operate together to form a human being." What the state and the industry labeled as
theory consisted of one hundred hours of biological and
mechanical facts, within the context of the medical model
of sickness and care. We were admitted into a profession
based on the knowledge of bodily systems. It was not a
theory of feelings, urges, desires, or needs. It did not address why nursing homes are organized the way they are,
who lives in them, or who works in them under what conditions.

Once, when the class was nearing its final weeks, a
friend asked me, "How can it take them that long to teach
you hand-holding?" I was forced to respond that hand-
holding had never been mentioned in the course. There
were no concepts taught or discussed that explored the
term *caring*. The school taught a language of germs and
disease.[9]

A note of pride was heard in many voices as graduation
day approached. Becoming a certified nursing assistant
was a goal achieved at considerable cost and effort. Many
spoke of graduation parties and presents families and
friends were to give. Some students organized a farewell
dinner at a restaurant near the school, and most of the
class attended.

Few groups of new professionals could have joined in
the main topic of conversation at that final banquet. After

sharing promises to help each other find jobs, our talk turned quickly to the heart of the matter: which patients we liked most and least during the clinical training, and the times each of us got closest to becoming sick to our stomachs or fainting while learning the work.

Most of the time was spent listening to graduates respond to the question: "C'mon, now, when did you come closest to losing it?" Each story was an attempt to top the previous one and was met with a louder chorus of "Oh, yech! How gross!" followed by an increasing release of raucous laughter.

It was a conversation, as Mrs. Bonderoid might have observed, less about septicemia than about bedsores, less about science than about mother's wit. But now, armed with science and certificates, we were off to see what awaited us on the firing line of health care.

2

"How Do You Make It on Just One Job?"

Four-thirty is close to the end of the administrative day in nursing homes, as elsewhere in the business world. Applications are filed and interviews held only during business hours. I had visited four nursing homes earlier in the day during a week of pounding the pavement in search of a job. At each home a nurse, stationed near the entrance desk, monitored visitors and residents coming and going through the doors. In two of the homes the nurse took my application and said they might call, for they had openings frequently. Two said they were not hiring. In one, the nurse was more specific: "We're not hiring because a lot of nurses just took the registered nurse exam and didn't pass, so they're working as aides."

With the hour growing late, I hesitated in making this one last application of the day. But an old, five-story brick building drew my attention because through the large glass window I could see a line of people going into the dining room. With its large lobby and dining room on the first floor and many small, evenly spaced windows on its upper stories, the building gave the appearance of having once been an elegant hotel. It was now a nursing home.

A young man stopped me at the entry station. While I was telling him that I wanted to apply for work, I scanned the lobby. At least forty people were milling around, most of them standing in line, others lining up at the coffee and soda machines or just sitting in the open room. The man directed me to the office of the head nurse.

Before offering her hand or asking my name, she quickly asked, "Do you have a certificate?"

I offered it somewhat proudly, knowing the time and expense that had gone into producing it and feeling that it would insulate some of the tense exchanges that might follow when I told of my dual purpose to work and to write about the work. After reviewing it, she said I could fill out an application but, glancing at her watch, she added, "You'll have to come back tomorrow for an entrance exam and interview."

The exam was similar to the final one in school: filling in appropriate numbers for vital signs, units of measurement for intake and output, some details about anatomy. Liza Martin, another applicant, was sitting next to me. Since the two of us were alone in the room, we helped each other with the answers.

We both passed, and we stayed to chat.

"How come you came here?" Liza asked.

"I just stopped in and took a chance," I said. "And you?"

"I came here from a place up the street. They only pay minimum wage. I heard this place paid more." She went on to say that she had been at her job for six months without a raise, and the rumor that this place paid $3.50 to start, fifteen cents above the minimum wage, was enough to entice her over for an interview.

The next day I showed up in uniform, with certificate, grades, and textbook under my arm, clutching whatever might lend legitimacy to my presence. While committed not to lie, I was not particularly eager to announce the whole purpose of my project, preferring the strategy of one step at a time. The interview was brisk. It seemed to be a routine event for this assistant head nurse, something she squeezed in among countless administrative tasks. On the application, after the section that indicated where and when the certificate had been obtained, was the typical slot for previous employer. Since I had spent the prior fifteen years in universities, my answer was scarcely typical. I wrote that I had been a research assistant at Northwestern University.

As I sat nervously waiting for an inquiry about my background, she glanced over my application and asked, "Is this the correct phone number of your previous employer?"

"Yes," I answered, ready to say more, but the telephone receiver was already in her hand, and she was dialing the number without looking at me.

At the Women's Studies program that I was affiliated with, the staff members were aware of and supportive of my project. Still, I had no idea how the director might respond to a telephone inquiry. As it turned out, she was asked a series of rapid-fire, yes-no, fill-in-the-blank questions.

"Is he punctual?"

"Yes."

"Is he honest?"

"Yes."

"Have you ever known him to steal?"

"No."

"Will he show up for work regularly?"

"Yes."

"Thank you for your time."

She hung up, and had only one question for me. "Can you work an evening shift?"

"Yes."

"Fine, we'll see you here tomorrow afternoon at three."

She hurried me out the door, and again I was faced with the disclosure dilemma. It was clear from her questions on

the phone and the rushed standardized interview that she
was simply screening applicants for laborers she needed. I
saw no reason to complicate this procedure. I had not
found job offers to be plentiful; no doubt many employers
were suspicious when they saw a white man apply, especially one with links to the university, even more so when
I told them of my research interest. This time I decided to
bring up the issue later. I needed a job, and took it.

"And How Are All Your Revolutions Doing Today?"

As the next day's 3:00 P.M. shift began, nine workers sat
and stood at the nurses' station. There was a registered
nurse, a licensed practical nurse, one social service worker,
and six nursing assistants, divided into two work groups,
one going off, one coming on.

"What's the patient count today?" asked the evening
nurse in charge.

"Well," responded her afternoon counterpart, "Lorraine
Sokolof fell, so she went to the hospital. That makes sixty-
three."

"Laina, take Diamond here and show him the ropes,"
the evening charge nurse said.

Laina Martinez was a Filipino woman in her twenties.
"Don't worry, once you get to know the people, it's not
that hard," she began. "Here's where you get the sheets,
over here you fold the clothes. On this shift you have to
give a lot of showers, so keep a fresh supply of towels
handy. After dinner I'll show you how to chart, that's the
most important thing. For now just change some beds and
assist some of them to the toilet."

Of the nine staff members who met each day at the
change of shifts, I was the only white man. There were
seven women, one of whom, the RN on the day shift, was

an American white. Three were American black women, two were from the Philippines and one from Jamaica. The one other man was from Nigeria.

While getting to know this group, I was reminded of a comment from a woman I visited in New Jersey during the early days of formulating my project. Flora Dobbins captured the international flavor of the group I was trying to get to know during these first few weeks of work. "How do you like it here in this nursing home?" I had asked her.

"Oh, I guess this place is as good as any of them," she said. "There's just one thing I can't get used to. It's like the United Nations in here."

Mrs. Dobbins's reference was distinctly about the staff, not the people who lived in the home. The staff were mostly people of color, residents mostly white. During the course of the research I worked with women, and a few men, from Haiti, the West Indies, Jamaica, Ghana, Nigeria, Mexico, Puerto Rico, India, South Korea, China, and many from the Philippines. Never before, or since, have I been so acutely self-conscious about being a white American man. At first the people who lived in the homes stared at me, then some approached to get a closer look, saying that I reminded them of a nephew, a son, a grandson, a brother, a doctor. This behavior made more sense as time went on: except for the few male residents and occasional visitors, I was the only white man many would see from one end of the month to the next.

As Laina was showing me how to fill out one of the charts, I noticed a small gold pin on her collar, embossed with the inscription, "St. Mary's School of Nursing." "Oh," said I, "my sister went to a nursing school by that same name, about twenty years ago." It turned out that while my sister's training had been in the United States,

Laina's was in Manila. She spoke of herself and her friends knowing throughout their training that they would work in the States after graduation.

"There were something like fifty nursing schools in Manila when I was there, and just about everybody was going to work in another country when they graduated, most in the States." Toward the end of her five-year training program, which awarded her a bachelor's degree in nursing, she and her fellow students signed contracts with an agency in Manila. The contract specified the particular nursing home corporation for which she would work, the exact city, and the starting date. "Some company has to petition you to come to work," she explained. "But there's always jobs."

Although it was easy to see that Laina was a highly skilled nurse, she was not yet practicing in this country as a registered nurse. To reach this level she had to take two different tests after she arrived in the States. She was complaining about this requirement when we met.

"Can you believe it?" she asked rhetorically. "Now they're talking about adding a third test. We have to study here more than we did in school." While she was studying for the tests and waiting for a license, she was employed as a "graduate nurse," doing work only slightly more skilled than the nursing assistant at only a slightly higher wage.

She joked about something we had in common during those first few weeks. She had been in the States only two months and had been working only about six weeks before I arrived. We both had loans to pay back, hers a loan for her plane ticket from the Philippines, about $750, mine about the same amount for my schooling. We were working side by side for the money to pay the loans that offered us the privilege to work. Occasionally we asked each other how many weeks we had left before we could start earning money.

These international workers were in many ways an exciting group to be among. They had traveled widely and spoke of countries all over the world. On the other hand, cultures often clashed in day-to-day living. It was not always easy to understand the speech of people for whom English was a second language. Even those well trained in nursing had studied a formal, written English and did not understand some local idioms. Many residents with impaired hearing or sight expressed anger and confusion at having people taking care of them who were from a different race, country, or culture.

In addition, these women and men were not just from "different" countries, not just the "United Nations" as Flora had suggested, but mostly from Third World societies—a dimension that started to become clear one day during lunch. Two Filipino nurses sat at a large table, offering homemade rice cakes to anyone who wished to join them. At the table were two other nurses from their country, one nursing assistant from Nigeria, and one from South Korea. A woman from Haiti approached the table, greeted everyone, sat down, smiled, and asked, "And how are all your revolutions doing today?"

The others responded with robust laughter, as though they had heard the question before. Throughout the 1980s every one of these countries was in intense political turmoil, and at least some citizens from each of them were calling it revolution. They went on to talk about the turmoil in their various countries. Revolutions aside, this joke they shared pinpointed a relationship between the advanced capitalist society in which they worked and a composite of developing societies from which they had originated. It illustrated that nursing homes expand as an industry within a world economic labor force. Sitting around that table in this seemingly autonomous nursing home, with its rustic, restful-sounding name, were nurses working in a multinational corporate context, in which the health care system of advanced capitalist societies depends on the work of Third World women.[1]

"How Do They Expect Us to Live on Two Hundred and Nine Dollars?"

In each of the homes where I worked, nursing assistants made up roughly three-fourths of the work force.[2] Since we were working on different floors and wings and shifts, we rarely got together as a group. There was, however, one day every two weeks when nursing assistants from all over the home assembled, greeted one another, and gossiped for a few moments. These meetings occurred as we stood outside the administrator's office, waiting for our paychecks.

Debra Moffit and I started work at the same time, two weeks before this particular meeting. We had been to the same school at different times, and on that first day of work enjoyed talking about the teachers and some of our mutual shocks at learning how hard the work was. Since that first day we had seen each other only in passing, as one of us went on a shift and the other off. On this payday we picked up our checks and met outside. Walking up the street, we pulled our checks out of their sealed envelopes and scanned them for the most meaningful entry, net income. Debra abruptly stopped walking. She had discovered that her take-home pay after two weeks of work was $209—$3.50 per hour, minus deductions.[3]

"Two hundred and nine dollars!" she shrieked. "How do they expect us to live on two hundred and nine dollars?"

The full impact of that question unfolded to me only slowly, after months of working at this wage. Debra immediately starting talking about looking for a job at a different home. As I listened to her, I understood why Liza Martin, with whom I took the test during the job application, had gone from one home to another in the hope of earning ten or fifteen cents more an hour. At these wages such differential can be significant. It also became clear why the assistant head nurse had hired me so quickly. Taking on new workers was a normal part of her everyday work in a revolving-door labor structure. As Debra and I talked, what we held in our pockets was less than what we paid for rent; we would have to work more than half a month just to meet that cost.

We collected $104.50 a week. It did not take long for that sum to take on a meaning different from that of the abstract notion of "minimum wage." Up to that point I had glibly assumed that this concept somehow actually reflected minimum survival expenses, but I was beginning to see that $104 a week was not going to come anywhere near meeting expenses even for a single man living alone.

Debra started to calculate whether she might be eligible for food stamps. Maureen Wilson had to move herself and her one child back to live with her mother, but since her mother lived off the public transportation route she had to take another part-time job to buy a car to drive to work. Ina Williams and Aileen Crawford worked six, sometimes seven, days a week.

Yami Loma, from Nigeria, was pregnant. I asked her how long she was going to choose to work before she was due to deliver.

"Right up to the last day. Got to. No choice about it. But don't worry," she said smiling. "When the day comes I'll teach you how to be a midwife."

Yami and two others once spent a whole week comforting Lottie Ganley, a mother of two, who was terrified that she might be pregnant and knew she could not afford another child. Lottie had been there almost six years and was up to $3.90 an hour. Toward the end of March in 1984 she brought her income tax forms to work trying to figure them out. That year after taxes she took home under $6700. For her and her two children this income was less than the official poverty level, even though she was employed full time.[4]

Raises came in tiny segments—fifteen cents or perhaps a quarter. Back in the coffee shop several months earlier, Ina Williams had muttered, "It ain't hardly worth our time to come out here. They give me a raise I can't even pay bus fare with." All her fifteen-cent raises in her ten years of work added up to just under two dollars above minimum wage, or about $5.25 per hour. The bus fare was a dollar each way. Her raises did not even add up to the cost of her transportation.

Rumors were rife about homes where they paid better. Solange Ferier, from Haiti, heard there was a home in the suburbs that paid $5.50 per hour. "There's a catch, though, they're only hiring part-time, so they don't give benefits." In some other big cities, it was claimed, they paid almost $5.00 everywhere. Yet, for every rumor of higher rates, everyone seemed to know, often first-hand, places where they paid about the same as here, sometimes less.

Eventually, the very concepts of job and wage versus unemployment and poverty that I had brought with me began to break down. What had been clear distinctions in my mind, and in the sociology literature, began to mesh together in real life. Everyday talk continued to center on not having enough money for rent or transportation or children's necessities. Full-time work meant earning less than the cost of subsistence; it did not alleviate poverty. In the 1980s and the early nineties public rhetoric centered on jobs as the panacea for poverty. The women I met were working at full-time jobs that created poverty. Their pay, slightly more than minimum wage, turned out not to be minimum at all. Nor did raising the minimum to $4.25 per hour in 1991 make much difference. The increase scarcely kept up with the rate of inflation; before taxes it brought an annual wage to $8840. If "minimum wage" ever did have any meaning historically, it seemed from this vantage to have become just an item of abstract political narrative, out of touch with the actual contingencies of these working mothers' day-to-day survival.

A simplistic solution to this apparent contradiction occurred to me initially as the most logical option: Why don't they get some other kind of job that would pay more? This was an abstract idea, removed from nursing assistants' realities. I discovered that to suggest it could be taken as an insult. No doubt many do leave the work for higher-paying jobs. Yet, even apart from the deeper structural issue that if everyone did so there would be no nursing home industry left, the nursing assistants I spoke with responded in a different way. First, there was the immediate retort, "What am I going to do instead?" The fact was clear to them that positions as nursing assistants were among the most available jobs of the eighties and were projected to be abundant through the nineties.

Erma Douglas had a more profound response to the issue. She was teaching me about how not to put soap anywhere near people's eyes because it has a way of creeping in that people who wash their own faces do not quite understand. I was mumbling about the low pay, wondering how some of the workers survived, and asked if she had ever thought about getting another job. Her back arched and her eyes blazed.

"This is what I *do*," she said indignantly, with a quick glance at the person whose face she was washing.

The few seconds of uncomfortable silence, coupled with her unblinking stare, left no lingering doubts that this was Erma's profession, something she had practiced for fourteen years. It included skills that she was now able to teach someone who had been to school learning the tasks but was only beginning to learn how they got accomplished. Among the many insults that nursing assistants absorb as they perform these skills, I came to think of none more naive than to inquire why they don't just get another job.

Debra understood the answer to her question, "How do they expect us to live on two hundred and nine dollars?" much quicker than I. She told me she had to work another week just to make her rent payment. The answer started to dawn on me when veteran nursing assistant Dorothy Tomason boasted of "knocking off two double shifts back to back" and needing only four hours of sleep. It became still clearer one day when Aileen and I met on the street by chance, and she asked me if they were hiring part-time evening workers at my place. Ina, she informed me, was doing evenings as a "private," a special-duty aide in someone's home, but Aileen had not been able to find an extra job and was still looking. Donna Jackson, whom I had met at the very first clinical training session, spoke of working the 7:00 to 3:00 shift at this home and the 3:30 to 11:00 at another.

The answer became more apparent when Erma, once she calmed down from my insult about her picking up another line of work, went on to describe her situation more fully.

"How do you like it here?" I asked.

"Oh . . . it's OK," she reflected. "They pay awful, but you'll be all right. You're young, you can get a second job. At home it's just me and my husband. If I had children I couldn't afford to work here. I'd have to go on welfare or get an extra job."

Even with Erma's analysis, the answer to Debra's question did not jell until once within the space of two days two people asked me the same question, revealing how odd my situation was to co-workers. A Filipino man remarked as we passed out trays together that this place had more hustle than the other place where he worked, on the evening shift. Then he turned to me to inquire, "Where else do you work?"

"I only have this one job."

He cocked his head and looked at me distantly. "Oh?" he said, and walked away.

Two days later I was having lunch with Solange Ferier, from Haiti. "You know, I've done this job for six years in my country. There's one thing I learned when I came to the States. Here you can't make it on just one job." She tilted her head, looked at me curiously, then asked, "You know, Tim, there's just one thing I don't understand about you. How do you make it on just one job?"

"Oh, ah . . . I . . . ah . . . do a little teaching and tutoring when I get the chance," was my fumbling response. Then I tried to explain my situation to Solange. Alone with my one job, I stood apart from the work force I thought I had joined. I was getting exhausted from doing just one of these forty-hour full-time jobs, working alongside people for whom this was only a point of departure. I appeared to the others as the odd one out—not, as I had feared, solely because of my status as a white American man but because from somewhere within that category I was mak-

ing it on just one job. Double shifts, part-time moonlight-
ing, two jobs—these I came to realize were not the excep-
tion but the rule for nursing assistants, the newest
members of the health care team, and by far the largest
work force in the emerging nursing home industry. For
most of the people with whom I was working, the answer
to the question, "How do you make it on just one job?"
was quite simple. You don't.

"Are You Done with Your Coffee yet, Fella?"

Under such conditions, the relationship between labor and
management was very tense. Holding more than one job
to make subsistence may have been the way most of the
nursing assistants coped with the situation, but they did
not do so without complaint. One of the earliest and most
forceful lessons of my participation in this industry was
that the lines between management and labor are strictly
drawn.

Comments about the bosses permeated conversations
during lunch and breaks. Carol Davis spoke of wanting to
be a union steward. She was upset at having lost a day's
pay when her daughter was sick. She had claimed a sick
day to take care of her, but management directed that sick
days were to be taken only when the employee was sick.
We belonged to a union and occasionally heard of its activity in other parts of the country, but though it had become
a source of benefits in our area, it was not a forum for
ongoing negotiation. Management kept a close watch over
its activities. Carol wanted to run for steward but did not,
for fear of losing her job.[5]

In this atmosphere, since the workers had viewed me
with some suspicion in the first place, it became increasingly impossible for me to reveal to management that I
hoped to write about my experiences. Given the tension, it

also became less feasible to do so. When I told Solange Ferier that I hoped to write about this industry, she responded, "Well, don't tell them that. They'll have you out on your ear in a minute."

The administrator of this first nursing home where I worked approached me after about three weeks on the job. "I see from your record that you're connected with Northwestern University," he began. I was ready for him to show me to the door within moments, and I had no intention of lying about my purposes, but after listening to the other workers, I had no intention of trying to win his approval either. "Are you doing some kind of report for them?" he inquired. Strictly speaking, the answer to that question was no, since at the time I was living solely on my wages and was only tangentially associated with the university, receiving no credit or money from them and doing no report for them. I assumed, however, that this was just the beginning of the conversation and that the more we talked the more he might think it was in his best interest to fire me.

Luckily, the conversation was abruptly terminated. It was an extremely hot August afternoon, particularly stuffy there on the fourth floor, where there was no air-conditioning and where thirty-five to forty people had been sitting all day amid the accumulating smells of leftover food, bodily messes, and cleaning fluids. The administrator emerged from the elevator, coming from his office, which *was* air-conditioned. He made a sudden leap in temperature, probably from 70 degrees to over 90. The heat and the smells hit him hard, as they did many visitors. He started to perspire and become visibly weak. Simultaneously, he was approached by three residents who had been eager to speak with him. As often happened, they all spoke at once, all standing just a little too close for his comfort. He turned to the drinking fountain, then backed toward the elevator, and our conversation on that stifling afternoon ended.

I never again pursued the issue, and neither did he. I proceeded to tell some co-workers and residents that I hoped to write, but I never told him. He probably suspected something, as did almost everyone I met, since I continued to be the only white man on the nursing assistant staff. But as the months wore on, suspicions seemed to diminish. Solange put it succinctly, "I knew if you were doing some kind of newspaper story you'd have been in and out and gone in a couple of days."

In later months, working in another home, I had a similar experience. When I first started, the administrator had been on a business trip to the Philippines. By the time he returned and was making one of his morning tours through the halls, I had worked four weeks on the day shift. One of the hardest things to get accustomed to in the work was the early morning regimen of getting people up and fed. When the coffee urn arrived with the breakfasts, I would pour a cup of coffee and leave it in a corner, sipping it on the run so the caffeine could help drive me through this timed and pressured work. Drinking coffee, I soon discovered, broke the strict rule that staff were not allowed to consume food or drink except on their breaks.

The administrator spotted me sipping coffee. Though we had never met, the violation caught his attention. He came up from behind me and put his arm completely around my shoulders, brought his face close to mine, and asked sarcastically, "Are you done with your coffee yet, fella? You know you could get a day of suspension for this. I just happen to be in a good mood. See that you don't do it again." He had spoken loud enough for almost everyone in the room to hear.

He was drawing the line between management and labor, talking to one of the laborers, and talking down. I was to serve as an example to the others. A cold sweat of inexpressible anger began to drip across my forehead while this man, younger than myself, wielded his power over this morning cup of coffee. This moment displayed the relations of labor and management from which he proceeded. Since understanding the relation was crucial to this study, just as it had been from the moment when a new rule had precluded Ina and Aileen from continuing our conversations, I decided not to challenge the lines of authority he was marking out with his arm around me and his face six inches away. It would have been foolish to start an argument; he had all the power. Besides, he was clarifying an issue that I was trying to resolve at every step—whether or not to reveal myself as a writer to the authorities. Solange's warning, "They'll have you out on your ear in a minute," underscored the suspiciousness of the climate and its divisions of power. This too close and too loud administrator was shouting at me, whether he meant to or not, that one could take the standpoint of labor or of management, but not both, at least not simultaneously.[6]

Erma Douglas, Dorothy Tomason, and Aileen Crawford were all seasoned nursing assistants, from whom I learned much about how to do this labor.[7] They were all in their mid-to-late forties. Among the other things they had in common, they had all worked between eleven and fourteen years as nursing assistants, and all at one time had mentioned retirement. They joked in wistful tones, imagining how nice it was going to be. Along the second line of the paychecks, in the slot for itemized deductions, there was a section called FICA, Federal Insurance Contributions Act, commonly known as Social Security. Like most other workers in the United States, nursing assistants had

a percentage of gross earnings deducted from each paycheck for federal retirement insurance.

In the next chapter some of the women and men who
lived in the homes where we worked speak about the
phase of their retirement that they spent in nursing homes.
What they had to say about them may portend what lies
ahead for Erma, Dorothy, and Aileen after they contribute
to FICA for another ten or fifteen years, working a shift
and a half or six days a week, wondering how anyone in
their profession could make it on just one job.

3

"Where's My Social Security?"

Helen View, age seventy-nine, was typical of the women and men who lived in the first two homes where I worked: a long-term resident, without monetary resources, tied financially to the nursing home through public aid. It was only after several weeks of getting to know her that a contradiction in my image of her began to make itself felt. If Helen was on public aid and if she had been so for years, as her comments and charts indicated, how was it that she sat in that day room week after week, her posture poised and elegant, wearing fine jewelry, including a gold ring, and dressed in one of her three perfectly tailored tan, brown, and maroon wool suits? Helen's was neither the dress nor the demeanor of a pauper.

After talking with her and scanning her charts while entering her vital signs, I learned that Helen had not always been impoverished. During her tenure in nursing homes, her financial resources—which had been considerable—had been depleted. After my workday I occasionally passed through the neighborhood where she spoke of having lived in her earlier years as a housewife and mother. It was among the wealthiest suburbs in the area. When we met, Helen had been in nursing homes almost nine years. She started in one that was in her old neighborhood, a posh, private place. She moved out of that home into a hospital, then transferred to this home, initially to the first floor, where private-pay people lived. Then she was moved to one of the public-aid floors, where she had been for

nearly six years. Under "prognosis," her chart read "no
release anticipated."

I could learn nothing more about Helen. Yet her nursing
home history seemed to beg for an explanation. What had
happened to her? Could it happen to anyone? Helen spent
a great deal of time sitting in the day room, walking the
halls, or lying in bed under a blanket, clearly bored. And
she was penniless. On the floor where she lived many
women and men were living under similar circumstances:
poor, but poor for the first time in their lives.

I was vaguely aware that I should work in some homes
where residents were paying privately and others where
they were on public aid, that is, Medicaid. I had this general image that there were "rich" and "poor" homes, and
had somewhat inadvertently started in a home of mostly
public aid support. While I was there, certain comments
from Medicaid residents helped clarify the design for my
project. They drew connections between private-pay and
public-aid homes. In everyday conversations they frequently talked among each other and to the staff about the
kinds of places where they used to live. Eventually I dis-
closed to some residents that I hoped to write about nursing home life. The advice of some public-aid residents was
precise.

"Oh, well then," said Anna Ervin, "if you want to write
a book, you should go to the place where I first lived. We
had carpets, radios, glee clubs. It was much better than
this." She called her time in that first home "the good old
days."

Luckily, I was eventually hired in a home where some of
these women spoke of having lived when they first moved
into a nursing home. It was listed in a magazine article that
described the best homes in the wealthy suburbs of Chi-

cago. So I worked in homes where the clientele still had their own resources, as well as ones where they did not. Over time, the continuity that Anna spoke of became clearer. It was not just that she "lived" in a nursing home, but that she had experienced a variety of settings, all related to her financial status.

"They'll Never Get Me Like the Ones Upstairs"

As a private industry, nursing homes are embedded in a market, and there is a stratification among homes depending on how much is paid for residency.[1] At the luxury end of the spectrum there are life-care arrangements in which one turns over an estate in exchange for housing and medical services. Though I did not work in such a setting, I heard a fascinating description of them one day on the way to work. A woman in her mid-thirties sitting next to me on the bus struck up a conversation. Seeing the white uniform, she asked, "Are you a nurse?"

"Well, not exactly," I responded. "A nursing assistant, the kind that work in nursing homes."

"Really?" she perked up, "My grandmother just went into one." She named a home highly praised in the magazine article, reputed to be luxurious and expensive. "It's the kind of place where you give over your estate and they take care of you for life. She had money, so they took her in."

"Oh, and how does she like it?" I asked.

"Well, she's ninety-three, and started to get worried about living alone. Now she likes to joke that she has joined a Jesus movement."

Knowing that this home was affiliated with a religious organization, I inquired, "Oh? Is that because it's quiet or because they say prayers there?"

"No," she responded with a grin. "Because it's like what Jesus said to the apostles: they tell you to give over everything you have and follow them."

Very few older people belong to the social class for whom this arrangement is an option, because the initial investment requires the kind of estate only a few possess.[2] A more typical pathway into nursing home life is to enter after being discharged from a hospital. Some come in for a relatively short stay while in rehabilitation. If they qualify, Medicare will pay most of the cost for a short while.

The twin pillars of long-term health care policy in the United States, called Medicare and Medicaid, were set in motion in 1965. Medicare is a federal program, part of which is designed for hospital stays and short-term, rehabilitative periods in nursing homes; it has limits in terms of time, place, and sickness. Medicaid is funded in part by federal taxes, in part by state taxes. Eligibility varies somewhat, especially regarding the amount of assets that can be retained by resident and spouse. In every state citizens are eligible for this system of nursing home reimbursement only after they have become nearly impoverished.

I met people who had lived under both public programs.[3] As staff, visitors, and residents walked by John Kelley's private room in the nursing home in the wealthy suburb, he often beckoned them, "C'mon in and sit down." John, seventy-one, had been determined eligible for Medicare after a stroke left him partially paralyzed. Medicare assistance is not determined by one's resources. John had some savings, and he was covered under a private insurance program that supplemented his Medicare expenses.[4] Flowers and greeting cards adorned the windowsills on these floors, some brought from the hospital, some newly sent in with best wishes for a speedy recovery. John had his own color TV and telephone; and, what he seemed most proud of, "I've got my own power of attorney." He felt secure in his ability to sign his name and continue to manage his own accounts, and he was confident that he would leave soon. "They'll never get me like the ones upstairs," he would say. The ones upstairs were the ones who had to stay and who no longer had such autonomy.

Down the hall lived Barbara Mahan, in short-term residence. At eighty-six, she broke her hip in a fall. After a hospital stay her physician thought it best that she spend some recovery time in a nursing home. She reluctantly agreed, as she told the story, on the condition, that she be allowed to be there with the services of a "private." Ina Williams from the coffee shop and many others did this service as their second job. Working through an agency that absorbed half of their hourly pay, privates tended solely to the person who hired their services. When Barbara was leaving the home after a two-month stay, she paid tribute to her private nurse: "I'd probably not get out of here if I hadn't had her with me." At the time it was too early for me to understand her analysis, but there was no denying the fact. She did leave, unlike the vast majority who lived in these homes.[5]

Some on this floor did not leave because of the severity of their illnesses. They were in the short-term, skilled-care wings not for rehabilitation but to spend their last days there. In several of the rooms on these Medicare and private-pay floors there were people in comas, with intravenous and oxygen tubes plugged into them to keep them alive, some who died only weeks after admission.

While these floors were designated as Medicare and private-pay sections in the posh suburban home, not all of the people who lived there were accepted for Medicare benefits. Jim McKeever suffered from an inoperable brain tumor and was classified as not capable of rehabilitation and therefore not eligible for Medicare. His family had to pay to keep him in the home. His wife, Betty, came to tend to him every day. She was shocked, as many were, to find out how little Medicare covers for nursing homes. At the rate of nearly a hundred dollars per day charged by this home, Betty was enraged to find that by the end of Jim's six-month stay their life savings were almost gone. She had lost her husband as a result of the tumor and her savings as a result of public policy.

Even for the people who had been accepted into the federal reimbursement categories, security was far from guaranteed. While Medicare covered most of their current bills, many residents expressed nervousness, feeling the economic ground shake underneath them. Medicare has time limits; coverage lasts less than six months.[6] In the private-pay wards, residents expressed fears that they might be moved after this time to a different ward or even asked to move out of the home.

Grace DeLong trembled when she spoke about this economic path. She had fractured her hip and, with no one at home to look after her, entered the nursing home for what she thought would be a matter of weeks. But after five months, with her Medicare limit fast approaching, she was still there: "My damn hip won't heal." She knew that because of her hip and crippling arthritis she would need more time before she could manage "on the outside." Each day when I helped her into the wheelchair to head toward the day room, she clutched her purse and made sure her bankbook was in it. Frequently she took out the book and studied it. She had worked as a secretary most of her adult life and now had between $20,000 and $30,000 in savings.

Grace complained loudly, sometimes screaming in her fear that this money would be drained from her. She lived on a floor where she had seen it happen to others. In the public rhetoric of the day, she was facing what was euphemistically called spend down, a process in which one must reduce assets to near destitution before becoming eligible for Medicaid. She often screamed, "I've got to get out of here soon, or I'll never get out of here." As I saw happen on two occasions, a passerby or professional who had only fleeting contact with her could quickly interpret these screams as senile behavior. Yet anyone who was around her day after day knew that these protests were lucid and rational claims against a social policy within which she felt trapped.

Mrs. Mosby, who shared a room with Grace, once summarized the phase of spend down. "You can lose everything you have before you know it," she observed. Personal resources were depleted within months, and residents became paupers, dependent for the rest of their lives on public aid. Some had to endure the pain of sitting in the home knowing their spouse or children were going nearly broke. Others were too confused mentally to understand the process, so their families had to manage financial negotiations on their own, paying the bills to the caretaking industry.

Many residents had no recourse but to stay in a nursing home. Some, like Grace, maintained their own homes for a while in the hopes of returning to them, but most had to sell them to pay the bills. Some were confused and unable to cope with life on their own, others were sick and frail and needed continuous care. Still others simply got caught in the vicious cycle: they ran out of money, then had to stay because they became dependent on the state. Most

entered from a combination of frailties that could have stabilized over time. But although their physical and psychic
states may have stabilized, their financial state did not.

Miss Black pinpointed the process.[7] A teacher of math-
ematics for seventeen years, she was in her late seventies
when we met. She was confined to a wheelchair, having
lost the use of her legs because of severe diabetes. Sitting
in the hallway, she occasionally burst into fits of anger directed at her living conditions. "Where's my Social Security?" she would yell. "They've taken it away from me and
I want it back! Get me the administrator immediately!"
She had the commanding voice of someone who had directed students for many years, and she knew exactly how
to gain the attention of staff. At least twice the administrators personally came to her room in an effort to calm her.
They explained as politely as they could that her checks
now went directly to the nursing home, not to her. They
also told her that the Social Security payment constituted
only a part of what it cost her to live in this home, the
remainder coming from public aid in the form of Medicaid.

Their explanation did not satisfy Miss Black. She demanded to move beyond the logic of that answer. Her yelling continued until she wore out or was given a sedative.
These outbursts were recorded on her chart as "acting
out": "Miss Black was acting out again today."

She had lived through the spend-down policies of nursing home residence. Medicare was a start, but a short-term
one. Her health care needs outlasted it, and they continued
after the depletion of her personal resources. She became
indigent and dependent on the public aid transfers. Her
Social Security had provided the initial part of the payment
of her costs. Medicaid supplemented the remainder of the
costs only after her other pensions were exhausted.

"I'd Rather Call It Poverty Aid"

Medicare and Medicaid are different, but interrelated, programs. Women and men who lived out the everyday consequences of these programs addressed their connectedness. Anna Ervin, speaking of the "good old days," remembered when she first started her nursing home life, while briefly eligible for Medicare. "When I lived on the first floor, it was cleaner and I only had to have one roommate," said the former licensed practical nurse. "I was on Medicare then."

The sequence of Medicare, spend down, and Medicaid involves progressive phases toward becoming a pauper. Once while shaving Ralph Sagrello I asked him if he were on public aid. "Public aid?" Ralph snarled, pretending to spit on the ground. "I'd rather call it poverty aid."

Under the public aid programs, the states, partly with federal monies, pay the nursing homes a fee for each resident. The public money, in other words, goes to the corporation, not to the person in whose name it is transferred. Residents receive a personal needs allowance. In the homes where I worked this allowance was twenty-five dollars per month.[8]

Less than a dollar a day didn't go far. Mickey Watkins, for example, spent a fifth of his monthly fund in just one call to his out-of-state relatives on the pay phone in the hall. Flora Dobbins, who spoke of "the United Nations in here," always asked her friend who visited her for the same gift: an ice-cream bar. Public aid residents continually asked nursing assistants to buy things or bring them from home: a writing tablet and pen, a magazine, candy, a drink. One of the more common requests was for an alcoholic beverage—a joke, or half-joke, for alcohol was strictly forbidden.

Rather than attempting to catalogue what people on this strict budget needed or asked for, it may be more straightforward to identify what the public aid payment covered. During the mid-1980s the average state Medicaid payment was $52 per day per resident, $1560 per month, about $19,000 per year.[9] The home was responsible for nursing, meals, laundry, and linen. Medications and physicians' visits were extra. No list of unmet personal needs can describe adequately the kind of life this system leaves in its wake. Following some people through their day-to-day lives illustrates the process more vividly.

During one day of every month the air was charged with excitement, for this was the day the allowance, called the trust fund, was dispensed. There was excited talk for days prior to trust fund day about how the money was to be spent. When it came, lines formed at the pay phone in the hall; debts of a dollar or two were repaid; paper, stamps, and envelopes were purchased; and amid the sharing of cigarettes, coffee, and candy from the machines downstairs, conviviality reigned. "C'mon, let me buy you a Coke" could be heard again and again.

As the month proceeded, however, this allowance of less than a dollar a day also got spent down. It was hardly the middle of the month when Fern Parillo, eighty-two, started asking workers for quarters as soon as we walked in the door. Once, in an irritated, if ill-informed, moment, I scolded her: "Fern, how could you have spent your money already?"

As I kept walking and she kept following, this former manager of a household and mother of two snapped back indignantly, "I told my roommate I'd buy us both a Big Mac dinner if she'd bring them in for us. That was six dollars, seventy cents. Stamps, a tablet, a toothbrush, two phone calls, some smokes, and a cup of coffee downstairs everyday. And I paid back two dollars." Just as she had probably managed her household to the exact penny for many years, now she gave me an up-to-the-minute accounting of every cent of that trust fund allowance.

Before starting this research I had been under the impression that nearly all people in nursing homes were bedridden. In fact, many were up and dressed, walking around, and free to leave the building during certain hours. "Free" may not be the best word here, for many were penniless; such freedom is sometimes mistaken for vagrancy. I made this mistake several times. One day while walking to work I could see a woman off in the distance rummaging through the trash. Upon getting closer, I saw that it was June Popper, one of the residents in the home I was heading toward. I soon learned why she was exploring the trash. It was nearing the end of the month, and her trust fund was spent. She was looking for something she might use, trade, or sell. Nearly two thousand dollars had passed from state to industry that month in the name of her health care, and she was on the streets to beg and barter.

In the homes populated almost exclusively by public aid people, the police got involved occasionally, often bringing someone back for a transgression common to indigents: loitering, shoplifting, panhandling. At one point all residents were barred from a local church because some took money from the collection plate as it passed across their pew. Ralph Sagrello's analysis of public aid as poverty aid became clearer: these people were trying to make sense of the contradictions of their situations.

Joanne Macon and I met on the street twice, once when I first started the project, once after I was well into it. The first time she was a stranger who approached me as I was walking to work. She stood too close for comfort, mumbling something I could not decipher that sounded like "Hamissagodakoda?" I gave her some change and passed on, happy to be out of her range. In her earlier years Joanne had worked in a factory to help support a child and a husband, both of whom were now deceased. When her health broke down she moved quickly into poverty along the economic course toward public aid. Among the expenses not covered in this program were glasses and teeth. Joanne, then in her early seventies, would walk outside some afternoons, dressed in the plaid shirt, striped pants, and white socks that she had been handed that morning from the general pile of laundered community clothing. She would plot how to get a cup of coffee or a smoke or both. Though she hated doing it, she would muster the energy to approach strangers on the street. Without glasses she walked too close to people, and, with teeth in disrepair, her articulation was far from precise. Inside the home those who knew her understood her, but strangers on the street misunderstood as I did when she first approached to ask, "Hey, Mister, you got a quarter?"

If the private-pay residents were nervous about impending pauperization, that did not mean that being a pauper was a stable state. It brought insecurities of its own. Some were moved to different wings or floors when management wanted to make way for more Medicare or private-pay people, who could pay higher rates than people on public-aid transfers.[10] Helen View, sitting in her well-tailored wool suits, spoke of having seen this happen to her friends. A social worker from the state would approach a resident and say that another home had been found. About the administrators Helen once said, "I heard they don't much care for welfare bums." She spoke from experience; when her personal funds ran out she was moved to another wing.

Helen's circumstance embodied at least three characteristics of the economic course of nursing home life. One is that it is a process, a journey. I brought into the project the stereotype that one "ends up" in a nursing home, that "it's the end of the road," after which follows a stationary, if not stagnant, way of life, then death. Helen and others demonstrated that it is not always stationary but often involves movement initiated by forces beyond their control. One of the skills demanded of this life is a certain readiness to move: out of the hospital, into a home, out of one floor or room into another, out of a skilled wing to a custodial unit, and from one home to another, especially out of a private-pay facility into one that accepted public aid people. Martha Craig, a public aid resident, once described it: "You think you're in your last place, and you're not."

It is also a journey through social class, and a rapid one. Whether or not anyone had ever used the term *welfare bum,* the fact is that Helen View had lived most of her life as a member of a wealthy, propertied class. In nine years her life had changed so rapidly that she was now trying to cope in a personal economy of dollar bills and quarters. She was physically healthy and well preserved, no doubt the consequence of the privileges of her class, and not altogether weak or frail, despite her impairments and intermittent confusion. Rather, like many residents, she was a skilled survivor, someone whose seventy-nine years were likely to stretch on for many more.

This social class journey is traveled primarily by women. Surely there are men in nursing homes, but in reference to this long-term class process, it is probably less precise to use the term *people* than *women* and *men*. Statistics indicate that at any one time, over 80 percent of those who reside in nursing homes are women.[11] Women live longer than men, and throughout their lives their incomes are less than men's; thus pensions and Social Security are less, and the drain is quicker. They are less likely to have the social support of a spouse as the years go on, because they have themselves been the social support for ailing and retiring fathers and husbands, who pass on, leaving them dependent on partial pensions, then public programs.[12]

In addition, when one arrives at the public aid phase, the journey through social class is not yet over. Just as one does not end up in a nursing home, so the public aid phase is not the end of the road but the beginning of an economic pathway of deepening pauperization. The people living through the various phases of pauperization were not just sitting idly, looking backwards; they were speaking with concern about their futures as well.

A major change includes becoming part of generic public aid categories and trying to live out the consequences. One of the misconceptions that broke down for me was that nursing homes house the elderly. Indigent residents of nursing homes might be old or young, disabled, retarded, mentally ill, or some combination of these. To live the public aid life on these wards was to be among a collection of people drawn from any of these disparate backgrounds of infirmity and indigence. Pooled under the generic category of patient, the women and men in it had little idea and no control over who might be eating or sleeping next to them. Private-pay people did not have much control over their roommates either. But under public aid, people entered nursing homes from other channels, and not all who did were elderly.

Some young people had been in accidents and became incapacitated, or had been from birth. Long-term residence, therefore, can involve a change in the age of the group with whom one lives. Over the years Anna Ervin's disabilities stabilized, though she also moved away from the good old days toward poverty with the result that there was nowhere for her to go on the outside, and the more she lived among people who fit under the generic public aid categories. In her three-person room were a sixty-year-old former state hospital inmate who had been classified as retarded, and a thirty-year-old former school teacher paralyzed and left speechless from an automobile accident. Ironically, the more time Anna spent in this environment and the older she got, the less she lived in a home for the elderly.

Some were former inmates of state hospitals living out the consequences of the deinstitutionalization programs of the 1970s, moved from state hospitals to the community and then to nursing homes.[13] All were lumped together under these policies for the indigent, and as a result all were together on the same floor.

Sharon Drake, in her seventies, had been a waitress at one of the area's finest restaurants for twenty-five years. On her public aid wing, she frequently complained about Bill Slaughter, who harassed her by continually exposing himself to her. He never spoke, he just flashed and grinned. Bill, then in his late sixties, had not spoken most of his adult life. During all the years that Sharon waited tables Bill had been an inmate of the state hospital. At the time I met them, both were relatively healthy survivors, having lived through different phases of nursing home life, Sharon still wearing her jewelry from an earlier day, Bill still leering at her. They were destined to remain on the same floor in the same day room for years, collapsed together under a social policy that abstracted two common characteristics of their lives, disability and impoverishment, and corralled them into the same living space. It was as though people who lived there had only two social characteristics: they were indigent, and they were patients.

Still another aspect of the journey as time goes on is that it becomes more multicultural, at least in larger urban areas. From the administrative point of view it is logical that the homes located in poorer sections and populated by indigent people would be more likely to rely on immigrant workers, who provide cheaper labor costs for the industry. As the residents get older, and their medical condition stabilizes for a period of time, they are more likely to live in a public aid setting and more likely to be cared for by a staff of a race, country, and culture different from their own. They move, as Flora Dobbins observed, to places that are "like the United Nations in here."

Finally, to get to know these people was to see them living out a continual process of dispossession, not one that stopped at the point of their entry into public aid. There was a political rhetoric in the 1980s that public aid provided a safety net. Yet possessions were continually being lost and not replaced, having fallen through the large holes in the net. Joanne Macon, begging for a handout, went without her glasses first, and eventually without her teeth.

What sometimes initially appeared as crazy behavior emerged over time as rational, desperate attempts to guard what was slipping away. Fred Murray wore three layers of clothes, which was a source of continual contention with the staff, but he claimed they were all he had left, and he was not going to lose them. His empty closet bore out the truth of his claim. Helen Donahue slept with her one remaining pair of slippers under her pillow. One of the survival strategies that they developed was the guarding of what little they had, even as their closets and chests of drawers became emptier.

On my daily walks to work, seeing poor and homeless, old and young, people rummaging around, I clung for a while to the notion that residence in a nursing home must at least be better than living on the streets or in the fleabag rooming houses that dotted the city. That thought was on my mind while I was waiting for the bus one day when, from behind me, came the question asked by the young woman whose grandmother had joked that she had joined a "Jesus movement."

"Hey, you a nurse?"

I responded again, "Well, not exactly. A nursing assistant, the kind that works in nursing homes."

The response was to a woman in her seventies, sitting on a step near the curb. Unlike the people I was heading for, she was not freshly bathed nor dressed in laundered clothing; like them, she lacked some teeth and was looking for a handout. We sat together for a few moments, Martha Sugarman and I, and talked of nursing homes.

"You see that place over there?" she asked, pointing to a four-story building with windows partially covered with cardboard and a half-broken sign, "Bro dv ew Ho el." It was an old hotel that had become a rooming house advertising for boarders by the month or week. "That's where me and my friends live. You know what?" she asked, with a certain pride in her upturned eyebrows. "They ain't never gonna get us in a nursing home. We'll do anything to stay out."

As we said good-bye and I rode off on the bus, I had to come to grips with the fact that still another assumption of mine had just been challenged. Initially it had seemed self-evident that a place that offered shelter, baths, food, and medicine was by definition better than one where all of this has to be a continual matter of struggle. Surely, I had assumed, nursing homes are better than the streets, or a run-down boarding house. Now Martha, with that pride in her eyes that lingered as I greeted my first sleepy resident, had opened even this assumption up for debate.

"My Daughter Won't Come Near This Place"

That very day yet one more concept was disrupted in the sociological framework of the study—the place of families in the lives of the people who lived in these homes. A nurse from a foreign country had just finished a contentious encounter with a resident, and frustration showed on her face while she tried to make sense of this most confusing social organization.

"Oh, these people make me so mad," she said. "But there's one thing that makes me even madder—their families! If their families hadn't abandoned them, they wouldn't be here. In my country we don't even have nursing homes. Our families take care of their old."

She was expressing an idea that was widely shared, by people native to the United States and its immigrants— that people live in nursing homes because they have been abandoned by their families. It is an easy explanation, but like my early preconception that nursing assistants should just get a different job that pays more, it rests on oversimplification. Listening to the residents' everyday conversations about their families did not lead to the inference that they were abandoned. Just five people who lived on the same floor where this foreign nurse and I worked, selected almost at random, could challenge this notion.

Violet Shubert, 82, never married. Once or twice she mused what it might have been like had she done so. Mostly, what she spoke about, with fondness, were her parents. She lived on her own for a while, and when they became frail she moved back in with them, first helping her mother tend to her father, then taking care of her mother. After they both passed away, she went on living in the family home until, in her late seventies, she broke her hip. Eventually she began a nursing home life course which brought her to the public aid place where we met. Far from being abandoned by her family, Violet was its last remaining member.

So, it seemed, was Jane Fox, in her late seventies, but she had had a husband and two children. Her husband had died first, then her son. Her daughter lived in California, thousands of miles away. It was likely that she was not able to take her mother into her home—a guess that came from the cards on the bedside table that read, "Wish I could be there." Jane used some of her trust fund money each month to call her; her daughter could not call because personal calls could not be accepted on administration phones, and there was only the pay phone in the hall. Jane clearly derived emotional support from those calls.

Will Baumer's seventy-nine-year-old wife took care of him in their home until his condition of extreme mental confusion, her own failing health, and their meager resources brought that family to intolerable strain, and he started his nursing home life. She came three times a week, weather permitting. It was not clear whether he recognized her, but it was clear that she did not abandon him.

Down the hall, Helen Donahue, who opens the next chapter, talked to her family all day long, someone named John and someone named Mary Helen, a husband or son and a daughter. At eighty-eight, Helen, like Will Baumer, was confused; she circulated a good deal of the time in her own private reality. John and Mary Helen were certainly not in the room, but just as certainly they were there for her, and she spoke affectionately to these people she had apparently outlived. If she had heard someone say that her family had abandoned her, she might well have felt insulted.

One last example leads into the final theme of this chapter. Muriel DuMont had worked in some kind of government office. Three years before we met she had a partial stroke. Then eighty-two, she had observed the course of her friends' lives, with their progressive impairment of bodily functions, and realized that in the future she might need a situation of constant caretaking, which she did not want to impose upon her daughter. Soon after, from what I could infer from her comments as she sat in the day room during long summer evenings, she disposed of her resources. Yet it seems not to have been soon enough. The statute was that one must spend down resources fully two years before applying for public aid or the state could lay claim to these resources as the beginning of payment.

"You know, you have no financial privacy any more. You have to lay your finances out on the line," she once said in dismay.

It's probably a safe guess that Muriel did not dispose of her assets exactly within that two-year frame, and it's probably safe to assume that she gave them to her daughter, whose picture sat on her table. I was to learn nothing about their relationship, except for one comment Muriel offered: "My daughter won't come near this place," she once whispered. "She's afraid they'll start asking her questions, and grab the money."

To assemble these various snippets of life history leads to the conclusion that there is no single family type engaged in a single set of activities, like abandonment. There are innumerable family relationships, and people who lived and spoke of their families were living through its multitude of possibilities.[14]

Before dismissing altogether the notion of abandonment, however, perhaps we might look for another agent in this process. If Muriel's daughter was afraid to visit because of the policies that ruled the public aid system, which in turn drove a wedge through her own family system, perhaps it is not the family that abandoned Muriel, but the society, as a consequence of its social policies.

The public programs of the late twentieth century in the United States are, in administrative logic, two separate policies of payment, Medicare and Medicaid. But in the logic of their lived experience they are related and continuous: through spend down, one moves from one to the other. The experiences recounted in this chapter alter the image of Medicare and Medicaid from the two pillars of American long-term care to two interrelated peaks of a roller coaster. The process involves a distinct progression: the longer the stay in long-term care the more impoverished one becomes and the more unstable is one's environment. Along the way, poverty and sickness get collapsed into what is just called sickness.

The accounts offered by these residents suggest systemic links among the whole nursing home population, regardless of whether they live in a private-pay or a public aid situation. A continuity can be discerned between the public aid situation and that of the women and men who live at any one snapshot moment in more luxurious settings. They are not as distinct from one another as a structural view of rich and poor homes might suggest. While the residents of the plush, private homes are not dependent solely on their government, they are part of a conglomerate of people who are. Both private-pay and public aid residents spoke of the insecurities bred by these policies. The former, even amidst their momentary stability and relative luxury, were part of a population in a state of flux.

The experiences collected in the foregoing accounts indicate that nursing home care in the United States can involve not just *a* home but home*s*. It can mean moving through a series of situations, a maze of different wards, floors and homes, not "ending up" in a home, but traversing a course set out by pauperizing public policies. The people who lived in all these settings, therefore, engaged in a rumbling, unsettled life even when they were just standing still. They got up in the morning and moved through the day, often with the strength of determined survivors that probably characterized much of their earlier lives, or they would not have gotten this far.[15] They went along practicing skills of survival that younger people had yet to learn. Far from rest or retirement, what the foregoing stories displayed was turbulence.

To judge from these speakers, nursing home life was not an altogether static or passive existence, not just sitting in a chair or lying in a bed "doing nothing." Each person sat in a chair, or lay in a bed, or waited in a line, often appearing motionless, but actually moving and being moved through a social and political process.

Part Two
Forming the Gold Bricks

The first three chapters explored how nursing assistants and residents conduct their lives within the constraints of economic and social policies. So far I have hardly mentioned tending to or living with chronic sickness and frailty. The strategy has been to introduce these people not foremost in terms of sickness or the work of tending to it, but as members of a society, in order to establish some significant features of their day-to-day existence.

Chapters Four and Five go round-the-clock to convey a sense of every day and every night life in a nursing home, illuminated by comments and incidents that occurred during the course of my work shifts. Each chapter follows a daily sequence, from morning through afternoon, evening, and night, sometimes with leaps across the hours; and the various homes where I worked blend together. The round-the-clock sequence provides a framework to move from the actual talk of the people in the homes toward general themes. Each chapter concerns one basic element in how gray is made into gold. Chapter Four focuses on the lives of residents, Chapter Five on the work of nursing assistants.

4

"Why Can't I Get a Little Rest around Here?"

By 7:00 in the morning the work day was under way for the nurses, the nursing assistants, the cooks, and the housekeepers, and it was time for those who lived in the homes to begin their day as well. The four waiting nursing assistants learned our assignments this way: "Today you have beds 201 to 216, you have 217 to 232, you have . . ." and so on until all of the residents had been assigned. Despite the words, this did not refer to the beds we had to make but to the people who occupied them. The first task was to wake residents, help them up if they were scheduled to get out of bed, and prepare them for breakfast and medications.

This early morning regimen was the hardest part of the day for many nursing assistants, a source of continual jokes and complaints. It was difficult, too, for some of the residents, and they frequently fought against it. The first moments of the day, therefore, were often spent in conflict.

"Bed 201" was Irene O'Brien. "Morning, Irene, rise and shine. Let's go," was a typical reveille on the firing line.

"Oh . . . no . . . ," Irene mumbled, pulling the blankets over her face. "Work all my life waiting for retirement, and now I can't even sleep in mornings."

I fumbled for an explanation. This was like a hospital, I told her, or at least she and I had to follow the early morning regimen of a hospital. At 7:15 in the morning this made little sense to her or to me, so we always started the day in tension.

It started that way with Helen Donahue as well. "Oh . . . I don't feel like getting up today," she moaned forlornly after I nudged her two or three times. "Why can't I get a little rest around here?"

For Irene and Helen, neither of whom was bedridden, to stay in bed was simply not an option, and if I had let them it would have been failing at the job and cause for reprimand. As I quickly learned from the other nursing assistants, the trick was to engage each person in some kind of conversation, something personal if possible, to execute the task and minimize the conflict. With Helen Donahue this soon turned into a series of delightful episodes.

Helen was nearing ninety and visually impaired, so it was a long, slow walk down the corridor to the day room. Since there was plenty of time for conversation, I often asked her to tell a story about some earlier time in her life, in part to get her animated so that she would walk down the hall to the day room without a fuss. She laughed and paused to think of some tale. Frequently, when we got to the third room down the hall, she interrupted her train of thought to yell into the room, "Mary Helen, Mary Helen, let's go, time to get up now, time for school." Mary Helen was the daughter that she had had to rouse out of bed for many years. There seemed little sense in demanding that Helen come back to reality. It made for a much smoother exchange when I leaned into the room and chimed in with her, "C'mon, Mary Helen, if you don't get up, you'll be late." I was stepping outside of the present reality for a moment but, after all, I had just chided Mary Helen's mother with a similar warning—that if she did not get up she too would be late—and we were both still trying to make sense of that.

As the long walks continued down the hall, Helen sometimes came up with rich stories of the first years of the century. My favorite was from 1915, when an excursion steamer, *The Eastland,* sank after catching fire in the Chicago River. She recaptured in vivid images the screams of the people, the chaos of the makeshift fire engines, the heroics of the volunteers, each of which was part of a different story on a different morning, each recaptured with the excitement of a teenager who had watched the whole thing, remembered by an elderly woman now nearly blind. On those walks, my sense of what was real and what was mental confusion was already being disrupted, and it was not yet 7:30 A.M.

The hour before breakfast went by quickly for staff, if not for residents. Each of the four nursing assistants on the floor was charged with waking and preparing fifteen to twenty people, each with her or his distinct circumstances, moods, stories, and needs. Grace DeLong was difficult to work with because when getting into her wheelchair, she always insisted on packing up virtually all her possessions to take with her into the day room. Bankbook, purse, small radio, wool sweater, an expired membership card from the American Association of Retired Persons, a greeting card from her nephew, an extra pair of socks—they all had to go with her in what she called her little mobile home. The difficulty arose from the pressure of time. On the other hand, Grace was invaluable in getting the work accomplished, for she would prompt her two roommates to get up and sometimes was more successful than the nursing assistants.

When all of the people had finally been awakened, dressed, and, if possible, helped into the day room to await breakfast there was, if the morning had been without unintended incident, a brief lull before the 8:00 A.M. breakfast trays arrived. It was then that I would look out to a roomful of forty to fifty people sitting in their assigned spots and notice, for the first of several times in the day, two characteristics of the group that continued as puzzling issues all my stay in the nursing homes. The first was to be seen, the second heard.

The first was the gender character of the group. The terms I had read and used to describe the people who lived in this setting had not accounted for what I saw. Residents, patients, people—all these collective categories are genderless. Yet in the day room those mornings, as in most homes throughout the industrialized world, the vast majority of those who sat there were women. This fundamental social fact could not be ignored.[1]

The second mystery was something heard or, to be precise, not heard. The room was filled with quiet. Forty women and ten or twelve men sat assembled together, not talking. In the few moments before breakfast that was easily understandable, with people still half-asleep in their morning daze. Yet frequently the same overarching quiet could be noted as breakfast went on, and after breakfast as well. It was present during the lull between breakfast and activities, and before and during lunch, and sometimes all day long. It was an intriguing sound of silence, what seemed like an absence where one might expect the presence of conversation, during mealtime for instance. It took several months of experiencing it at more than one home before I was able to piece together some ideas about this mystery.

There was little time for speculation on the issue before the trays arrived for those forty or so who did not go to the main dining room for meals. Indeed, it was a rare morning when waking people and the time for serving breakfast trays did not overlap. Accidents of incontinence or other unplanned episodes of sickness needed attention, one or two who refused to come to the day room had to be coaxed or forced, an argument between residents had to be adjudicated, a new admission had to be given orientation—any or all of these could make eight o'clock come too early for the nurses and nursing assistants.

By contrast, it never seemed to come too early for residents. From the way they stared at the elevator door waiting for the trays to appear there could be no doubt that their overriding concern at that moment was hunger. In the language and records of the authorities who directed food production, there was little room to question its validity: three meals and two snacks were served each day, all scientifically designed for adequate nutrition. From the standpoint of living out this scheduled and documented design, the result was often hunger.

This morning hunger was expressed pointedly in the Australian film *Captives of Care,* a film about living in a hospital for handicapped persons, in which actual residents have the major speaking parts. One resident explained it clearly, "They give us our three meals all right, but they don't understand that it's fourteen or fifteen hours between the close of dinner and the beginning of breakfast. By the time breakfast comes around, we're weak with hunger." This explanation made the silence during these moments slightly less mysterious. Most were waiting and watching for the first sign of the elevator doors to open so they could break their fourteen-hour fast.

After breakfast, vital signs were taken—blood pressure, pulse, temperature, and respiration. They were taken frequently during the day, so it was easier over time to understand why the proper procedure had been drilled so repetitively in school. "Vitals" is a word drawn directly from

the Latin word for "life." In medical settings, ~~bodily func-~~
~~tions are defined as vital, and they are measured and re-~~
~~corded~~ as life signs.

Many people had identical vital signs day in and day out
for the years of their residency, as their charts indicated.
When residents lined up for the procedure, it was often a
time for levity, for over the months and years many had
built up repertoires of jokes that mocked the process and
set it off more as a ritual than a requirement of health care.
It was a rare morning that I did not head for the charts to
record the day's vitals with an inner smile, reflecting on,
for example, Irene O'Brien's feigned excitement—"I went
up a whole point today, wow!"—or Jack Connelly's favorite crack as he rolled up his sleeve, "I guess you got to
make sure I'm alive again today, huh?" "Vital" might have
come to mean many things, like emotional state, personal
biography, or social environment. Here, because everyday
life was molded into a hospital environment, ~~vital meant~~
~~the physical survival of bodies.~~

After the vitals were taken, they were recorded. This
task was a welcome relief for nursing assistants, for it was
the first chance to sit down after several hours of standing
and bending and running around. It was also an opportunity to become acquainted with the residents through their
formal documentation. Vitals were recorded in the formal
record of residents' existence in the home—the chart. This
set of documents began at the first moment of one's residency and was continually updated all through the day,
week, and month by various health care personnel. The
specific sections of the charts varied slightly in the homes
where I worked, but they always contained at least the
following eight sections: diagnosis, drug regimens, consultations with medical specialists, bath and bowel record,
restraint and position sheet, social and medical history, vi-

tal sign record, and nursing notes. In one home the head nurse urged the nursing assistants, "Get to know the patients better by reading their charts as much as possible." To get to know them better through the charts was to get to know them primarily through their sicknesses and medical care.

Interspersed in these records were bits of information about personal histories that served as jumping-off points for conversations while the assigned tasks proceeded. This information was especially helpful during the intimate contact that was next on the agenda: showers or bed baths.

A midmorning walk into the dayroom where most of the residents had been kept since breakfast was again a walk into a notable absence of conversation, even as thirty or forty sat in their assigned places, some with heads slumped over in sleep. By now it was not silence, however, since one of the staff had turned on the television, and the game shows or soap operas were blaring away, with some residents watching them. When a particular person was notified that it was her or his time for a shower, one-to-one relations began. The collective non-talk so characteristic of the day room gave way to conversation, and an initial element of the puzzling quiet began to unfold. While it may have been a silent collectivity, in one-to-one encounters these women and men had a lot to say.

Sometimes the conversations that followed were not pleasant. "I've taken baths all my life, and I gave them to all my children," Marian Gregg used to retort. "Why do I have to be told when to do it now?"

When Marjorie McCabe was told that it was time for her regularly scheduled shower, she got up with reluctance. "You keep washing me this often and pretty soon there's not going to be anything left of me."

"Three times a goddam week. Three times a goddam week!" Margy Anderson began, before her convulsive emphysemic cough overtook her in this moment of agitation. "Soon I'm not going to have any skin left!"

Trying to change the subject I once asked Mrs. Anderson, "Do you prefer to be called 'Mrs. ' or 'Miss?' "

" 'Mrs.,' my boy," she chuckled. "I've never been missed!" And it was off to the shower to begin the cleaning and to converse about her twenty-two years as a furniture saleswoman.

"I Gotta Get Going"

As time went on, such conversations challenged another image I carried into the research—that what was being lived in nursing homes were lives of passivity. I had thought of residents as on the receiving end of human activity, acted upon rather than acting. The training had reinforced such an image, with its focus on what we as caregivers were to do for them, the patients. The charts reinforced the same image. Mrs. Gregg's records had only a fleeting reference to the fact that she had mothered for twenty-five years, and Mrs. Anderson's had no mention at all of the saleswork that characterized her entire working life. Instead, their charts, the formal record of their membership in this organization, named them in terms of sicknesses and diagnostic categories. Everything that followed from this first page was about what health-care goods and services were rendered to them, about what was done to them, not about what they themselves did in the home or what they had done before arriving there.

It can easily appear as a passive existence to outside observers, as it had to me in the early days of the work. A quick visit to most day rooms will yield a snapshot image of people just sitting and is likely to convey the sound of silence. Getting to know the residents, however, dissolved that notion. From the conversations, even from the whispers, grunts, and babbles of those who seemed less coherent, my image of passivity gradually transformed into one of some activity. My research questions soon turned away from issues like "What can 'we' do for 'them?'" That very question contains within it the seeds of reinventing passivity, with its "we" as the active ones and "them" as the objects of action. I began to wonder "What is it that they are doing?" then "By what criteria does it come to be viewed as doing nothing or just sitting?" Ultimately, these questions came to center on one issue: "What kind of human activity does it take to live in a nursing home?"

Hazel Morris was one of the people who did not spend her days just sitting. Hazel was the first person I helped into the shower on certain days. In her tennis shoes she roamed all over the floor, from her room to the day room and up and down the halls, sometimes quite rapidly. "I gotta get going," she said when I caught up with her. With her full head of black hair and robust energy, I took her age to be about sixty-five—until the second time I assisted her to the shower. On that occasion her wig fell off; she was bald. An African-American woman with three children, the oldest of whom was herself sixty-five, Mrs. Morris was in her early nineties.

The chart labeled her a wanderer, which meant that her roaming was to be seen as a manifestation of her disease, Alzheimer's. She shared her room with three other people and did not like staying there, nor was she content sitting in the day room, so around and around she walked. To judge from her specific direction and comments, where she wanted to wander was out of the place. She headed for the door at every opportunity.

While the chart noted this wandering tendency in more

than one place, it did not note that the shower was assisted by a man. Yet this gender difference permeated our interaction. As I blushingly proceeded to help Mrs. Morris, she seemed to sense my embarrassment and attended to it gracefully with questions like "You're new here, aren't you? How do you like the place? Don't worry, you'll get used to it."

It is not as though it was planned that a man should give women showers. What was so shocking during the first weeks, however, was that it was not planned that a man should *not* give them. It was as though, given the age differences, the available labor, and the dictates of the shower schedule, gender did not matter. It did matter, as several residents observed. Sometimes they would make sexual remarks, tell a joke, even venture an overture, if not a serious one.

"How ya doin' in there?" I asked Mrs. Ryan as she showered.

"There's only one thing I want from you, baby," this eighty-eight year-old fired back, with a twist of voice that left no doubt about the innuendo.

Maggie Kuhn, founder of the Gray Panthers, said in a public address just before her eightieth birthday that as far as she could determine, "Sexual desire doesn't stop until sometime after rigor mortis sets in." [2] Shower time confirmed this observation more than once, though never in an overtly tense way, and almost always in a way that mitigated the embarrassment with humor, as Hazel Morris had done with poise in the face of this institutional insult. Nevertheless, the entire interaction was made asexual when the encounters were entered into the records. Shower given. Check. The documentation procedures, which drove us into those delicate encounters in the first place, now rendered them invisible.

Not surprisingly, many men residents expressed relief when a man was assigned to tend to them. They had had to become accustomed to being tended by women, since almost all nursing assistants were women. Generally, though, men seemed to appreciate men, at least in domains like shaving. Resident Lito Esparza thought there should be many more men around. "They won't let me shave myself because they're afraid I'll cut my face. But look at it!" he muttered, while scratching various cuts on his cheek. "Women don't know how to shave a man."

There was not much time to pursue conversation in any given cleaning encounter, since eight or ten people were on the morning schedule. Between showers there were others in the day room waiting to be assisted to the toilet. Many needed help not only because of their own lack of mobility but because they were unable to move from the chairs in which they had been placed after breakfast. They had been secured in the chairs by restraint vests. In effect, these functioned as the opposite of a vest, which is by definition a piece of clothing that opens at the front and gives freedom to the arms. These garments were tied behind the chairs and made escape virtually impossible, even though many residents spent much of their day in that effort. Anyone who tried and failed to get out of the restraint was, by the time a nursing assistant arrived for the trip to the toilet, in a state of disarray, with the vest wrapped around shoulders and neck, half in, half out of the chair. Sometimes the disarray was total: chair, vest, and person all tipped over.[3]

Nursing assistants had to snatch time when they could to take people to the toilet, and the time did not always coincide with residents' bodily needs. Often an accident happened, and a nursing assistant arrived after the fact. Yet this was not considered an organizational disruption, nor did it mean that messes would be on the floor, for most people were secured with a diaper first thing in the morning. The toilet trip included replacing the diaper, returning the resident to her or his chair, and making the restraint vest secure.

"Nurse, Nurse—are you my nurse today?" Bernice Calhoun beckoned, "Hurry, I've got to go!"

One of us would yell back from across the room, "No, Bernice, Laina is assigned to your section today. You'll have to ask her to take you." Bernice already knew that, but she had developed a timing and a way of asking that at least half the time one of us yielded to: "Well, all right, here I'll take you, but let's be quick about it."

"No problem, you don't have to worry about me," she smiled wryly, proceeding to strike up a conversation, which had been at least part of what she wanted in the first place.

Though we did not have to worry about Bernice, by now, about 10:30, we did have to worry about filling in the Restraint and Position sheets in the charts. It was a Board of Health directive that for each person these had to be completed and signed every two hours of the twenty-four hour day. For the bedridden this involved the crucial gesture of turning them to one of three rotating positions so as to make at least a formal attempt at circumventing bedsores. For about half of the people on the floor it meant noting that they were "up with restraints." "Up" meant out of bed, but the only real up was there on the records; in actual practice it meant down, that is, secured into the chair. In writing this into the records down became up, just as tied from behind became vest and the person a bed. It was difficult at first to learn these administrative terms, when the meanings seemed so firmly rooted in their opposites.

Active Range of Motion, known by its acronym AROM,

was a program of exercises conducted in the late morning. It was mandatory for every resident who was up to participate. Conducted most often by the activities director, substituted occasionally by a nursing assistant, it involved a set of hand, arm, and neck exercises usually timed to music. The leader was likely to elicit only varying degrees of participation. Some residents were asleep in chairs; a few were absorbed in TV, a book, or a crossword puzzle, and they resented the interruption. A few were frustrated that their infirmities allowed them only limited engagement in the exercises, and some were insulted by the whole procedure. "I don't know why they make me do this foolishness," Mrs. Karlaski griped. "It's not my arms that need therapy, it's my legs." Despite these reactions, AROM was conducted twice daily, once in the morning, once in the evening, six days a week. It was over by about 11:20, forty minutes before lunch.

For residents there was a lot of time for which activities were not planned. At first it seemed that they spent such time just lying in their beds or sitting in the chairs. As I got to know them, however, their everyday lives became more complex than this image of passivity might indicate.

Grace DeLong sat in her little mobile home attending to painfully arthritic hands. When there was time during the late morning a nursing assistant cleaned the brace that kept her fingers from clenching inward and wiped the perspiration that had accumulated. Grace seemed continually engaged in a relationship with her hands—one of struggle, quite unlike those who take their painless, working hands for granted. She tried to make light of her shooting pain, in part to instruct the staff how to deal with each hand. The pain was so much a part of her existence that her hands took on a life of their own. "Watch the baby, watch the baby!" she admonished when we got near her left and more troublesome hand. "You know she doesn't like to be disturbed at this time of day."

Robbie Brennan, 46, liked rolling his wheelchair around, but sometimes his paralyzed foot fell to the floor, immobilizing him, and he would spend a lot of time trying to lift it. He insisted on going to the toilet by himself, an activity that could take up to an hour while he struggled to position his body in and out the chair. He understood the workings of his body and had to correct the staff when they did not.

David Forsythe wandered around, glancing into the ashtrays for leftover cigarette butts, then turned to a staff member to plead, "Hey, give me a cigarette, will you please?" Often his monthly allowance had run out, so his nicotine dependency was compounded by his financial dependency. He spent a lot of time in economic activity, in his case carrying on with the work of being penniless.

Elizabeth Stern, ninety, diagnosed with Alzheimer's disease, sat tapping her fingers on the table, sometimes raising them to wipe her face, for she cried a lot while sitting there. It became evident eventually that her crying had a focus.

"What's wrong, Elizabeth?" a staff person might ask.

She looked up and asked from some distant sphere of thought, "Are we going to the funeral?" Then she stood up as though en route. "He was a very good man, you know." Elizabeth was still actively grieving for her husband.

"No, no, he's gone now, Elizabeth. Lunch will come soon."

She was confused about time and place, but she knew something about grieving: "I'm still in mourning, you know. You think it's going to get easier as time goes on, but for some it gets harder. I'm one of those. I miss him more than ever."

These residents were active in their own way, like most others, with their physical, economic, and emotional wants and needs. While there were some people who seemed completely out of consciousness, for many more than I ever imagined, living in the home began to appear less and less like sitting doing nothing.

Next door to Elizabeth Stern, Mrs. Herman, nearly blind, sat at the side of her bed, waiting for someone to orient her, as with "How are you today, Mrs. Herman?"

"Not bad. Is it day or night?"

"Day."

"Oh good." With that she stood up and reached for the washcloth and towel that she always kept neatly folded within reach. She taught the staff something about how to ask "How are you today?" At first I said it too loudly. She snapped back, "I'm blind, you fool, not deaf!" Later she instructed, "It's not that I can't hear you, it's that I can't understand you. You don't speak slow enough. Most people around here talk too loud to the blind."

Many mid-mornings Mrs. Herman reached out her hand, palm down. At first it seemed that she was reaching for support. But when I put my hand under hers, change dropped out. "Here, get me a cup of coffee on your break, will you?"

"Sure, but there's sixty-five cents here, Mrs. Herman, and coffee is only fifty."

"I know. The rest is a little tip."

Her gesture presented a dilemma. It was against the institutional rules to accept money from the residents, but it was an insult to her not to do so. I accepted, more gladly all the time, for it became increasingly clear that the rule was part of a larger organizational ethos many struggled against: that the people who lived in this institution were not there to give; they were there only to receive.

Photographs that feature old, frail people in nursing homes frequently portray caregiving through pictures of hands. Typically, the hands of the caregiver are on top of those of the resident. In day-to-day operations, both parties sometimes had their hands on top; both gave as well as received.

Many were involved first and foremost in their own caretaking. Grace DeLong taught us how to situate her in the wheelchair, how to get the sand out of her eyes, how to adjust the hand braces, how to place the bedpan. In her jovial yet commanding manner, she was an active participant in her care. And she was fond, as well, of getting us out of her way. "I'm fine now that I'm in the chair. You go tend to the other girls. I can take care of myself." Moreover, she tended to her somewhat confused roommate, especially in waking her, talking her through getting dressed, and guiding her down the hall.

In fact, many took care of fellow residents. "Rose," yelled the charge nurse from across the room, "take care of Georgia, will you?" That meant getting Georgia Doyle's shoes off the table, a habit she had picked up in the course of her senility. Rose Carpenter tended to Georgia, coaxing her slowly, knowing well her capacities, often able to deal with her better than the staff could. This involvement in caretaking was a logical extension of the earlier lives of these women. Grace and Rose had raised children and taken care of husbands, one of whom was in a deathbed for nearly two years. Mrs. Herman liked to remind everyone that she had been a field nurse for many years as well as a wife and homemaker. Their orientation and skills at caretaking work did not abruptly change in the last part of their lives, even if the institutional definitions of them had.

This orientation extended into observing and caring for staff as well. Part of the activities of surviving in this environment seemed to involve studying the staff. "Tomorrow's your day off, isn't it, Tim?" asked Bernice Calhoun.

"Yes, how did you know?"

"Oh, I know everybody's day off," she chuckled.

"How's your mother?" Irene O'Brien once asked, "I heard she was sick." It was true, although I had not told her.

"You're new here, aren't you?" asked a resident from another floor, who made it her business to know every staff person.

Many could account precisely for the staff who came and went. On my last day of clinical training a man who often sat in the hallway pulled me up short. As I brushed by him I tossed off the cliché, "Hey, Roger, see you later." But this was where he lived, and he knew I was just passing through. "No you won't," he retorted coldly. "Don't tell me you will."

When residents got to know staff, they often expressed interest in and concern for them. Rose and Irene both worried aloud about nursing assistants' overwork and high blood pressure, and they urged one of the cleaning women to find other work, knowing that the constant exposure to disinfectants was making her sick. At the end of a day as I slumped in a chair, Fern Sagrello put her hand on my shoulder and advised, "You know, you're too skinny. You should eat more." Hazel Morris, diagnosed with Alzheimer's disease, had not lost her capacity to evaluate nursing care. "You see that one," she observed, pointing to one of the nursing assistants, "she's too rough on these girls." Pointing to another, she said, "But look at her. She's kind. I can tell by the way she washes their faces."

In addition to involvement in caretaking, part of the efforts of residency involved clinging to some benchmarks of time and place, not an easy task amid such repetitive monotony. "Is this Wednesday?" Laura Blumberg asked as she sat waiting for lunch. Volunteers often came in on Wednesday to offer a bake sale. Notwithstanding the large calendar at the entrance to the floor where activities and birthdays were posted, the days folded into one another, so that special strategies of concentration were needed to keep track of them. For Mrs. Blumberg Wednesday meant the bake sale, and the bake sale meant it was Wednesday. Questions about what day of the week it was were voiced by staff too. It seemed a particularly odd measure of reality orientation when a psychologist or social worker tested residents by asking them what day of the week it was. Nursing assistants used to joke about how lucky we were that they never asked us the same question.

"That's the One Thing You've Got to Learn around Here — to Wait"

When members of the floor began to assemble in the day room for lunch, and the minutes dragged along, silence descended on the room once again, and eyes turned toward the elevator that would bring the trays. Marjorie McCabe, seventy-two, who had been a housewife and part-time singer in earlier years, gave the lie to the apparent passivity. "C'mon, will you? Let's get lunch up here!" she urged.

"Just wait a minute, will ya, Marjorie?" someone responded.

"Yeah, wait," she muttered. "That's the one thing you've got to learn around here—to wait."

Her observation was revealing not just with regard to the continual waiting endured by so many, but also in the emphasis on learning to wait. True enough: one had to learn the skills and efforts required to practice this life of patienthood. Once when Marjorie was handed her lunch tray, she thanked the server, then turned almost immediately to her neighbor at the table and said, "You know, I get so tired of saying 'thank you' all day long."

People had to learn to eat on schedule food that had been planned and prepared elsewhere. If the butter was missing, the coffee cold or the milk warm, they had to learn the chain of command to request corrective action.

"Nurse, nurse . . . I didn't get any hot dog in my bun."

"Nurse, nurse . . . got any second helpings?"

"Just wait a minute, will you" was the regular response from nursing assistants, themselves enwrapped in a tight chain of command and having little say in the production of meals, or in the number of people hired to help serve them. People learned to stop asking and to eat what was available. Not to eat meant not only waiting until the next meal but risking being charted as one who refused to eat. Such a label was not looked upon kindly, and force-feeding was not beyond the powers of the organization.

On the other hand, many learned to take delight in the food, and for some it was the high point of the day. William Argyle smiled as the jello slid down, a soothing relief in the midst of his speechless, post-stroke days in bed. Jennie Carver's eyes lit up when she talked about the holiday dinners. "If you two are still here at Christmas," she told a pair of nursing assistants, "wait till you see what we have. Turkey, stuffing, cranberries, the works!"

Meanwhile, there were lessons to learn on how to carve out some creativity and social life. Sharon Drake dove into her novels, among them the six-hundred-page *Woman of Substance* that she was reading when I met her. She was always looking for sweepstakes contests to enter, and she spent much of her trust fund on stamps for them. Her constant companion, Mary Reynold, pored over crossword puzzles and her Bible. Some maintained an interest in conversation or in the television, which was on all day. Many appeared to curl into their own worlds, sometimes nodding off. A woman I met in a home in Switzerland, Tina Keller, a resident who was also a psychiatrist, summarized the action that may often be behind what appears like a passive life. "I spend much of my time in here," she observed, "learning how to *not* do."

Some actually worked for the places where they lived— not that their work was recognized as such. Sonia Franklin delivered trays to some residents, and she picked them up and cleaned them afterwards. Every day Marian Hughes gathered charts to take to the clinic for those who had appointments. Peter Olson used to sit out in the lobby, especially in warmer weather, to stop errant residents from wandering out the door, and he was quick to notify the nurses should someone stray too far. Paul Morris emptied the wastebasket regularly.

"Is there anything I can do for you?" I asked Paul before I realized what this work meant to his sense of self.

"Yes," he fired back indignantly. "You can get out of my way. I've got work to do."

David Forsythe, like many, wanted to work. "You know, I used to help in the kitchen at the halfway house where I lived. Do you think if I asked they might let me help with the dishes here?" The answer was no. Over time he was to learn that whatever he did, it was not to be considered work. His reason for being in this institution was to be worked on; it was the defining characteristic of his patienthood.

A planned activity often came along in the late morning to provide social stimulation. A paid staff person coordinated the bingo game or sing-along or seasonal party, often operating with very little budget. The success of these events depended largely on the participation of those who lived there, who frequently could be seen feigning excitement or appreciation to help carry them off as social events. Some participated happily, while others resented the intrusion of these activities, organized by younger people, into their lives.

"Now why would I want to go to a sewing circle," Katherine Stack protested. "I sewed for a living for too many years."

The social production of activities bore a certain resemblance to the social order of food and cleanliness. Directed by those in authority, who did not live there, activities were presented to recipients, those acted upon, who tried to make sense out of the social order that had been created elsewhere.[4]

One learned, too, to rest within the schedule. Nursing assistants were instructed to discourage morning naps. "They'll be up all night," was the rationale.

"But it's 11:30, and I got up at 6:30—I'm tired," Lorraine Sokolof countered.

Many slept a great deal, often not so much for needed rest as for something to do, some way of surviving, coping, working through this way of life. "Guess I'll go take a snooze," was the way David Forsythe posed the option. "Ain't nothing else to do."

After the noon meal, the dayroom tables were quickly cleared and residents returned to their assigned chairs so that the maintenance workers could mop and wax the floor. The nursing assistants washed residents' faces and assisted them in their toileting needs. The time of day was about to begin when visitors came in from the outside.

Who came to the homes in the afternoon varied from place to place, in some ways corresponding to the life course of the residents. Most of the visitors flowed through the short-term, rehabilitation sections of the private-pay facility to see residents they were related to personally or professionally. In this area, greeting cards and flowers decorated the windowsills, and private physicians would drop in for post-hospital checkups.

Long-term residents, especially those on public aid, could look forward on those afternoons chiefly to visits by volunteers. These were outsiders, mostly women, who came to participate in lunches, games, or parties coordinated by the activities director. Joanne Macon made clear just how crucial an organizational task these women performed in creating some social bonding and festivity.

"How was your birthday party, Joanne?" I asked one day.

"Oh," she responded glumly, "not too good. Nobody came."

"Nobody came?" I reacted with surprise. "What do you mean? At least fifteen people from this floor went down to the cafeteria to help you celebrate."

"Yeah, I know," she concluded, "but nobody from the outside came." No volunteers had attended. [5]

Visits by medical professionals were also likely to vary between the private-pay and public aid sections and homes. One physician, who visited once a month, explained his own bind under the Medicaid regulations to a group of nurses and nursing assistants who were busy lining up people and stacking their charts for him to sign.

Pointing to a section of public aid forms, he said, "If I want to come here more than once a month, I have to justify it on all these forms."

Public aid policies thus discouraged medical consultation, with consequences for everyday life. Physicians came rarely. When they did appear, it was in rapid-fire fashion, such that I occasionally wondered whether this was the firing line of health care that the vocational school owner had in mind on that first day of class. When the floor nurse was alerted that the doctor was on his way, she lined up the residents in a row of chairs and opened the charts in the order of the lineup. On a given day, the heart doctor came to check the hearts, on another the foot doctor to see the feet, and on a third the dentist to survey the teeth. They signed the charts, having visited the heart, the feet, and the teeth.

Helen Donahue had some thoughts on this kind of contact, for she had been within the public aid mode of medical consultation for three of her five nursing home years. She felt badly that her original doctor had recommended a nursing home merely on the basis of her failing vision and "a little arthritis." Once I asked her what she might have done differently now that she knew the consequences of that recommendation.[6]

She thought for a long time. "Well, I'd have gotten a second opinion, that's for sure."

She complained frequently about the 7:00 A.M. rising, having to wear a diaper, sit in the hard chairs, and endure the monotony. It must have been chiefly the monotony that made her say more than once, "I think I'm going to smother in here." When it came time for the momentary monthly interaction she had with the physician she seemed well aware that her situation was beyond the purview of this person passing through to certify her charts. Standing behind her, he would put his hand on her shoulder and ask, "Is there anything I can do for you, Helen?" Though she talked freely to us about her situation, her only words, as he stood behind her with his unsolicited touch, were "No, Doctor."

While Helen withheld her opinions from the physician passing through, she expressed them continually to Doris Quinlan, who sat next to her. In time, as I watched them share quiet comments off and on during the day, another dimension of my original perception of silence broke down. Not only did the people in the day room have a lot to say to the nursing staff, but quiet friendships bloomed throughout the room.

Helen and Doris regularly shared complaints, Doris seeming to have the most difficulty living with the constant odor of cleaning chemicals. Still, she responded graciously to passersby. During the afternoon, a visiting minister or student or someone else's relative might walk by her with a smile and ask in a voice sometimes too loud, "And how are you today, Doris?"

"Oh, fine, and you?" she responded, except that her response was different from the normal answer to this common question, not in words but in cadence and pace. Hers was extremely slow, a result no doubt from a combination of factors, her confusion, sedation, perhaps boredom among them. So her answer came back with pauses between the words. "Oh ... fine ... thanks, ... and you?"

Whatever the circumstances of her life, these visitors' smiles and snapshot courtesies were far removed from her ongoing situation, as that question usually is. When asked, she responded to the gesture politely with "Fine, thanks." But the passing visitors, living and talking at a faster pace than hers, unaccustomed to her slow, spacey manner, and full of assumptions about the institution, seldom saw it that way. More than once they could be seen walking away with practiced smiles, then shaking their heads with a vaguely focused sympathy: "Poor Doris, it's a shame she's so out of it."

"Out of it" was a slang phrase used by outsiders, visitors, and some of the staff to describe the mental state of residents in all the homes where I worked: "Tomorrow you have to work on the fifth floor, but there's nothing to it, they're all out of it up there." "You have to talk loud to Rita, she's completely out of it." "Most of our people were out of it before they got here." "Go wash Alice. She's so out of it she doesn't even know when her face is dirty."

Alice McGraw, eighty-nine, was indeed confused a good deal of the time and did get dirty. There was usually no one nearby to wash her chin, and some cereal or mashed potato may well have dribbled down unnoticed during the meal. She did not look in a mirror often, and perhaps did not know the food was there or perhaps did not care. Yet to all appearances, Alice was not an unhappy woman, for she sang to herself a good deal of the time. That is, when we first met I thought it was to herself that she was singing. The songs were mostly Irish melodies: "My Wild Irish Rose," "Galway Bay," and "When Irish Eyes Are Smiling." She wove in and out of coherence often enough to make clear that the audience for the songs was a fellow by the name of Jack or John, or maybe two fellows, that she had loved. She stopped singing abruptly during our initial encounters, but after a while kept on and got me to chime in with her, which made the whole cleaning procedure much easier for both of us.

Alice seemed still very involved in this relationship with John or Jack, even though death had most likely ended his life, just as Elizabeth Stern was sitting in the day room ever

ready to go again to her husband's funeral and Helen Donahue was calling to John and Mary Helen. The opening
line of Robert Anderson's play, *I Never Sang for My Father,* is "Death ends a life, but it does not end a relationship." In speaking out loud to people who were not physically present but with whom relationships were not yet
over, Alice and Elizabeth and Helen faced severe consequences, for they became widely known and treated as
"out of it."

When the clock finally crawled around to 3:00 P.M. and
the day shift drew near its end, we held our breath, hoping
that Nancy Block and Rita Plumber would be nice to us in
those closing minutes. Neither was happy with her situation, and both had a habit of expressing that unhappiness
to the nursing assistants in one of the few ways that was
available to them: purposely defecating. After the first two
or three times that one of them made a mess precisely at
ten minutes to three, we began to realize more was going
on here than the categorical "incontinence" that their
charts listed among their diagnoses. Incontinence, by definition, means out of control. The label did not account for
the sardonic laughter with which Rita followed her "accident," knowing it would keep one of us past three. Nor
did it explain Nancy's apology when she realized the
wrong person was going to have to stay late. "Whoops,
sorry," she grimaced.

Faced with the mess, but also with Rita's laugh or Nancy's apology, nursing assistant Vera Norris grudgingly advised me as she resigned herself to those extra ten minutes,
"I don't care what anybody says. I know these two. Don't
ever let anybody tell you either one of them is out of it."

Still, when they were nice to us, which was most of the
time, we joined the rest of the three o'clock departing

workers amid gleeful jokes. Edna Stanzone, who worked in the kitchen, had a favorite quip as we stood in line to punch the time clock: "There's only one out of it I want — out of here!"[7]

Back at my own home by 4:00 P.M., washing my uniform spotted with the day's soils and trying to soak away the day's odors, I realized that I was only visiting this life, not living it, either as nursing assistant or resident. I called up an image of Hector from the Philippines, who had asked me where else I worked, backing away from me with his curious "Oh?" Somewhere across town he was just starting his second shift of the day. I called up one as well of Yami from Nigeria, working up to the last day before giving birth "because I got to." Dorothy Tomason was still back there too, perhaps boasting to someone else about needing only four hours of sleep. While I was washing my uniform, these three were changing into their second one, ready to start their second shift or second job. And Alice McGraw, still singing to Jack back there, once again was challenging the validity of the slang. In the sense of Edna's joke, it was now I who was out of it, while Alice was still very much in it. For these four the day was not over. Its second phase was just beginning.

"I've Got to Have My Purse"

The 3:00 to 11:00 P.M. shift presented its own challenges for those living and working in this environment. At the nurses' station the charge nurse held her chart and queried the day crew regarding earlier events, "Anything happen today?" The answer she hoped for and usually received was "No, not much. Just a few cuts and bruises." This exchange was prompted primarily by a form, the Incident report, that had to be filled out if any accidents occurred for which the home might be liable. Everyone dreaded having to fill it out, so all were happy when what had happened could be reported as "not much."

Standing in the circle behind the nurses' station, in addition to the RN from the day shift, the LPN who took over for her in the evening, and the nursing assistants, was a social worker from the home's department of social services, who monitored the Medicaid records. During one meeting she admonished the new nursing assistants that "the more you get to know these people, the more you know there is always something for them to improve upon." She was concerned with individuals as cases, each with her or his file, and her advice went like this: "Miss Black was acting out again today. We've got to work on Eddie's socialization skills. Frances, the new admission, is having delusions again. I want one of you aides to keep checking her reality orientation, and try to calm her down." [8]

Frances Wasserman, in her early eighties, was sitting alone in her room, extremely agitated. She had just come from a hospital, having been in a different nursing home prior to that. My task was to make sure she had clean linen and to take her vital signs. The delusions of which the social service coordinator spoke were immediately apparent. She was calling out for Jimmy, who I later learned was her son, warning him not to go so far out from the shore or he would drown. She was very frightened, as though she were living through a nightmare or still sorting out a real-life event. Yet the source of her agitation was something different. In the transfer from hospital to the home she had lost her purse: "I've got to have my purse. I've never lost it before. Get me my purse. Please find it."

Riveted on this issue, she had little interest in cooperating during the vital signs procedure and even less in getting into bed in the middle of the afternoon. What she wanted was her purse. I assured her we would try to track it down, but it was a thin promise that she could see through. First I had to discharge my own medical tasks, so I took and recorded her blood pressure. It was a bit high.

Back at the nurses' station, the nurse said that she would call the hospital, but like me, had little hope that the purse would be recovered. Frances had traveled through a maze of hospital wards, to a discharge waiting room, an ambulance, a nursing home, perhaps all the time talking to her son Jimmy. It was impossible to identify the people along the way who may have perceived the delusions she was suffering but would not notice the absence of her purse, and at any rate there was no one who could retrace those steps for her. It was weeks before she stopped asking those in charge of her to keep looking for her purse. This loss no doubt contributed to the severe psychological decline that followed her admission.

Out in the day room thirty residents sat, some watching television, some sleeping, some gazing off into the distance, some fighting their restraints. As I was en route to the clean community laundry to sort the women's clothes from the men's, the charge nurse abruptly changed my task: "Go to 246 and make sure it's clean. His family is on its way."

The news was a relief to us. Fred Murray, sixty-four, was a bother to the staff because he insisted on wearing layers of soiled clothing. He eagerly anticipated Tuesdays and Thursdays when his daughter walked in with a bag of clean laundry. Until she came, he hid his soiled clothes or refused to take them off, fearing that he would lose them to community property. This behavior was annoying because of the smells and the odd appearances it created, but eventually it seemed less irrational. I was, I realized, en route to sort the clothing that represented precisely what he detested: clothes that were clean but no longer personal—for men a shirt, pants, socks; for women a top, a skirt or slacks, and socks. Socks were imperative; no one was allowed to go without socks. It was a Board of Health rule. Nursing assistants joked about being able to spot a nursing home resident on the street: "You can tell by the socks." Sometimes the clothes fit well, sometimes not; the overriding mandate was that they be clean. Though not exactly a uniform, neither did they resemble personal property, and it was to personal property that Fred clung.

He was one of the fortunate ones in that he had someone who would convey his complaints to the charge nurses. Sometimes his daughter's attempt to mediate would spill over into heated discussions, because his daughter, in questioning Fred's treatment—why this? why that?—occasionally threw out an indignant "I've paid out almost his whole estate to this home. How come I have to supply his laundry and cigarettes?"

Yet, like so many of the complaints discussed earlier, these issues were being raised with the charge nurse, who had little power to alter the situation. She had to mediate between everyday living and administrative mandates. She could no more say "Yes, it doesn't make any sense to me, either" than I could let Helen Donahue roll over and go back to sleep in the mornings. All she could say was what she had been instructed to say: "Everybody gets the same trust fund. If Fred spends all of his money during the month, that's his problem. What if everybody thought they could just be handed cigarettes all the time?"

She was charged with presenting the rationale that everybody should be treated alike. No doubt this generalization made sense, in another part of the home, as an abstract administrative principle, as though the idea of egalitarianism would minimize conflict. In actual practice, for the nurse, the nursing assistants, Fred, and his daughter, it did not.

By 4:30 the group that had been sitting in the day room began to thin out. It had been four hours and a half since the lunch meal and was now thirty minutes before dinner. For those mobile enough to go to the cafeteria for dinner, the line started forming at its door. In time I understood why the line was there, even if it meant standing in it for half an hour. In addition to the fact that waiting was "something to do," as David Forsythe put it, food at the beginning of the line was hotter, fresher, and sometimes more plentiful. During the day, food was a major topic of conversation: what was going to be for dinner, what had been for lunch, who was and was not able to go to the cafeteria. "Oh, you don't get to go downstairs, do you?" Lorraine Sokolof asked her roommate Monica Stewart sympathetically. "I'll try to bring you something." It was not that different food was served on the floors. It was the same food, but it tasted different. By the time some of it, which had been prepared as early as when Lorraine appeared first in line at 4:20, finally reached the fifth floor at 5:30, something had happened to its temperature, texture, and taste, something over which the eaters had no control.

This lack of control over the food actually ended up drawing Mary Karney and me together into a slightly conspiratorial friendship. When the trays arrived at 5:30, the nursing assistants handed them out by name. On hearing her name Mary stood up from her assigned chair, came forward, took the tray from me, and offered a smile that had an ironic twist to it, the meaning of which emerged only over the course of several weeks. A clever, humorous woman of seventy-eight, Mary's diagnosis was vague: "Post-cataract. Arthritis." Dismissed from a hospital after having spent her entire resources for that care, she was able to receive her necessary aftercare only upon being accepted onto the rolls of public aid and into this home. One day she extended her meaningful snicker into words while I handed her the tray. "Thank you, Mommy" she giggled, with a slight curtsy.

Mary had raised three children; one was dead, and two lived in distant parts of the country. She heard from them periodically, and she spoke of them fondly. She also spoke about the planning and cooking of meals that had occupied a large part of her life as a housewife and mother, and one of her favorite pastimes in the nursing home was verbally sharing recipes with the other women sitting in the day room.

There seemed something oddly inauthentic to me about passing the tray, as it was called, to her. Mary, who knew more than I about the planning and executing of meals, now became reduced to a recipient, removed from any part of the process of preparing the food. She seemed to sense my feeling of awkwardness. Whether or not that was why she initiated her little joke, my handing her the tray was now transformed from an inauthentic gesture into a thoroughly amusing one. "Thank you, Mommy" turned this odd inversion of a man passing the tray to a woman who had mothered for years from a potential insult into an odd twist of fate that we shared and that became the basis for many future jokes. If she shared this little joke with me, one could only speculate what she shared with the other mothers as they ate their sandwiches and dishes of pears off plastic plates, sipping from cardboard cartons of milk, talking of recipes.

There was an occasional rumor that nursing assistants stole food from the homes. It was true that an apple, orange, or cookie did make it into a purse, pocket, or mouth during the course of the day. Yet in all of the homes where I worked, the staff conveyed a more pronounced relation to the food—mockery and distance from it.

Dorothy Tomason saw the tomato soup and said, "Ah, water soup again today, I see."

Vera Norris snickered, "By the time that stuff gets up to this floor, it's time to throw it away."

Lottie Ganley liked to joke to the new staff, "Hey, watch that juice, you know they put drugs in it, don't you?" When there was an alternative, nursing assistants were not likely to eat the food, much less steal it.

While food was a constant topic of conversation, sometimes evoking delight, sometimes disdain, staff and residents shared a common attitude regarding its production. By the time the food was delivered to the ward, the nursing assistants and the women and men who lived there had only to serve and consume, having had nothing to do with any of the prior steps in the chain of production. The vast majority of the people in this room had been mothers and housewives, just as the nursing assistants still were, which means that both had been intimately involved in producing meals, not just serving or consuming them. Mary Karney's "Thank you, Mommy," were the words of a clever woman playing the child and seeing herself created as one in this exchange.

Nonetheless, most residents eagerly anticipated dinner. "Where are you running off to, Edith?" I asked.

"I eat downstairs," she retorted quickly, "and I have to make sure I'm not near the end of the line."

The absence of conversation during meals that had seemed so curious at first became less so as I realized the central importance of eating as an event in this setting.[9] With comments about food permeating everyday talk and with the silent voraciousness with which it was consumed, another answer to the question about what it took to live here began to emerge. To eat meant learning how to eat in this setting: learning to receive meals, though not participate in the planning of them, to eat on schedule, to eat institutional food. Some new arrivals balked at the food at first but gradually accommodated themselves to it. Some studied the menu cycle carefully. "Hey, that wasn't bad," said Edith on her way back from the cafeteria. "Let's see, is tomorrow Tuesday? Oh good, chocolate cake."

When the evening meal was over at 6:00, the nursing assistants had to make two records of it. First, the cards on each tray were collected and returned to the kitchen. These cards contained a name and a listing of the nutrients: a separate listing for protein units, carbohydrates, starches, and a line for special comments on special diets, like "no salt." The cards, which were turned in after each meal, were essential to the certification process that a nutritionally adequate meal had been served.

The second recording procedure was on each person's chart: a space to check that she or he had been served each meal and a line for comments, used whenever the meal was "refused." "Refused to eat" was an option and was recorded as such on the cards and charts.

There was no place to indicate any reason for the refusal. For example, David Sabin, sixty-nine, refused hot dogs every time they appeared in their seven-day food cycle. "I hated them when I was a kid, hated them in the army, and hate them now. Get them out of my face!" David "refused to eat."

Nor was there a place to record refusals when they occurred as widespread actions of a whole group. If the mashed potatoes had become chunky or the eggs solid and cold and almost everyone left them on their plates, or if no one ate the pancakes, which had had syrup ladled on them down in the kitchen and were now saturated like wet sponges, there was no place to record that no one ate the potatoes or eggs or pancakes. There were records only for the behaviors of separate cases, each in a file.

The next formal events on the schedule were exercises, evening medications, and a snack. "All right, everyone," a nursing assistant announced at 7:30, while turning off the television, "let's get together for AROM. I'll put on the music. Okay, those of you who can stand, stand, those who sit, sit. Now, up with the arms: one, two, three, four. Good. Now roll your heads around to the beat of the music: one, two, three, four. Now the fingers: one, two," and so on. The participants received stars next to their names on a large board that hung in the day room.

By 8:00 P.M. the time had come for medications. Unlike food, it was not an option to refuse medications, and every resident had a drug regimen. Everyone who could walk was lined up outside the nurses' station, after which meds were delivered to the bedridden. LPN Pearl DeLorio dispensed the prescribed, presorted drugs. "I hate giving drugs to strangers," she complained more than once. "You have to get to know these people so you know how they react to these things." She felt there was too much distance between those who tested and prescribed these medications and those who took them. "You know they test these things on forty-year-olds and give them to eighty-year-olds."

Rose Carpenter and Mary Karney agreed with this assessment. Rose frequently asked if she could take her drugs later in the evening. "These things make me so sleepy. I like to stay up at night." The answer was no; in fact, it was part of the staff's duties to watch that each person consumed each pill when it was given.

Mary also fought the stuporous effects of the sedatives.

One night when she was standing in line, sleepy and about to become more so, she turned around to Rose, who was standing behind her, and said, as she leaned against the wall, "You know, Rose, this place drives me up the wall."[10]

During my months of witnessing the medications procedure, one of the oddest moments occurred in response to a request from a resident that Terry Arcana, the nurse on duty, was not able to fulfill. David Forsythe approached with a runny nose. He had a cold, and the nursing assistants had to remind him continually to blow his nose or help him do it. "Nurse," he asked as his turn came up in line, "have you got a Vicks inhaler there so I can take care of my cold?"

He caught her at a particularly tense moment, while she was struggling to match a variety of pills with the names on her list. She snapped at him, "Of course I don't. What do you think this is, a drugstore?"

David went away silently, and she caught herself in time to apologize to him and glance with embarrassment at the nursing assistants when she realized the reasonableness of the request and the logical absurdity of the answer she had to give back. Amid a vast array of prescribed drugs, she was unable to nurse a common cold. Another way of saying this was not a drugstore was that this was not a place that dealt with short-term sickness episodes, nor was she, after her years of training and three of work, able to respond to his request. The drugs were prescribed by authorities who were not present, and her nursing role was to dispense the drugs. Both parties to the exchange had to disregard the practical needs of the situation and figure out how to live and work around the documents that determined their health care. "If you still feel bad tomorrow," she said to David later, "go to the clinic." He sniffled for days afterwards, until finally one of the nursing assistants bought him a Vicks inhaler.

After medications there were snacks, a glass of juice and some cookies, the latter sometimes shared as a gift. Cookies could be shared, but other things that residents attempted to exchange were scrutinized and sometimes forbidden. During snack time one evening Paul Labruetto and Elaine Morrow got into an argument with the activities director. Paul, fifty-five, had become fond of Elaine, a paraplegic in her late thirties. The feeling seemed to be reciprocated, and they had become known as a couple. Paul was walking down the hall with his portable television in his arms when he was interrupted.

"Where are you going with that?" asked the activities director, who had been filling out her charts just prior to her 9:00 P.M. sign-out.

Paul answered, "I'm giving it to Elaine for a present."

"I'm sorry, Paul, but you can't do that," the director said. "It's against the rules for patients to give things to other patients. You've been here three years. You should know that by now."

Paul became infuriated and started arguing, and Elaine wheeled herself down the hall and took his side of the debate. It was not really a debate. Confronted with this rule, they had no choice.

"Take it up at the residents' council meeting if you want to," offered the activities director, "but in the meantime, take the television back to your room." Later, Paul and Elaine returned to the day room and sat together, not talking to each other or anyone, silently simmering.[11]

Soon after medications and snacks, some of the mobile residents drifted off to bed while others stayed in the day room to watch television. Television was on almost all day and evening. For some it seemed a source of entertainment, and certain programs were eagerly anticipated. For others, it was not the distraction that younger people, the staff for example, might have imagined. Sally Massington, ninety-one, a woman I met while visiting homes in England, put this in some perspective. "Around here you have to make your own fun," she said. "There's the television, but I don't much care for it. I'd already lived most of my life before they started watching that thing."

Grace DeLong also had a story about television and nursing homes. She was an avid fan, always eager to hear the latest news. In her little mobile home, the wheelchair in which almost all her worldly possessions fit, she carried a radio, and listened to both radio and TV at the same time. The local TV channel aired a special news segment on pet therapy for the elderly, which showed residents of nursing homes becoming spirited when presented with puppies or kittens. The show celebrated the therapeutic value of pets.

During the commercial, Grace turned to her friend Bernice, saying, "Yeah, I used to have a dog, till I came here. Of course, they said I couldn't keep it. What made me mad was when my neighbor brought her to see me one day. They said she couldn't bring her in because it was against the Board of Health rules. So she had to stay in the car. All I could do was wave to her through the window. Of course, she didn't know who I was." For weeks Grace talked about this show, bitterly measuring its rhetoric against the reality of her life.

She did, however, seem to enjoy the conversations that occupied the last hour of the evening. She and Lorraine and Rose and others talked about many things on those hot July and August nights: recipes, what their kids would and would not eat, what their parishes were like, and what they imagined they might do once they got out of the nursing home, when, for example, Lorraine was "really going to get into some cooking."

"Okay, folks," one of the nursing assistants said to the few who remained in the day room at 9:45, "let's start thinking about turning in." One by one then they would drift to their rooms or be wheeled to them.

"C'mon, Georgia," said Rose, as Georgia mumbled and played with her shoes over in the corner, "let's turn in now." Lights were out at 10:00. Soon it would be time to start another day. Before that came another night.

"Is that You, Alice?"

Ten-thirty meant room checks. We started at room 401 and worked our way all around the floor, unless 11:00 P.M. came first, which meant the change of shifts. In room 401 Harriet Bowler lay, not moving, rarely speaking, barely blinking. She shared the room with two others. We checked to see that they were in bed and that bed restraints were securely fastened for two of the three, then tiptoed toward the door and clicked off the light switch. More than once there was a scene that Mrs. Bonderoid must have experienced often in order to teach us that hearing is the last to go. What was for us the end point of that room check was for Harriet the beginning. Something aroused her as we clicked off the switch. Thinking that the room had changed from dark to light instead of light to dark, she spoke, probably for the first time since her daughter, Alice, had visited her earlier in the day.

"Is that you, Alice? Come in. Are you there?"

There were only the two of us to cover the whole floor, so there was no possibility of staying with her. "No, Harriet, we were just leaving. Try to sleep now," was all we could say, half-hoping she could hear us, half-hoping she could not.

By 11:00 P.M. two nursing assistants reported to replace the evening workers, as did one licensed practical nurse, who rotated between two floors. After the changeover, the night shift assistants completed the room checks begun earlier and recorded them in the charts, while the LPN reviewed nursing notes from the day and evening shifts. After a few minutes of group discussion behind the nurses' station, the evening shift departed and the night crew began. The first question at night from the supervising LPN to the nursing assistants was "How did it go at room check?"

"Good," was the typical response, supplemented with stories about which residents occasioned some concern. One such situation involved an odd set of twists. The nurse from the earlier shift had written, "Claudia went in with her mother again." Through some unusual circumstances both Claudia Moroni, sixty-nine, and her mother, eighty-nine, lived in this same home. The elder Mrs. Moroni was an immigrant and spoke only Italian. Mother and daughter lived on different floors, separated by different medical categories. Claudia had a habit of going upstairs to her mother's room and crawling into bed with her. This was severely frowned upon and was charted as inappropriate behavior. The chart registered the suspicion that they carried on sexually: "Claudia and her mother exhibiting lesbian behavior." In this environment it was interpreted as a deviance that a mother and daughter would want to cuddle in the same bed. One of the first jobs of the night was to go to get Claudia, bring her back to the floor, and put her in her own bed.

Family members got separated, sometimes by categories,

sometimes by events. Eddie Sokolof and his wife Lorraine shared a room. One night Lorraine twisted her ankle and was taken to the hospital. Eddie was beside himself, crying profusely.

"She won't come back. She's gone," he wailed.

"There, there, Eddie, c'mon, she'll be back, don't worry," we chimed in, trying to console him.

"No, she won't. You don't know what it's like around here," he insisted, as though from some insider's knowledge.

In this instance he was incorrect. Lorraine returned the next day, and they had a grand reunion. Yet Eddie's fear stemmed from two years of living there. Various market forces swept people out of the home, often to the hospital, and when they were gone they were replaced. In a place defined by bed occupancy, an empty bed was economically unproductive. Eddie had seen people leave and get replaced quickly, and he felt powerless to ensure that this would not happen to his wife.

"Whew." The nursing assistants sat down as midnight approached, having checked all rooms and responded to contingencies along the way, like Eddie's fears or someone who needed cleaning and a bed that needed changing. There were usually a few moments to sit down and mark the appropriate boxes on the room check report, but even those few were often interrupted. "Nurse! Nurse! Hurry!" It might have been a call prompted by a need for toileting, or a scream from an awakening dream, or a complaint, or concern about a roommate, or just a call for a nurse for any apparent reason. The night had begun, and these calls were to be a constant part of it. In an image from the outside of nursing homes as rest homes, it might seem that the nights would be characterized by sleep and quiet. Not so. They are very much alive at night.

Frequently just after midnight Joanne Macon came strolling down the hall. "What time is it?" was always her first question, rarely her only one.

"Twelve-thirty."

"What y' got to eat?"

"Nothing."

"I can't sleep."

"What's wrong?"

"That stupid 'Hey, hey, hey,' man and his screaming! He thinks he's dying." We could hear his screams cascading down the halls, "Hey! Hey! Hey! I'm gonna die. I'm gonna die!" They continued until his roommate, Peter Olson, managed to talk him out of his fear or until a staff person turned up to tend to him.

"There, now, Henry, you're not going to leave us yet." one of us said, putting our hand on him and hoping we spoke the truth. "Easy now." He calmed down, but he had awakened several others. With only two aides available, another tending act was truncated.

Occasionally people passed away in the night. At the first sign of imminent death an ambulance was called, but often it was too late. "Is there anything you would like?" I once asked Nancy Block as she lay nearly powerless from a stroke.

"Yes," she responded immediately, "to die." Two nights later she got her wish.

"She saw it coming long before any of us," said veteran nurse Marian Moran, "Most of them do."

Whether or not the ambulance attendants had arrived before the moment of death, the person was whisked away to the hospital, where death would be formally pronounced. If there was a death, it was noted in the nursing home in a very subdued way, often not announced at all. It might have been recognized silently, known by staff and residents alike, but unspoken, except in whispers. "The Spanish man must have died last night," Flora Dobbins observed. "They've got the doors closed today. That's the only time they close the doors during the day."

At another time the question circulated, "How's Frances Wasserman?" She had been taken to the hospital one night. "We don't know, we haven't heard," said the charge nurse. When ten days had gone by, the word finally came back to the nursing home that she had died a few days after leaving the home. "Go tell Irene O'Brien and Miss Black," directed the charge nurse to one of the nursing assistants, "and break it to them gently." These three had been friends for over a year. Irene asked a few others if they cared to join in a prayer. Beyond that there was no recognition on the floor of Mrs. Wasserman's death, no formal observance, no ceremony or public ritual.[12]

Although several residents spoke of having lived in church-affiliated homes earlier as private-pay residents, the homes where I worked were not religious, in the sense of their ownership and formal organization. The practice of prayer, however, was very much in evidence. Many of these people had been involved in religious activities in earlier years, particularly wakes and funerals. Now they lived in a place where there were no such ceremonies. Deaths occurred as silenced, hushed events, as though they were failures in this secular medical system. Yet another lesson for residents to learn was that praying and mourning for the deceased were done primarily alone.

In stark contrast to the absence of religious ritual, symbolic gestures pervaded the days and nights devoted to the display that this environment was hospital-like. The formal terms that shaped everyday activities related to sickness and disease, medicine and nursing. As each night unfolded, there was much chart work to be done. Reflecting on the information contained in these various documents yielded some explanations for events that had seemed incongruous earlier in the day. These pages were composed of diagnoses and medical treatments, filled with coded and quantified measures of the care that was being provided. They did more than simply reflect what was provided; they also created the conceptual boundaries that defined life inside.

One night charge nurse, Florence Castenada, asked me, her pen poised over the Nursing Monthly Summary, "How has Monica Stewart been eating lately?"

"Oh." I paused to think about some of Monica's comments on the food, which she often disliked and often chose not to eat. "I guess 'fair,' but sometimes she goes on complaining and won't eat at all."

"No, no!" Florence interrupted. "I mean on this scale. Is she 'independent, requires assistance, dependent on staff, or a tube feeder?'"

"Oh, well . . . ," I paused again, trying to decode her scale, "someone is always trying to talk her into eating more."

"Okay!" she cut in, noting, moving on. "Requires assistance."

Florence moved quickly through the precoded questions and answers, trying to get her paperwork done so she could catch time to study for her RN test. Occasionally resident Sharon Drake would put in an appearance around 2:00 A.M.

"How y' doin', Sharon?" one of us asked.

"Not bad. Can't sleep, though."

It was Sharon that Bill Slaughter had exposed himself to. According to her chart, she had been manifesting extreme agitation. This diagnosis related to her heart problems, but it also described her social life. Some time after

Sharon started complaining about Bill, all staff members, including nursing assistants, had been invited to attend a psychiatric consultation. Bill had been manifesting "exhibitionist behavior" again. The psychiatrist and head nurse agreed that Bill's sedative should be increased by fifty milligrams per day. After this intervention, Bill's behavior actually did change. He became much more subdued. He was quieter, sleepier, and he did not expose himself to Sharon. He only stood by her and followed her around and grinned a lot.

Sharon offered a different kind of strategy for the situation. "They should get him the hell out of here!" was her cry. She was more interested in changing the social context than the psychopathology of Bill's behavior. However, the medical authorities primarily attended to their cases and diagnoses, not to the setting. So Sharon was at the nurses' station manifesting "agitated behavior," while Bill was down the hall sleeping off his "exhibitionist behavior," arrested by tranquilizers. Their interaction, which in another context might have been called sexual assault, became analyzed as the behaviors of two separate individuals. Sharon's suggestion to alter the setting by getting him "the hell out of here" was neither responded to nor recorded.

In separate slots on the shelves behind the nurses' station, were filed the charts of the residents. Each person had her or his own record, beginning with diagnosis, followed by medical consultations, prescriptions, vital signs, weights and other physical measurements, and behavior. The process of charting treated the residents as individual entities isolated from the personal relationships within which they were enmeshed in daily life. In the charts, the formal records of their existence, they were taken out of their local contexts and the relationships that were an indispensable part of their everyday survival strategies.[13] In

the documents they became patients, identified by their
pathologies.

Earlier the head nurse had instructed the nursing assistants to "read their charts to get to know them better." In
the charts none of the actual interactional stories that contextualized these days and nights came through. The settings vanished, overridden by cases: patients, diseases,
medicines, and measurements. The process involved the
ongoing creation of phenomena the organization could
service.

Toward the back of the chart there were several categories in which boxes were checked: toileting, feeding,
bathing, mobility, continence, behavior, and mental status.
This group taken together was called functional needs.
The first four taken as a group were called activities of
daily living. In fact, the activities framed in this chart referred to how much nursing help each person required to
execute them, so it was actually nurses' activities, not residents', that were involved. Once again, despite the words,
the person in question was not the actor but the acted
upon.

Under mental status, one could be "oriented, in need of
orientation, semi-disoriented, or disoriented." According
to the census on the wall, sixty-one of the sixty-four living
on the floor were in one of the last three categories. These
statistics tended to create a "them" on the floor, as though
all fit into a generic category. As I was heading to the ward
my first day, one of the staff tried to put me at ease by
invoking one of the "out of it" generalizations, "Oh, don't
worry about that floor. They're all out of it up there." Anyone who proceeded from the chart as the point of departure could come to the same conclusion.

Under behavior, one could need frequent intervention,
need occasional intervention, or could be judged no prob-

lem. The best one could be was no problem. This word pervaded charts and staff conversation. "Any problems today?" "Is she a problem?" "Oh, no, you won't have any problems with her." To live there was to be defined in terms of sicknesses, behaviors, and problems.[14] It made more sense after "getting to know them better" through the charts, as the social service coordinator instructed the nursing assistants, to "remember that the more you get to know these people, the more you know there's always something for them to improve upon." Being defined in terms of physical and mental problems in the first place, the people who lived here could only be judged as showing improvement, or no change. Meanwhile, words like *impoverished, insulted, powerless* or *angry* did not appear anywhere in the writing.

Marian Cregg, eighty-two, who had suffered a stroke months earlier, was bedridden and had lost speech. Sometimes about 3:00 A.M. when we went to turn her she muttered unintelligibly with what seemed like some agitation, while her eyes moved rapidly. Of all the efforts put forth by people living here to get through the day and night, maybe Marian worked the hardest, just learning how to survive while constantly bedridden. Occasionally saliva or particles of food dribbled down her face and neck. It was apparent from the ruffled pillow and top sheet that she had tried to remedy this herself; she may have spent a good part of the night at the job before one of us arrived to turn her.

Another resident conveyed the experience of living through the night in this virtual absence of caretakers. Also bedridden, Sara Wostein, eighty-five, had lost much of her physical but none of her mental agility. One night at room check I breezed through her room and leaned toward her, asking, "Is there anything I can do for you,

Sara?" It was a polite question, but I had no idea how empty of meaning until her response put it in perspective.

"Yes," she responded propping herself up and looking straight into my eyes, "stay with me."

Were I to continue with my assigned tasks this was the one thing I specifically could not do. "Gee, I'm sorry, I've got all these rooms to check," I responded feebly. Sara and I began our acquaintance with a reasonable rapport, but after this exchange she talked very little to me. It was clear she was turning away, turning inwards. She was also unfolding yet another form of the permeating silences that were becoming less and less mysterious. Silence was one of the few ways she had of expressing an emotion. In her feeling of rejection, and forced aloneness, she carried on thereafter by actively not talking.

As 4:00 A.M. crept around, most charting was complete, the laundry and linen were sorted, and there were more requests emanating from the rooms—for a drink, or the toilet, a tissue, or some holding. Someone might be coughing, breathing heavily, or, asleep or awake, calling out a name from some other place and time. Many asked for something to eat, having finished their last meal over ten hours earlier, with four more to go until the next. Food was not available. In effect, neither was holding, since it was rarely only one person making such a request, and the two nursing assistants and one LPN were floating around "putting out brush-fires," as Pearl DeLorio used to say. Staffing was structured as though very little happened at night, but this was often not at all the situation. If most lights had been put out by 10:30 P.M., they did not stay out; many came on again before dawn.

During the night, residents worked through various kinds of physical and emotional demands: fighting insomnia and pain, ironing out confusions, dealing with thirst or hunger, struggling with a colostomy bag or a nasal tube. Whatever kinds of demands intruded on residents through the night, they had one thing in common. Family and visitors were not on hand, and nursing assistants, assigned at a thirty-to-one ratio, were not able to cope with multiple needs and requests. Those who lived there had to learn that whatever they had to cope with at night was to be coped with alone.

Night nurse Terry Arcana once made mention of a new idea circulating in some nursing homes, one she thought would spread to other homes. All of the people diagnosed as having Alzheimer's disease were being moved into the same ward. She did not like the idea at all. Her sentiments were very similar to a discussion I later heard while on a tour of nursing home facilities in England and France. Two nurses, one social worker, and two physicians, all from England, became engaged in a rather heated argument about this relatively new category of disease. One of the nurses began to speak about some special care that was provided for "the confused" at her long-term care center. She was corrected by the physician who suggested that most confused people are afflicted with some form of Alzheimer's disease. The nurses and the social worker, who had apparently been in this debate before, fired back that "confused" remained a preferable term since it encouraged an awareness that senile disorientation was widely varied and, for many people, more intermittent than constant and categorical. As the discussion became more intense, one nurse said emphatically, "The last thing we need in nursing care is another disease label." The physician disagreed, saying that identifying diseases was the first step in finding their cure.

Disease labels are important for medical research and diagnosis, but they often seemed extraneous to the practice of nursing during those nights. In this particular home a move to assemble those with the Alzheimer's diagnosis would bring together Hazel Morris, who wandered; Alice McGraw, who sang; Frances Wasserman, who called out for her son and her purse; Elizabeth Stern, who mourned for her husband; and Georgia Doyle, who put her shoes on the table. Some diagnosed with this disease were indeed beyond communication of any perceivable sort. But to get to know many of these residents was to get to know very different kinds of people, many of whom were only inter-mittently confused and who, despite their confusion, con-tributed to the ongoing social life of the place. Were these five cordoned off together, what was already a disease-driven model of organization would be further accen-tuated. Such a development would not only respond to their confusion but would contribute to it, crystallizing their disease labels for them and those who worked with them, insuring the attitude that "they're all out of it up there." [15]

To be sick, frail, confused, disabled, or old is not the same as to be a patient. In becoming a patient in a nursing home one enters a social organization; patient emerges in the meeting of person and institution. Day and night as boxes got checked and records reviewed, these people were entered into the administrative language and codes of what services were rendered to them. In turn, these terms and categories and codes came to be viewed by many staff and outsiders as the ultimate reality itself, rather than a small part of it. The status of patient begins only in sick-ness. There in the nighttime was a glimpse of another facet of the production process of this industry. As they lay in their beds, another blanket was being folded over their lives, a blanket of paper that defined them as patients. These documents did not merely reflect needs, they defined certain needs as well, and they erased others.[16] Most basically, they erased identities of the people whom they described as being social actors. The women and men living here did not write in these documents, nor did they read them. They did not speak in the charts. They were spoken about.

It was determined that the intervention needed in the case of Claudia and her mother was that they be separated. As they cuddled together in that bed and spoke, mostly in Italian, they did not know that someone was writing about them as separate cases, separate beds, with separate behaviors and diseases. When they were placed back properly in their own beds, just as when Bill Slaughter or Miss Black were back in theirs, intervention had been accomplished and recorded. Things were quiet again, as a successful product of this institutional order. Each was in her or his own bed, each one's separate chart slid back into its slot. In the process residents were transformed from acting beings into beings acted-upon, to be given the goods and services of this health care industry, and formally turned into passive voice. Patients were produced.

By 6:30 A.M. another day was about to begin, living in the land of patienthood.

"Good morning, Irene."

Even if grumbling every step of the way, Irene O'Brien did get up. She worked her way into her wheelchair, and into the bathroom, washed, came back to make her bed—she insisted on making her own bed—and cleaned around her area before wheeling herself into the day room to wait for breakfast.

The close of the night shift just before 7:00 A.M. was usually made easier by waking Sharon Drake and Mary Reynold and being cheered by them. When the curtains rolled open they were often ready with some morning quip. "Good morning, boy. Today we'll have breakfast in bed, eggs over easy, and two Bloody Marys, please." Sharon, having waitressed in a hotel restaurant for twenty-five years, had delivered many room service meals, and knew exactly how to mimic the speech of the leisure class. These two did not like being rushed; it took them the full hour to get ready.

Mary put on pearls and makeup, as she probably had done all her life. "Mutton dressed like a lamb, that's me. You know what my problem is? Parkinson's disease. You see, me and Katharine Hepburn have something in common after all." Off she and Sharon sauntered to begin another day in the day room.

Eventually an answer began to unfold to Helen Donahue's question about why she couldn't get a little rest around here. This institution was organized around rules appropriate for a hospital. Even though there was very little curing going on, the organization seemed to draw legitimacy by demonstrating that it was a place where medical personnel, practices, and terminology were the repository of authority. Helen had to get up for the same reason that the day shift had to start at 7:00 A.M., because this was the hospital-like order of things. Helen thought she had entered a rest home. She had not. She had entered a patient home, and now she had to live under its rules.

Food, cleanliness, activities, movement, warmth, rest, communication—it is not that people did not participate in these basic human processes. They were not passive in the face of their needs: they ate, kept clean, took part in activities, rested, communicated, and for the most part complied with the social regimen in which they were encased and, in so doing, helped accomplish its production.

The narrative of formal documentation was about isolated units, bodies, and behaviors, while the financial resources of the people were continually being drained. Taken together, these forces fostered passivity. *Patient* is a word close in origin to the word *passive*. Under such conditions the silences became less mysterious and emerged more as a logical consequence of this set of social circumstances.

There is a word even closer to *patient* than *passive*: *patience*. As Marjorie McCabe implied when she spoke of learning to wait, it had to be practiced here. Poet Adrienne Rich begins her poem "Integrity" with the line "A wild patience has taken me this far." [17] It seemed an appropriate description for Marjorie and her fellow residents as they sat waiting for breakfast to arrive.

"Sit over here in your assigned chair, Marjorie."

"Here, now, Elizabeth, you're over here. Wait, now, until I put a bib on you."

Next to Marjorie sat Miss Black, ever ready to talk about Social Security. Next to her was Sharon Drake, the former waitress, eager to direct the serving of the food, and at a nearby table Mary Karney, the former mother who now played the dutiful daughter. Each woman has spoken several times in these chapters. There each sat before breakfast, bib in place, eyes glued to the elevator. They waited quietly, with a wild patience, practicing patienthood, actively practicing the skills of silence.

5

"If It's Not Charted, It Didn't Happen"

As the minutes sped nearer to 7:00 A.M. the nurses, nursing assistants, cooks, and housekeepers all rushed into the locker room to hang up coats, then back upstairs to get in line to punch the clock. Punching in with coats on was against the rules. Seven A.M.—click! "Whew!" came from most, except those still in line, those who came at 7:03 or 7:04, and were therefore late. In effect, we had to be there earlier than seven just to get in line. Three times late past two minutes meant one day of suspension, no work, no pay. Edna Stanzone, who worked in the kitchen, underlined the seriousness of this rule. "You start pulling suspensions, and before you know it you start cutting into the rent money." There was some cooperation, like hanging up someone else's coat if the supervisor was not watching. There was also some unpleasant pushing and shoving. It was a serious, sometimes tense, beginning of the day.

We went off to our respective floors to sign in and receive assignments. One registered nurse or licensed practical nurse coordinated our activities, while she prepared and dispensed medications, charted, and intervened in emergencies. "Beds 201 to 216 for you today, showers for half of them," she instructed.

During the orientation in one of the homes the assistant head nurse stressed two fundamental responsibilities for nursing assistants: to sign the restraint and position sheets every two hours and to "remember that your most important job is to get them up and get them ready to take their meds." She handed us a booklet that set forth our duties, then pointed to a sign over the nurses' station that made the consequences of our work clear and matter-of-fact. It read: "If It's Not Charted, It Didn't Happen."

We were told to read the booklet before reporting for the first day of work. Its contents were similar to the textbook. The first page welcomed nursing assistants to the health care team and outlined their duties. The booklet itemized the work as a series of tasks: wake patients and prepare them for meals and medications, change beds, change clothes, pass trays, take vital signs, measure weights and heights, conduct AROM, give snacks, conduct room checks, and "assist as needed." This last category was left vague. It was not long before I found out that "assist as needed" would take up the bulk of the day and constitute the most complex part of the work.

"Don't Worry, You'll Learn"

Mornings began with waking residents. For most nursing assistants it seemed that a certain way of greeting each person developed, not always successfully, but always bearing some relation to the person in bed. Juanita Carmona typified the approach. "You've got to watch that Sagan," she warned. "He's a rough one."

"And what about Mrs. O'Brien?" I asked her.

"Oh, just ignore her, she'll go on griping about having to get up whether you're there or not." These grumblings about wanting to stay in bed were more subdued than disruptive or violent. While they did make for some conflict during those early morning hours, there was no real debate about whether or not the complainant could stay in bed. It was not as though a right was being claimed.

Waking some was complicated, because it involved immediately cleaning up messes made in the bed during the night. One early lesson in the rigors of the work revolved around such an incident. I approached Monica Stewart, who announced with caution, "I'm afraid I've made a mess today."

"Oh, no problem, Monica, it happens to the best of us," was my naive response. But as I folded back her sheets, now confronted with the real work of "getting them out of that," Monica could see me get weak and pale. "Um . . . I'll be right back." I sputtered, rushing off first to the toilet, then to Mrs. Johnson, a co-worker and veteran of ten years. "Mrs. Johnson, ah . . . I don't feel too good today, and Monica has made a terrific mess. Could you help me?"

"Sure," came her reassuring response.

"Good morning, Monica," Mrs. Johnson began with an uplifting chuckle. "C'mon, let's get you up and rolling!" Without hesitation, continuing her talking, she folded the blankets down to the bottom of the bed and with her right hand rolled Monica over on her left side, deftly wrapping the soiled bottom sheet toward the center of the bed, then turned to me with, "Here, hand me that Kleenex box. Quick! you got to be quick about this!" and turned to Monica, talking and cleaning, "Okay, up once, okay, now over," and lifted her lower half completely with just one arm, folded the clean parts of the old bottom sheet under her to help finish the cleaning, unwrapped a new bottom sheet and another for protection and slid them down the side of the bed where Monica was not lying, simultaneously turning to me, "Now that washcloth and towel, quick! You've got to have these right at your side before you start," and to Monica, "There you go," rolling her over onto the new bottom sheets and folding a new top sheet and blankets over her. I gasped in amazement. Mrs. Johnson had executed the entire operation, turning it into one continuous fluid motion, in little more than two minutes.

"Don't worry," she said, scurrying out the door, "you'll learn."

I did not learn, even after months, in any way that matched the orchestration, agility, timing, strength, speed, compassion, or rapport that Mrs. Johnson demonstrated in her expertise of "getting them out of that."

Little by little, however, I did pick up on the skills of the next task on the agenda, feeding someone. As with cleaning, the actual work of feeding had not been described in class or in the text, nor was there any code or guide in the charts other than a box to check as to whether the patient ate or refused to eat.

"You feed Alice today," came an early instruction. Alice McGraw sat confused, still groggy from sleep, mouth tightly closed. Somehow the food had to get into it to stimulate her taste buds. Mrs. Carmona advised, "Try doing just like we do everything else with Alice. Try a song." "Okay. Ahem. Alice! Hello? When Irish eyes are smiling, all the world is bright and gay." Eventually, recognition dawned, and with some egg held long enough under her nose to smell and see, she opened her mouth a crack.

Learning how to become someone else's tastebuds, how to vary portions and kinds of food and drink, was a complicated puzzle, the more so for being slightly different for each person. "Keep looking in their eyes, especially the ones who don't talk," Mrs. Bonderoid had taught us in

als, these skills slowly began to develop. Some residents, unable to perform all the complex tasks of eating, needed assistance. Feeding someone began by selecting a portion of food, or more likely drink, since thirst was frequently intense. Then the food: a piece of the scrambled egg to begin, how much or little depending on the person, then offering it, waiting for it to be chewed and swallowed, then some milk, and more waiting, then toast, dipped in the milk for easier chewing, a pause to avoid regurgitation or a choke, and another piece enhanced by the single pad of jam, then coffee. With some it could be a pleasant exchange, feeding someone and watching them smile.

But there was always pressure when several people needed special help. It was considered a bad day when it fell to a nursing assistant to have to help more than two or three, because it was intrinsically a very slow process. "C'mon, will yah, Ellen, eat the damn food, and let's go!" I urged under my breath, while residents urged back, "C'mon, will yah, I'm hungry, let's go!" Buried underneath this pressured moment was the delicate, sometimes frightening process of feeding a frail, sick person. It often seemed one of the most refined nursing skills of the day as I watched a seasoned nursing assistant sensitive to the slow pace of an old person's eating, knowing how to vary portions and tastes, how to reinforce nonverbally while feeding—a refined and complicated skill, but unnamed and suppressed when forced into a forty-minute task.

Because the rush was on to finish by 8:40 when the kitchen worker arrived to pick up the trays, the work involved juggling: feeding one person, handing a drink to second, grabbing a third to sit her back down, dodging the nurse and her cart as they moved along dispensing the morning medications. By 8:20, with feeding not half done, the requests began. "Toilet, take me to the toilet." "Is someone free? I need to go." "Got any second helpings?" "Nurse! nurse!"

One day Suzy Drepardieu from Haiti snapped at me sarcastically. "Ha! Sorry, Meesta Dyaamund," she drew out with a feigned formality, "but you are never going to make it on time." Suzy disliked me, or perhaps distrusted me. No doubt many staff and residents in whom I did not confide could see right through me and knew that something was going on that I was not telling.

I disliked her right back, mostly because she never showed me her masterful skills at feeding the frail. Ellen McMahon, ninety-eight, was strapped to her chair and fed mashed food through a plastic squeeze tube. Her brittle bones, her bobbing head, and her inability to speak made her frightening to me. When I mashed the food into the tube and squirted it into her mouth, she screamed and kicked and choked and cried. When Suzy served her, Ellen cooed with contentment, swallowed slowly, and opened her mouth for more. I was jealous. Suzy expressed something more intense. "Sorry, Meesta Dyaamund, but this isn't as easy as it looks," she sneered. "There's more to this work than they teach you in that school." On the records, the same box was checked whether it was Suzy or I who fed Ellen. The check mark certified that someone had been fed, but it erased the fact that in the doing they became different acts, as part of different relationships.

At first it seemed odd that all of this had to be done by 8:40 A.M. But by 8:45 the reason was clear: there was a lot of work on the schedule. After breakfast one nursing assistant was assigned to beds, one to showers, two to day room coverage and toileting. Some residents made their own beds, but many did not. Changing and making forty beds seemed at first a simple enough, menial task that anyone could do. After a while such a perspective seemed simplistic, a view that could be maintained only by someone who did not do the work. It is simple enough for someone with a lower back strong enough for three straight hours of constant bending at the body's center and a blood pressure low enough to avoid dizziness at each quick rise.

Dorothy Tomason was convinced that over the years this constant up-and-down motion contributed to her high blood pressure. Vera Norris associated it with chronic back pain.

"You got beds today?" I once asked Vera.

"Ohhh . . . ," moaned the four-year veteran, placing her open palm against her lower back, "my back hurts just hearing myself say yes to that question."

While Vera agreed with Dorothy on the health hazards of this task, she preferred it to the alternative. "I get weak doing beds, sure, but I'd still rather do them than showers."

Each person who lived in the home had to take a shower every third day. Showers were going on continually through the morning and afternoon hours. Vera's reason for not liking to give showers was straightforward: "I can't stand the screams."

Sometimes the screaming was about water temperature, which dropped as the day went along. "You get in here and try it," Marjorie McCabe protested. "You know testing the water with your hand isn't the same as being here." A few of the more frail were frightened just by the shower itself. For many, with brittle bones and highly sensitive body thermometers, it was an effort just to stand or sit underneath it, and for the nursing assistants it was a challenge to provide adequate support and force, while managing to stay out of the shower.

"You all right in there, Hazel?" I inquired of Mrs. Morris.

"Yeah," she yelled, thus freeing me to get a towel and check on Harriet Bowler in the next stall. Within thirty seconds Hazel fell to the floor. Luckily, she had fallen first against the wall out of dizziness, and only slowly drifted downward. After that, maintaining those delicate balances took on new meaning as an integral part of the work. It took a constant anticipatory vigilance to keep ahead of potential accidents.[1]

In the charts, boxes were marked after each shower. There was no space to note the work of nervous monitoring or residents' fears, not to mention their screams. Hazel Morris. Shower. Check. If it wasn't charted, it didn't happen, but much more happened than got charted. What happened to the work that wasn't charted? It seemed as if much of it was being made invisible. The chart makers needed to have certain information. I began to wonder whether, in order to accomplish their objectives, they also needed to leave certain information out.

In the late morning one day after I had worked for about two months, I was assigned to clean and change linen for Bill Hackett. Bill had spent his life as a bartender. In his late sixties he got liver disease, and he did not have long to survive. At first it was frightening and embarrassing for me to be with him, and no doubt he felt the same, as I bumbled along trying to clean him, get accustomed to the smells, avoid sickness, and feign a smile. Most days I tried to bear in mind the advice of registered nurse Mary Collins. "There's one good way to get beyond your feelings of embarrassment. Think of theirs." Over time, as we got to know each other, the encounter became easier. Bill held on to the humor that must have made him an excellent bartender, and he came out with great quips about nursing home life. It was something of a turning point in learning this work when one day I left Bill's room and realized that while cleaning him I had not even noticed the assault on my senses that had so dominated the encounter when he was a stranger.

By 11:45 A.M. it was time to serve lunch. "Get your babies ready in here," Vera Norris beckoned from the day room. In this instance she was using the term "baby" to ridicule the rule, which many residents made fun of as well, that bibs had to be tied on to each resident for each meal. "Baby" was used often, and in more than one way. In some contexts it was used to create fictive family roles. Dorothy Tomason put her arm around Joanne Macon when she cried. "C'mere, my baby, now what's the trouble?" Florence Castenada did the same with Frankie Sorento, thirty-seven, a former inmate of the state hospital with brain damage. "Here, my Frankie, come to mama." Those words of comfort, with a hug, seemed to soothe him.

"Baby" was also used more broadly as a designation of the impersonal, referring to infants who were incompetent and unaware. "Oh, you work up there on the baby floor," observed a first-floor nursing assistant. Another advised, "Oh, don't worry about these people; when they get old they all start acting just like babies."

In fact, it was a highly controversial term, creating some conflict between the staff and the people who were called, or made to feel like, babies, and generating some defensive reactions. Bedridden Frances Wasserman protested, "Just cause I have to lay here in this gown doesn't mean I'm a baby." The same protest came up at mealtime in the same tone, in part because of the bibs but also for the reason expressed by Mrs. Herman, who was blind. "You know, I was a field nurse, too. I'm no baby just because someone has to help me eat." She spoke to this point as more than one noontime meal arrived, underlining the delicate balance between service and insult that was involved in helping blind people, especially if there was any undertone of infantalizing.

"Here's your spoon, Mrs. Herman," I offered.

She snapped back with all the ferocity that she called

upon when I had spoken too loudly, "Leave me alone, I'll get to it."

It was one of the pleasures of the work to help a blind person with a meal. Nursing supervisor Marian Moran summarized it, "If you don't do it right, sometimes they just don't eat." Still, it was easy to overstep boundaries. To get to know Peter Prince, who was also visually impaired, was to realize that he resented many offers of service, especially relating to food. He had just finished telling me to get out of his way when Robbie from the next table asked him, "Hey, Prince, what did you get for dessert, cookies or peaches?"

"I don't know," said Mr. Prince, his fingers creeping around his tray. "I haven't found them yet."

"In Here They Get Their Feelings Hurt Awfully Easy"

After lunch when there were free moments, nursing assistants washed residents' faces, which was for some a sensual delight. Eyes slowly closed while the cool cloth swept across a forehead, and slid down into the crevices where the sand collected. "I've been waiting for an hour for someone to clean my itching eyes," Grace DeLong once sighed. As the cloth moved down across the cheeks and neck of someone whose hands were no longer capable of such an act, it cooled as it cleaned, and it picked up the last crumbs missed by the quick stroke of a napkin.

Combing followed. This gesture involved giving some attention to style, even for the older women and men who had little hair. Age distinguished people markedly in this area. Hair served as a reminder that wholly different generations were housed together physically in these homes, lumped under "the elderly" or "the aged." The women in their seventies, more likely with fuller heads of hair, were the younger women in the day room. At combing time, many commented on the twenty- and thirty-year age differences in the group. "Oh, don't bother with me," insisted Hazel Morris, at ninety-four. "Go take care of the younger girls."

Dressing someone was another skill that took some practice to coordinate, especially with people who could not help much. Ellen McMahon, for example, had almost no power of movement, so lifting her took some strength. Yet at almost a hundred years old, her bones were eggshell brittle; one false move while coaxing her fingers and arms through the sleeve of a blouse or sweater could mean a broken bone. To lift her in and out of the wheelchair took holding her bobbing head and her limp legs while trying to secure her pencil-thin arms at her sides. These tasks required both strength and delicacy and knowing how to distinguish which among her almost inaudible utterances were deep breaths and which were muted grunts of pain.

Her roommate, Edna Barrett, showed that the act of dressing involved some emotional delicacy as well. Edna was in the public aid phase of her nursing home life when we met, but the fine wool and cotton clothes in her closet suggested that in her earlier days she had been a woman of some wealth. It was not easy to lift her spirits. When approached for the afternoon face washes she responded glumly, "Who cares?" and "What does it matter?" So one day I decided to help her dress up in one of her finer suits, with a necklace and bracelet. "There, you look good, Edna," I said. Smiling, she followed me into the day room. Then to the nurses' station. Then into someone else's room. Then down the hall. Much of Edna's time in the home she wanted to follow someone around, but now following had taken on a different dimension. She was engaged in being dressed up, and she wanted to continue sharing the occasion. The problem was that she stayed

about two feet behind me for almost an hour. I could neither get the work done nor persuade her to sit down or go
back to her room. Eventually, I had to sit her down and tie
her up. That hurt her feelings.

In this work it was difficult to learn when to hold back,
how not to offer too much. LPN Pearl DeLorio, a veteran
of several years' work, understood the dilemma. "It's
tough," she said, "you just never know when you're going
to hurt their feelings. In here they get their feelings hurt
awfully easy."

Anna Ervin got her feelings hurt regularly in the course
of one of the nursing assistants fulfilling her assigned job.
At some point between 1:00 and 2:00 P.M. Bessie Miranda
approached Anna to persuade her to go to the bathroom.
On Anna's chart, which Bessie held in her hand during
these encounters, it was recorded that her bowel activity
was irregular, and Bessie was carrying out orders designed
to correct the problem. The idea was that if Anna could be
encouraged to go at a regular time each day her intermittent difficulties with constipation and incontinence could
be avoided. The regimen was called bowel and bladder
training. Anna disliked the training, as did Bessie, as was
obvious from their loud yelling.

Bessie coaxed, "Did you go yet, Anna? C'mon, let's go.
I don't want to fight with you today."

Anna screamed, "Get away from me! I was an LPN myself, you know. I don't need you telling me when to go to
the bathroom. Besides, I tried earlier. What do you expect,
miracles? Get away from me!"

Bessie could not get away, not without failing at her assigned task. "C'mon, Anna, it's time, let's go," she insisted,
while pulling her along. The argument raged daily as Anna
was escorted to the bathroom, usually under duress.

By 2:00 P.M. interpersonal clashes were subdued. It was

the peak period for visitors. Nursing assistants' instructions for this period were succinct. They were based on maintaining a good appearance to the outsiders, with special reference to physicians or Board of Health inspectors who might happen to drop in. The assistant head nurse told us, "When you are in the day room never stay in one place. Keep moving. You never know when they'll pop in for an inspection. If somebody comes in, grab a chart or fold some sheets, or take some blood pressures. Look busy." Looking busy was hardly difficult: there were beds that needed making, more showers, orienting a new arrival, being interrupted by an emotional crisis, helping the registered nurse change a catheter or bandage, cleaning tables, washing faces, sorting clothes.

The family members on hand during the afternoons were appreciated not only by those they came to visit but by nursing staff as well. They provided crucial caretaking services. They also contributed material support that kept the operation going, contributions not limited to their own relatives. When John Kelley's wife Carol brought his clean laundry every week, she brought some for his roommate as well. When Fred Murray's daughter brought cigarettes she brought cartons, some for Fred, some to give away. Family members brought other things, tidied up the rooms, and made contacts with others over the course of their visits. To watch these wives and daughters and nieces and husbands circulate through the halls, with their particular greetings for particular people, remembering a birthday, a nickname, a specific problem with sickness, was to see them create an integral part of the social fabric of these homes.[2]

The fabric was also partly woven by volunteers. As with relatives, they were primarily younger women caring for older women for free. This small cadre supplied the major base of personnel for outings, games, and parties, through the coordination of the activities director. The boundaries of caretaking work between paid and unpaid labor in this developing industry were by no means fixed, and no small part of the work was done by women outside its formal organization.[3]

Nursing assistants went about trying to organize their day as best they could. It took continual mental work to balance the tasks from above with the contingencies of the moment. Schedules were completed, if sometimes late: beds got made, showers given, vitals and weights taken, diapers changed. Yet if these activities were all that happened, all that the work consisted of, the contours of the day would have been very different from what they actually were in the everyday world.[4]

The official tasks were difficult, sometimes unpleasant, and took some skill. But there was also a host of unspoken, unnamed demands before, during, and after the tasks that presented problems, both physical and emotional. If the orders from the rational plan had parceled out the tasks into a time-motion calculus that made sense in the abstract, carrying out the orders continually came up against the unplanned, fluid, and contingent nature of everyday tending.[5]

On the way from one specified task to another, there were always two or three quick cleanups that demanded immediate attention. In addition to cleaning people, nursing assistants were involved with the cleaning staff in keeping the place sparkling, and though never formally mentioned as part of the job, housekeeping was a regular part of it, one never fully completed. I learned ways to keep doing it while doing something else. These lessons did not come from the authorities but from those who did the work. Dorothy Tomason advised us to keep a rag handy

at all times, pointing out another simple tool of this complex trade. "We're nurses' aides," she said. "We clean
everything."

As the afternoons went along, moving around meant
passing in front of a row of people sitting in their chairs,
sometimes coming upon someone who had slid down or
fallen over and needed repositioning. In such a circumstance, the fact that there were still six more beds and two
more showers before shift change had little bearing on the
immediate need. Often at this time of day the pace of the
staff and their duties came into conflict with the pace of
the people who lived there. "C'mon, c'mon, will you, I
haven't got all day" was a legitimate plea of a nursing assistant trying to tend to her eighteen or twenty people.
That plea contrasted with the slow pace of the people who
lived there, who kept asking, "What did you say? I can't
hear you" or "Please walk slower. I can't keep up with
you" or who, in answer to a question like "How are you
today?" Doris responded "Oh ... fine ... and ...
you. . . ?"—by which time we were halfway down the
hall.

Nursing also meant trying to learn each person's pecu-
liar mental and physical problems. This skill was not
static; it evolved as personal relations developed. "I hate
changing strangers," Vera complained when she returned
from a day when she had been switched to another floor.

When nursing assistants described their work, they
often referred to gaining experience or skills in terms of
getting to know people. In getting to know someone, the
knowledge of anticipating their needs and desires took
shape. Being able to sense in advance who needed water,
moisturizing lotion, or a change of clothing took experience in the work and knowing the people. "Arthur needs

changing," Dorothy Tomason could point out, even from across the room.

"How do you know?" I asked, standing next to him, oblivious to this need.

"Oh, I don't know," she tossed off. "I guess it's just a sixth sense you get in this work."

"Don't Ever Tell These People You Know How They Feel"

~~By the start of the 3:00 to 11:00 shift, many of the medical tasks were done for the day, but a lot of person-to-person work lurked ahead.~~ Perhaps the most difficult part of the caretaking work was just keeping up its necessary conversations. When the shift began, nursing assistants left the nurses' station with some objective in mind, perhaps to gather a pile of clean sheets or clothing. The objective was reached only slowly, ~~for to leave the station was to be met with a barrage of conversation from a few of the residents.~~ Some expected a nod of recognition as soon as we came on duty, some a handshake or other touch that meant a greeting, and they were quietly insulted if we walked by without making it. Moving out from behind the nurses' station meant fielding many overtures, sometimes simultaneous: "Hi! What's for dinner?" "Can you fix my belt?" "Have you got a quarter?" "Guess what I did today?" and most of all, the ever-ready "How are you?"—often made in the hope of more than just a one-line response.

The barrage of overtures received a blitz of responses: "I don't know what's for dinner." "Here, stand over here so I can fix your belt." "No, you know we can't lend money to the residents." "Fine, Lorraine, and how are you?"

My friend Cheryl once inquired while I was working the evening shift, "How did it go in the spider web today?"

Her imagery captured those first few moments in the late afternoons. Amid the rushing, changing, and charting, there was the never-ending listening to comments and questions that accompanied them. Frequently, the questions were not easy. From Edna Barrett, who was slowly dying with cancer, "Am I going to die?" From Elizabeth Stern, "My mind keeps wandering. Am I crazy?" From Sharon Drake, far along the path of poverty, "You know, you have to believe you won't be here forever. Do you think I'll be here for the rest of my life?" Regardless of the prospects, a cool yes to any of these questions did not work well, but neither did a transparent no. It took something in between, including some knowledge of the person asking the question.

"Above all," advised veteran Mrs. Carmona, referring to Robbie, confined to a wheelchair, "don't ever tell these people you know how they feel. You don't."

In the training manuals and records the tasks appeared as discrete acts, as though they were performed one at a time, but the actual work always involved more than one focus, at least mentally. Arriving at the end of the hall to sort out some clean clothing meant simultaneously listening to the day room several yards away, attentive to its potential incidents. The rule was "coverage"; someone had to be present in the day room to oversee the thirty to forty people sitting in it. With three nursing assistants on the floor, and recurrent emergencies calling us away, it was a rule impossible to follow. Usually, just as soon as we left the day room for an instant, we had to rush back, for someone was likely to have seized the moment of our absence to wiggle partly out of her restraint vest.

"Nurse, nurse!" yelled Bernice Calhoun, who kept a vigilant eye out for such potential catastrophes. "Mary

Ryan's out again!" At that instance the clean clothing was dropped for the more urgent demand to rush back to reposition her or another of the eager escapees; that is, reposition and try to negotiate.

"Mary, please stay put this time, will you?"

"Stay put?" Mary Ryan screeched back. "You're all crazy in here. I don't trust anybody in white anymore. Look at my arms!" She pointed to black and blue marks on her arms, the result of continuous struggle with the restraints.

"Just try to relax, please; dinner will be here soon," I said, as if I had any idea what either "relax" or "soon" meant to her.[6] Then it was back to get some changes of clothing and fresh linens, and perhaps to squeeze in one of the showers that had been delayed earlier. En route Robbie Brennan often reached out for a handshake and a snippet of conversation. He got a handshake.

"Hey, catch y' later, OK, Rob?"

"Sure."

Or someone might have asked to be cleaned. "Hey, wash me today, will you? I feel grungy," urged bedridden Sara Wostein.

"Well, I don't know," I answered when I was first learning the job. "You're scheduled for a bed bath tomorrow, but I guess it's okay." It was not okay. Nursing assistant Solange Ferier spotted me proceeding to wash her and scolded me.

"You're supposed to keep to the schedule," she said. "When I first got here I'd give a bedbath to anyone who wanted one. Then I didn't get my beds done, and I got bawled out. Now I give baths only on their bath day."

"Well, Sara, looks like I got to finish this up tomorrow." While I folded the blanket back over her, we exchanged quizzical expressions and had nothing to say. Though we both had to absorb it, this externally imposed formal rationality was beyond our rational comprehension.[7]

By 4:30 visitors, family members, and volunteers filtered out. It frequently fell to the nursing assistants to encourage this, subtly at first, more strongly as the dinner hour approached, since we had to rearrange the day room into a dining room for the thirty or so residents who did not leave the floor. When the visitors departed they sometimes left an emptiness that could be seen on their relatives' faces. This was especially true of those for whom visits were rare. It was part of the work to be there when the visitors left, to try to fill the vacuum made by their absence. "Hey, they'll be back, don't worry." "Hey, you like to watch television?" "Hey, guess what's for dinner?"

And always there was a push and pull, the balance of getting close enough but not too close. Residents had much to teach about the latter. Some pointed out rules of touch and protested their breach. When the evening meal approached, nursing assistants seized whatever moments were available between 5:00 and 5:30 to attach the bibs, which involved their moving toward people from behind, not always announcing the approach. Marjorie McCabe once let out a shriek when the bib came around her neck. "Didn't anybody ever teach you not to come up to somebody from behind?" she reacted with rage. And Elizabeth Stern scolded me when I touched her back once without any prior eye contact. It seemed like a friendly gesture as we waited for the trays to arrive. Instead it was an insult. "Don't ever touch me like that," she insisted indignantly. "It's not natural."

Usually staff members were either moving or standing, while the people who lived there were sitting or lying down. Consequently, even with the best of intentions, it was the staff who became the touchers, those in the chairs the touched. Marjorie and Elizabeth seemed especially sensitive about this asymmetry, as though part of their practice of patienthood was learning how to deal with staff's unsolicited touch and how to avoid their invasions of presumed familiarity.

Dinner trays arrived between 5:15 and 5:30. Another strict regulation from the Board of Health was that plastic hats and gloves had to be worn when food was distributed. "Don't get caught without those gloves and hat," warned Kenny Obaku, a co-worker from Nigeria, "or at least have them close by so you can grab them. If the administrators or head nurse see you without gloves and hat, it's suspension for sure." Meanwhile, the work of serving included encouraging people to eat. These negotiations sometimes meant inventing ways to make food palatable and trying to generate appetite for someone, especially when the materials at hand, the tepid hot dog and chunky mashed potatoes from the steam tables, did not lend themselves to the challenge.

After the meal the formal responsibility for nursing assistants was to mark on each person's chart whether the food had or had not been eaten by each person. We leaned on the counter of the nurses' station and checked the boxes. That is, we checked the boxes and conversed.

"Will you help me make a phone call later?"

"Yes, Mickey."

"Can I borrow a quarter?"

"No, Joanne."

"Can I have a cigarette?"

"Yes, Fred."

"Will you fix this?"

"Okay."

"How are you this evening?"

"Oh, not bad. You?"

"Katherine, you're scheduled for a bath tonight."

"I know," snapped Katherine Stack, 79. "I've done it all my life. I don't need you to remind me." Perhaps this re-action of indignation restored some self-dignity for Kath-erine and the others who made the same response to this directive. Yet the fact remained that Katherine did need us to remind her, or at least the institution did, for another aspect of our job was to remind the people who lived there of their place in the schedule.

"Whoops, I'm sorry, Mickey, I almost forgot your phone call." Mickey Watkins, nearly blind, sat in his chair clutching the change he had saved from his trust fund for his twice-monthly call to his niece in Alabama, waiting for a staff person to tend to his request. Nursing assistants were his essential link to the outside world. First we helped him sort the correct change, then dialed from the number written in his notebook, then spoke for him to the opera-tor because Mickey, his teeth in disrepair, was often mis-understood. Then we spoke to his niece, who inquired about his well-being, and finally turned the phone over to him, staying nearby, while tending to others, to make sure he did not go overtime, which he usually did. We waited for the phone to ring to announce the overdue charges, fished for the coins in his purse, dropped them in, and waited for the mechanical "thank you." The procedure took about fifteen minutes, yet another quarter hour of activity that was unnamed and uncharted.

Mickey was one among many for whom the searching for change in his purse was a source of irritation not just because of his blindness but because of his poverty as well. "Hey, you know I worked all my life, what the hell is this?" he mumbled as we separated the quarters from the dimes. "How come I ain't got no money?"

"Well, it depends on how you handle your trust fund."
I repeated that official response regularly, until about the
third time Ralph Sagrello, who preferred to call it "poverty
aid," feigned a spit on the ground in the face of that logic.

"Well, it costs a lot to take care of sick people these
days." This explanation was less easy to debate, but it
wore thin, too. There was no opportunity for the people
to raise the issue of money in a forum more public than
there on the floor with the staff. It was up to the nurses,
nursing assistants, and other residents to absorb and reflect on this continual complaint, and try to mediate some
reasoning as to why chronic frailty had come to mean living the life of a pauper.

"You got any aspirin? I've got a splitting headache," said
Rose Carpenter one evening about 7:15.

"No," was the answer. "Wait until medications at 8.
The nurse might have some then." The key word in that
response was "might." It's worth repeating that ordinary
over-the-counter medications were, oddly enough, rare in
this environment. It was forbidden for nursing assistants
to offer remedies like an aspirin. Meanwhile, the registered
nurses had to be conscientious dispensers of pills that were
prescribed on the basis of categories that appeared in the
charts, with little local control in this process.

Both nurses and nursing assistants found the need to
bring into the homes an assortment of health-promoting
aids. "Damn," said Vera Norris, snapping her fingers, "I
forgot to bring those Epsom salts. Now Violet is not going
to be able to soak her foot." And since dry skin was one of
the pervading problems for those who lived there, many
attended to this condition of their own accord. Mrs. Bonderoid had emphasized this need in school. "Dryness is a
terrible problem in nursing homes. Keep some lotions
handy, for their skin, their lips, everywhere." Salves, balms,

lotions, even olive oil—such remedies came more often from the nurses' purses than from the medicine chest.

One evening Dorothy Tomason called Joanne Macon over to her, disturbed because Joanne had been scratching her dry scalp. "C'mere and let me oil that hair, Joanne," she said, pulling out her own hair oil. To another resident she said, "C'mere, Mirium, I'm gonna take care of that bee sting. I brought you some snuff." Whereupon she opened a chewing tobacco tin, moistened a fingerful, and spread it on Mirium's arm.

Besides bodily aids, the workers brought in old magazines, puzzles, and toys. One brought an old tape recorder and a tape so that a man who sang to himself could listen to his voice. Another was convinced that dolls were meaningful for some, so she brought them in for particular people. Such a gesture was appreciated, to judge from the dolls placed carefully by those residents under their pillows.

Delivering these health care aids was not enough. The residents usually required some encouraging, monitoring, or guarding. Putting lotion on bedridden Charlotte Walsh who suffered a chronic itch meant staying there to encourage her not to scratch before it penetrated. We once debated where to find some boxing gloves to keep Juan Loperez's hands away from his postsurgical eye patch. Offering Violet Shubert her walker so that she could get some exercise out in the hallway meant stealing time to watch her and staying close enough to stop a fall. This ongoing surveillance work of monitoring required some mental coordination while tending to one or two persons at a time, but thinking of the others as they scratched, picked at a bandage, or crept along the hall. We often needed to watch someone taking a precarious walk while we were doing something else as well—cutting someone else's nails, fixing clothing or hair, perhaps giving a shave. "Jack, I'm trying to juggle three things here, do you mind if this shave takes a while?" I asked while lathering Jack Connolly's face.

He understood the frenzied pace, in contrast to his own, and responded, "Go ahead, I don't care if it takes all day. I got nothing to do." A leisurely shave was a scarce resource because during the evening shift there was a full schedule of medical tasks to complete. After dinner there were showers and linen changes which had not been finished earlier, and vital signs of all the residents had to be taken.

The crucial significance of the vital signs procedure was brought into bold relief one evening about seven o'clock. Taking blood pressures, temperatures, and pulses was a five-minute task, barring interruptions. Mary Karney's turn came up, and on this particular evening she sat at the edge of her bed, head slumped over, crying—not at all typical of her usually jovial, if cynical, demeanor.

"Mary, what's the trouble?" I probed. No response. Wait. Responses sometimes came very slowly. "Can I check your pulse and blood pressure?" She offered her arm and looked away. Her blood pressure was a bit high, but within a normal range. Pulse, normal, check.

What was charted happened, but was the nursing care over? I waited, fiddling around with some blankets at the foot of the bed, apparently idle, waiting for Mary to speak. It was clearly idle to the charge nurse who was rushing down the hall. Seeing that I had completed the task in Mary's room, she called me out into the hall, beckoning me to get going on the appointed rounds. Looking at her watch, then at me, she said, "Let's get back to work. You've got sixteen more vitals to do." She rushed off to change a dressing, and while Mary continued to sit silently,

I moved on to the next room to the prescribed and enforced work of measuring life signs.

The blood pressure cuff, nicknamed the sphygmo (for sphygmomanometer), was an important piece of technology in the homes, continually in use and frequently in demand. While finishing the vital signs one evening, I was alerted by one of the staff: "Bring the sphygmo! Bring the sphygmo, quick!"

Lorraine Sokolof had stumbled on the freshly waxed floor, twisting her ankle and nearly fainting for an instant afterwards. The charge nurse alerted the nursing supervisor downstairs, who called an ambulance. The charge nurse then rushed with the two nursing assistants to Lorraine's aid. "Here, give me that," she instructed, grabbing the blood pressure instrument. As Lorraine regained composure she sat on the floor while the nurse wrapped its slip around her arm. She studied the gauge, then recorded Lorraine's blood pressure. That accomplished, the three members of the staff and three curious and helpful residents waited with her for the ambulance. Eventually the other nursing assistant, Kenny, asked, "Is there anything you would like?"

"Yes," Lorraine answered, "a glass of water."

In certain contexts, when someone nearly faints, the first gesture is to offer a glass of water. At that moment it was an afterthought, after the prescribed emergency measures for an incident had been executed. It was not permitted that any of us, including the charge nurse, deal directly with Lorraine's ankle, as, for example, by wrapping it with an elastic bandage. "We don't wrap without doctor's orders," explained Kenny. The primary health care delivery consisted of measuring and recording Lorraine's vital signs and waiting for the ambulance to arrive. Off she went for X rays and a hospital stay, at considerable cost, leaving her husband to worry if he'd ever see her again.

While the residents lined up for medications and then for their many requests afterwards, Dorothy Tomason carried on with her work. She was able, all at the same time, to converse, fix a bandage, improvise a belt with her ever-present string, oil someone's hair, and keep control over the many people competing for her attention. At its best her booming, laughing voice could control half a dozen simultaneous requests, "All right, quiet down. Now, one at a time, what do you need?"

At its worst, establishing control brought out behavior that came across as cruelty. Some of us, including me, slipped into this mode. As 10:00 P.M. came, it was time for lights out. "C'mon, now, off with the TV."

"Oh, just a little while longer."

"No. You know the rules." If they were not obeyed there was force to be wielded. We had the power to press the rules, even in the face of residents' opposition. I became amazed at my own capacity as an enforcer.

"Turn that off now. Do you hear me, Rose?"

"Yes," she mumbled.

"Do you hear me?" I barked again louder.

"Yes!" she repeated on cue, also louder. I had demanded that yes be repeated just to hear my own power through someone else's acquiescing voice.

"Can I have an extra cookie for snack?" was a common request.

"Let's see, have you had any bad behavior this week?"

"Oh, no, not me."

"All right, then, just one extra cookie." Within such relations of power and powerlessness it became easier to understand how Mary Karney came to derive and deliver her ironic "Thank you, Mommy."

I was fast enough at picking up on the power to lord it over my charges and efficient in deploying the drilled technologies. The learning that came later, and slowly, was how to think, listen, see, feed, touch, change, clean, and talk. These skills were buried deep within the complex of "assist as needed." Within this vast dimension was the knowledge most of the women brought to the job from their skills as mothers, wives, daughters, and other kinds of caregivers. I had none of these skills, as I came to realize daily. It was not a lack of emotions or concern; like the other staff I had these in adequate supply. What came so slowly were the actual skills of performance.[8] It became clear there was a base of skill behind that which was named, stemming from experience in unnamed domains, that was simply presupposed and written into the job.

That is, written out of the job. Just after most residents had gone to bed, and before the night shift arrived, we hustled to finish our charting of the bedmaking, bath schedule, bowel and bladder regimens, restraint and position sheets, weights and vital signs. Then nursing assistants were considered by the authorities to have performed their tasks. But these documentary requirements had little to do with how the night closed, or with much of what had gone on during the day, in terms of human contact. The coming of night meant coaxing brittle bones into night clothes, while negotiating with those who wore them to get into bed, calm down, and try to sleep. Then it meant slipping out the door and turning off the light as quietly as possible. Soon the shift would be over and we could go home, usually exhausted, not just from the physical labors that were officially specified for the job, but quite as much from executing the invisible skills of caretaking on which they depended.

There were numerous distinctions among the ranks of the nursing staff: different training and income, different racial, ethnic, and age groups. Still, before and after the 11:00 P.M. shift change, these distinctions paled, to judge from the general conversation. These workers were women. They had to cope with the stalking ghouls of the dark before and after their jobs. Their talk at this time of night centered on common apprehensions, strategies of how to negotiate the parking lots and bus stops. They offered to walk with each other and warned each other where to be particularly on guard. Vulnerability transcended rank. It was up to them to work around the organization, which followed the factorylike structure of shifts. There was no challenging that structure itself as the problem. So nurses and nursing assistants alike spent time before, during, and after shift change discussing the menacing dangers of the night.

"You've Got to Practice Hallway Amnesia"

When the night shift got under way, room check was the first designated task to complete. On a good night this meant a passing peek into the rooms. Occasionally it required changing someone's sheets, offering a drink of water, some turning, some noting of danger signals, like heavy wheezing, for the charge nurse. It may also have meant cleaning a body, wiping a nose or mouth to clear away phlegm, patting a perspiring brow, quieting a scream, a fear, a cough, a shiver.

Often it involved work that was more intensely interpersonal. "Oh . . . ," moaned Edna Barrett one night when she heard the door open. "Please stay here for a while, will you? I can't sleep. It's awful to be in the dark and not know anyone."

"Ah, I'll be back, Edna, just as soon as I check on the rest of the rooms." Upon my return in half an hour, Edna was still awake. She liked it when one of us could stay long enough for her to fall asleep—past just the closing of her eyes, which she did often during the day and night, past a few minutes of silence, until ultimately her deep sigh and slight snore signified that she was calm.

One evening, Dorothy Tomason and I returned from room check about 12:30 when the charge nurse stopped us at the nursing station. "Diamond, go put some lotion on Charlotte." Deferring to Dorothy's fourteen years on the job, she asked rather than ordered, "Dorothy, do you have time to change Arthur?"

Dorothy responded with an ironic smirk, "Honey, I'm a nurses' aide. I don't *have* time for nothing. I just make time to do what's got to be done." Then she turned to me with an instruction regarding Charlotte. "Don't ever put lotion directly on their skin. Old people are too sensitive for that. Always put it on your hands first and rub it around. Warm it up."

Charlotte Walsh's skin itched incessantly. Moisturizing her skin with lotion could have been done continually for her through the day and night. Various parts of this work brought the pleasure of knowing someone had been comforted, like being fed or quieted. With Charlotte the rewards were immediate. She seemed to calm down just seeing the lotion coming, just hearing it on the hands. As the rubbing proceeded, watching her hands gradually open up from their clenched fists was to see itch and anxiety dissipate as the cool lotion salved her skin.

Back rubs were not the order of the day, however. The organizational design for preventing bedsores was a schedule of turning bedridden people over on their sides every two hours. At the bottom of the restraint and position page was the physician's signature, indicating that all was approved and certified. Meanwhile, on Charlotte one could almost see bedsores in the making, as her ongoing need for lotion was transformed into a task on the daily schedule.

"Oh . . . I got to sit down," moaned Dorothy around 2:00 A.M. most nights, with her hand on her sore lower back. "Pain don't know no time."

"Yeah," said I, "me, too." Her eyes darted at me, expressing doubt. It was my only shift of the day, and Dorothy's second.

"God, how do you get some of these people out of your mind?" I asked her, with Charlotte's moans still echoing in my ears.

"Well," she said after a moment's reflection, "you've got to treat everybody a little different. But when you walk out of the room, you've got to leave them there and start moving on to somebody else. You've got to practice hallway amnesia."

We sat tidying up some charts. As I glanced over Mary Karney's vital signs, I remembered the incident when she was crying on the bed and I was told to keep moving. Here were the records of her life signs; they made it clear that formally the nursing assistant's job had nothing to do with talking with Mary. It had, in fact, been more efficient and productive not to do so, the faster to collect the measurements. In an early lecture in the school we were told "Nurses do the paperwork now, your job is to do the primary care." It turned out that often it was our job as well to walk away from primary care. To stay to give Mary Karney an emotional outlet for her trouble was supplanted by the act of taking vitals and moving on. Who was the giver and who the taker got confusing as I kept taking Mary's vitals. Tasks produced numbers that, rather than folded in as part of human relations, were extracted out as though they stood apart; then they dictated the form that interaction took between staff and residents.

Documentation reflected the physical life of the people who lived there and, in turn, generated a conception of nursing work as physical. Staff continually cursed at being overwhelmed with paperwork. Kenny once waved his hand at the whole row of binders containing these records. "Oh, they're just a formality," he said. They were a formality with a force—made of forms, and forming the contours of the job, both in doing the prescribed work and in certifying that it had been done.

Sometimes they formed the way we spoke. A new nursing assistant once approached a charge nurse who had been at work at this home for two years. Resident Frances Wasserman, who lost her purse, had now been at the home for two months and was crying out loudly in her room. "Is there anything I can do for her?" asked the nursing assistant.

"Oh," said the nurse, her mind immersed in the medications checklist, "don't worry about it, it's nothing physical, just emotional." Here in the night it was easy to see how readily such a comment could be voiced, for we were all thinking in physical terms: "Did I get the right vital signs? Is there enough linen? Is the place clean? Are we looking busy?" These were the issues monitored by the authorities and thus crucial to keeping our jobs.

Thinking was also shaped in terms derived from disease categories. Among Frances Wasserman's diagnoses was Alzheimer's disease. One time she was babbling and crying and moaning. "Oh," said the same charge nurse, "that's the way Alzheimer's people are." Frances's actions became explained as a manifestation of her disease, as though they were devoid of any personal, emotional, or situational content, and flowed purely as a consequence of knots in her brain. What would have explained her crying had this category not been readily available? Might her lost purse have come into focus? Or her son, who was going too near the deep water? Whether or not these might have had a place in a different context, they were considered irrelevant in this intellectual climate, permeated as it was by concepts

At 3:00 A.M. one morning, Frances started to wheeze heavily and vomit. The nurse assessed her condition. Fearing death was near, she called the ambulance immediately. Both nursing assistants rushed to tend to her. Vera Norris kept repeating: "Oh, c'mon now, sweetheart, don't die on me now, please!" To calm Frances's shivering, Vera put her hand on her brow, looked into her eyes, and kept saying "There, now, calm down, you're gonna be all right, there, there." Frances looked back at her, touching her once. Meanwhile, I was changing the linens, searching for a clean nightgown for her hospital journey, and trying to cooperate with Vera's strategy for soothing Frances.

"The ambulance is here. Help them," the charge nurse instructed. The ambulance attendants arrived at Frances's doorway, one fixing the portable cot, the other calling me out to the hall, where she held a chart with pen at the ready and asked one question before going in. "Is she alert to verbal stimuli?" I did not understand the question and had to ask her to repeat it. She replied, "I mean does she talk and understand what we say?"

"Well, she's not talking, but she seems to understand— at least Vera. I don't know if she will understand strangers." She checked a box and walked into the room, where Vera continued to talk to Frances, knowing as part of her nursing, as Mrs. Bonderoid had known, that hearing is the last to go. "There, there, sweetie, everything's going to be okay." The attendants moved Frances to the cot, wheeled her down the hall and out the door. It was the last we saw of her. Later we heard of her death. We suspected she did not long remain alert to verbal stimuli.

By 4:00 A.M. lights were on in many of the rooms. The

nursing assistants had thirsts to relieve, conversations to carry on, pain to acknowledge if not alleviate, nightmares to banish, sleep to coax back. "Go see what Henry wants, will you?" asked Dorothy around 5:00 A.M. one morning. He had awakened with his recurrent chant, "I'm gonna die, I'm gonna die."

"No, no, Henry, you're not! Please try to calm down," one of us appealed, while offering a cool cloth, or a hand, and a presence until he was quiet. After this it was back to the charts, where none of that happened. It was just another physically and emotionally draining moment of non-work.

More specifically, it was another moment of non-job. The work still got done, it just was not named or paid. Once I marched with a group of nursing home workers on strike in New Jersey. The marchers repeated a union slogan: "Our work is more than our job, and our life is more than our work." This distinction between the job and the work captured the difference between our tending to Henry and the official record. It clarified the question of whether or not it happened at all. As necessary work it did happen. As a job, beyond the vague notions of assist as needed or coverage, it did not.

"Hey, you got anything to eat?" Joanne Macon often asked just after 5:00 A.M., her night's sleep over.

"No, Joanne," responded Dorothy, "but here's a dollar. Go to the machine and get us both a cup of coffee." With the coffee, Joanne's hunger was abated for a few hours, as was Dorothy's weariness. Unless Dorothy had actually been seen at her work, whether on her double shifts or only one, her tiredness, high blood pressure and ongoing reference to feeling "hot all over" might seem unrelated to her job, for the way in which her work got documented erased most of what she had done during the night.

In one of the orientation lectures we were told that nursing assistants were the backbone of the place. In an impromptu speech by the administrator of another home we were called its muscle. Occasionally a friendly volunteer or relative called nursing assistants the heart of the homes. Workers spoke of all these body parts, too—but literally, not metaphorically, most often within the context of their pain. "I'm just worn out," Dorothy would say as the night came to a close. But she could not rest.

"Oh, now I've got to go clean Arthur," she said. "I can hear him moaning." It was a moan she had become sensitive to, as a mother does her baby's, while as we sat there I could not even hear him. Off she went to calm and cajole, clean, cuddle, and comfort Arthur, and he went back to sleep. She came back to mark in the small space in the nursing notes that he had been cleaned. The work of it all was distilled into one word, as the work was made into the job.

It made a certain kind of sense as those nights were drawing to a close that in the schooling and textbooks there had been no vocabulary of caring. There was no place for it in the records. Words that concerned how to be gentle with Arthur, firm with Anna, delicate with Grace, how to mourn with Elizabeth and mourn for Frances, how to deal with death and dying, loneliness and screaming, how to wait in responding to someone else's slow pace—these constituted much of the work as it went along, but nothing of the job. In the documentation there was nothing relational, no shadow of the passion, only a prescribed set of tasks a doer gave to a receiver.

Shortly after 6:00 A.M. it was time to begin preparing people for the day to begin. En route down the hallway I began to anticipate two of the forthcoming encounters. One was surely going to be a struggle, while the second hardly unpleasant at all. Yet both involved almost the same physical activity of cleaning and dressing someone. Erma Douglas's advice from the clinical training came to mind. Her prompt response when I approached her with trepidation about cleaning George was "Just go in there and pretend he's your father." By calling on this trick of fictive kin, she was telling me to put the exchange into some kind of personal context, even if I had to pretend one. In the early mornings I headed toward Mary Ryan and Alice McGraw. With Mary, unceasingly bitter and enraged, it was going to be difficult. With Alice the encounter would be partly in a fantasy world as she sang lullabies to people who were not really there. Erma's other lore began to make more sense as well. "After a while when you get to know these folks, it's like your baby" she said with a smile. "You'll find out whose shit stinks and whose don't." Erma's advice, besides being graphic and funny, was usually framed in a narrative of relations. Relationships, good and bad alike, were not something distinct from the work but integral to how it got accomplished.

But what Erma was telling me to do to get the work done, the charting process was prescribing *not* to do. Just as Erma's instruction was to put the tasks into a social relation to carry them off, the chart demanded that whatever happened as a human encounter be eliminated from the recording of the event. Recording the work in the charts came to be no more than jotting down numbers and check marks, transforming it out of social contexts into a narrative of tasks. Just as patient emerges into a social status in the meeting of sickness and institution, so the job emerged as a set of menial, physical tasks in the meeting of the actual work and the documentary products of it: the menial tasks were only a part of a larger human context in their actual execution, but they became simply menial and mechanical as recorded.

After rolling back the curtains to let the light into Sharon Drake and Mary Reynold's room, there was work to do, and much of it involved talk. "I'm dizzy when I first get up, you know," Mary grumbled, "so don't rush me."

"Yeah, I'm dizzy, too. Sorry, no Bloody Marys today. We're out of Tabasco."

"Sagan, rise and shine," as I tried to rouse him from sedated sleep. He awoke kicking, screaming, and cursing—always a rough one, as Mrs. Carmona had warned. We went along, waking, actively listening, filtering, and guessing who needed the most attention. We learned to cheer and to be cheered by Jack Sagan's two roommates. "How are you this morning, Juan?"

"Useless in here, thank you. I just hope my kids don't get a taste of this."

"Oh, c'mon, it's not so bad. The sun is shining. Get ready for breakfast, you'll feel better."

The third man, Art Jacobs, cheered the staff with his early morning renditions of "You Are My Sunshine." Even waking somebody was often more than just a mechanical task; there had to be some personal exchange to carry it off.

Like the residents who had to learn to live within that institutional order, nursing assistants had to learn to work within the people's specific visions of reality. Many were senile and spoke in their own obscure idioms that became understandable only after a time. Every day Jack Phillipson got up and put on his coat and tie, ready to go to work as he had for forty years. We called on nursing assistant Mimi Girard, who knew best how to reason with him. "No, Jack, no work today, breakfast first," she coaxed, "then a shower, okay?"

He paused, trying to figure this out, then asked, "Is the car in the garage?"

"Yes, Jack," she assured him, "the car is safe and

sound." Somewhat settled, he walked to the day room. Getting him there was more than "assist residents to day room," as listed in the job manual, and coaxing him to take off his coat and tie to take a shower was more than "give shower." To carry it off took knowing each other and an exchange based on familiarity within partnerships of caretaking.

In time I concluded that supervisors and other passing authorities often did not know the work. Even if they knew the skills, they did not know the relationships within which they were accomplished. "My Frankie" was distinctly not someone else's Frankie. Aileen Crawford's "I'm gonna miss that old goat" was about someone she had tended for two years. Feeding Helen Donahue's memories of her daughter or Sharon Drake's of her restaurant developed only with time.

Yet in the narrative of the charts a clear line was drawn between giver and receiver, and what was given was measured. The social and emotional work was distilled into measures of productivity, and a responsive job was made over into a prescribed set of tasks. The process erased work such as waiting for someone to make an endlessly slow walk down the hall or knowing how to touch someone in the right spots and not to touch someone else in the wrong ones, just as it erased work that was not named or even noticed until left undone, like making the sheets clean enough to be called dirty. No terms connected with caring, relations, or emotions found their way here to muddy up the smooth, carefully calculated records of care. The job was organizationally produced as menial and mechanical, industrially streamlined to complement the making of patients.

As those nights ended and as we waited for the next shift to relieve us and start a new day, the sign over the nurses' station reminded us that if it's not charted, it didn't happen. Still, even if not charted, a lot had happened. The nights and days moved along, aided by the intricate skills, including the mother's wit, that caregiving involved. Erma Douglas's position had now become a little clearer from the time when she stood across that bed explaining the complexity of her work with just five words: "This is what I do."

Part Three
Melting the Gold Bricks Down

The women and men who lived in these homes, and those who tended to them, went about their physical, mental, emotional, social, and economic lives within an organizational context and a set of rules about how caretaking was defined and accomplished. The previous two chapters highlighted ways in which these rules and the ideas behind them turned the people who lived in these settings into patients and turned the complex work of caretaking into quantifiable tasks.

Chapter Six continues that line of analysis, concentrating on the language that reflects how caretaking has been turned into a commodity and managed as a capitalist industry. This chapter is more analytic and less descriptive than the previous ones. Chapter Seven, by contrast, is fanciful, a wish list based on the comments of residents and staff. Both chapters attempt to decode and deconstruct, or melt down, certain words, concepts, and phrases that lead to making gray gold.

6

"There's Nothing Wrong with the Scale, It's the Building That's Tipped"

Each morning after breakfast we measured and recorded weights. Each resident was weighed twice a
week. Fern Parillo's turn had come up. "Fern, step up here,
will you please," I asked. "It's that time again."

"Sure," she responded, without much expression, used
to the routine after her three years of residency. A factory
worker for most of her adult life, an immigrant to the
United States in the 1920s, Fern was of relatively strong
constitution at age eighty-two, but she was a small, thin
woman. After a few times taking her weight, I turned with
curiosity to Dorothy Tomason, who had worked in this
home for several years.

"Dorothy, how can this be right?" I queried. "Fern
keeps weighing a hundred and fifteen pounds on this scale.
Look at her. Can she really weigh that much? Are you sure
this scale isn't screwed up?"

Dorothy replied without even turning around, as though
she had answered the question often. "Oh, there's nothing
wrong with the scale," she said, with a nonchalant wave
of her hand. "It's the building that's tipped."

Moments later she pointed toward the center of the
large room to show how the floor tilted toward the middle.
The building had been constructed as a hotel in the 1920s,
when Fern Parillo was just arriving in the country. Over
the intervening sixty years, crowds of people had walked
on the floor until it began to sag toward the center. With
growing populations in need of long-term care, nursing

home corporations bought and converted many old hotels; their small rooms and large public areas were compatible with the building dictates of institutionalizing several hundred people. Dorothy's explanation, that the scale was fine but the building tipped, resolved the momentary dilemma, and Fern was recorded at the weight indicated on the scale, as were the others. Irrespective of accuracy, the measures on the scale prevailed.

This incident may serve as a metaphor for how nursing homes are being organized in the United States of the late twentieth century. They are arenas of caregiving, but they are also bureaucratic organizations founded on specific relations of power.[1] In the context of being made into a business, caregiving becomes something that is bought and sold. This process involves both ownership and the construction of goods and services that can be measured and priced so that a bottom line can be brought into being. It entails the enforcement of certain power relations and means of production so that those who live in nursing homes and those who tend to them can be made into commodities and cost-accountable units.[2] Using a much looser round-the-clock framework than before, this chapter reviews some of the situations encountered earlier, adds some new data, and traces processes through which caretaking is made into a business.

"A Nursing Home Is a 24-Hour-a-Day, 365-Day-a-Year Business"

The very first instruction of the day keynotes this inquiry. Upon reporting to the nurses' station at 7:00 A.M., the nursing assistants were assigned to their tasks with the words, "Today you have beds 201 to 216, you have 217 to 232," and so on. That instruction—that the assignment was to beds and that beds meant persons—was reiterated frequently during the day. It is a commonplace item in the everyday terminology of medical settings. However efficient this figure of speech may be, it requires a leap of logic even as a metaphor, for it makes persons into things. Central questions for this chapter are how and why people in nursing homes get made into beds.

After breakfast one morning, the administrator of one of the homes summoned the nursing assistants to his office. He had called the meeting to reprimand the staff for not working faster and to inform us that he had a new plan for organizing our work. His first words set the tone for the meeting: "I hope I don't have to remind you that a nursing home is a twenty-four-hour-a-day, three hundred and sixty-five day-a-year business." His emphasis was on the full-time demands of the work; his message was that we needed to keep working harder. He was not pointing out that this was a business; he took that for granted.

He went on to outline a plan that was to make us more productive and avoid the need for increases in staff. We had been four nursing assistants on a floor, but he had figured out a way to cut that to three and a half. "You used to work together. From now on, you're on your own. On each floor I want one of you on toileting, one on showers and beds, one in the day room for coverage at all times, and the fourth will now float between floors. The nurse in charge will tell you who does what. Are there any questions?" There were none. He stood up from behind his large oak desk, with its gold pens and four-line telephone, walked to the door to open it for us, passing en route his wood-paneled walls lined with licenses and state certifications. "Okay," he said as he opened the door, "let's get back to work."

We walked out quickly in a line, passing the air-conditioned computer room, down the carpeted first floor where the private-pay,and Medicare people lived, to the elevators that would take us to the long-term residents. It was not until the elevator doors closed that reactions began. "It's simple," was the instant analysis offered by nursing assistant Solange Ferier from Haiti. "We do the work, they make the money."

Some chuckled, but comments were subdued, for among the nursing assistants on the elevator, one worker was now present who was brand-new. Solange initiated a greeting, "You're new, aren't you Brenda? Are you coming up to our floor?"

"Yes," the new worker responded, "but only for meals. They told me that for now I can only work part-time."

Solange and I glanced at each other, rolling our eyes. It was not that we wished to be unfriendly, but now another task would complicate our serving of meals. The administrator had exercised one of his management mandates to cut costs by breaking the job down into smaller segments of labor.[3] But we had to introduce someone to the residents and routines who would not get to know them for weeks since she would be around only at meals. It was not exactly as though Brenda was a new worker; she was almost like piecemeal labor. She was going to help serve the food, but she was going to make more work for the nursing assistants than she would contribute.

Predictably, one of Brenda's first questions when she started concerned the cards on the trays. "What are we supposed to do with these?" she asked.

"Take them off each tray," was the answer, "and put them over at the nurses' station. We'll turn them in after the meals." Great emphasis was placed on this procedure; it was important that she do it correctly. The cards served as documentation that the meal had been served and that it contained precise quantities of nutrition.

In the late morning the administrators usually came on the floor for inspection. Immediately nursing assistants and other staff started to move, grabbing a chart or a comb or a rag to clean tables—whatever we thought would adequately constitute looking busy through administrative eyes. One issue the authorities brought up continually on those mornings was the importance of staff wearing identification tags. "Where's your tag?" they asked. "We want to see it clearly displayed at all times. We catch you twice without it, and you can expect a day of suspension." As though our white uniforms were not enough to demonstrate that we worked there, the tags, with our photographs and worker identification numbers, were reminders that we and our work belonged first and foremost to the organization.

The head nurse was present on these internal inspections. On one tour she instructed us, "It's important to keep them in the day room after feedings and not let them go wandering around. Sometimes there will be only three of you instead of four on duty when we're short on another floor. We like to know where they are at all times. So keep them in here after meals. It's more efficient."

"Efficiency," was a favorite word, as it is in all businesses, and in these settings, as elsewhere, it was tied to the labor force and the abilities of the administration to produce the product with the fewest employees, within a specific calculus of labor costs. Upstairs as the day went along we coped with demands far exceeding our capacities— "Wait for me, will you?" "Water, please give me some water," "Are we going to the funeral now?" "Stay with me"—a constant stream of requests cascading down the hallways amid the clamor of the call buttons.

Downstairs it was a different story. Applicants were told, "No, we're not hiring right now." The administrative efforts were focused on cutting labor costs, mostly by hiring part-time staff, as Brenda the meal server exemplified, and "floating" the fourth nursing assistant on more than one floor. All of these efforts met state standards and were, by some criteria, good business.

Occasionally the head of maintenance was also along on these tours, and he gave orders as well. "Remember to keep them and their chairs at least three inches out from the wall—state regulations," he said, winning a nod of approval from the administrator. Once he looked out over the day room, with its twenty to thirty people sitting in chairs along the walls and mused to a nursing assistant, "You know, I should be running this place. I know exactly how they should look."

On the day the head nurse finished speaking about efficiency she stood waiting for the elevator. I happened to be passing her en route to Alice McGraw, who sang Irish lullabies to the delight of several who worked there. Since I had not been at this home long, the nurse paused to ask, "How are things going for you up here?"

"Oh, not bad," I responded with a slight chuckle, nodding toward Alice, anticipating lullaby time. "I kinda like a lot of the people."

As the elevator doors opened and she backed in, she nodded in apparent agreement with me. "Yes," she said, as the doors closed between us, "they're a good team. Very professional."

The maintenance supervisor's reference to how they should look and the head nurse's assumption that by "people" I meant staff served as examples of a certain attitude that dominated the settings. Those living there were the receivers of service, more acted upon than actors, whose ability to act was reduced not only by their own incapacities but by administrative definitions.

By mid-afternoon resident Jack Connolly frequently sat in his wheelchair trying to help Betty Slocum get something to eat. She may or may not have finished her lunch. Her appetite waxed and waned and was very unpredictable. After two or three hours of sitting in the day room, she was ready for a snack. Though tied to her chair with a vest, she often nudged, chair and all, toward the snack cupboards, which were locked. Seeing this, Jack often entreated the staff. "Give Betty something to eat, will you? She's hungry as hell."

Mr. Connolly's observation may have been true or false. In either case it was of no consequence. It was uttered by, on behalf of, and to persons who had no agency in the activity of eating in this setting. Even the naming of food was outside the control of the eaters. Lito Esparza, who had been a chef in his earlier years, regularly commented when the ground beef concoction came up on the cycle. It was not so much that he disliked the taste, it was that they gave it the wrong name: "I just wish they wouldn't call this stuff meat loaf. I know meat loaf when I see it. That ain't it." Margaret Casey made similar comments: "I wish they wouldn't call this stuff by all their different names. It's all potato goulash if you ask me."

No one asked her. The labels and measures that named and quantified the food and fed the documents their needed information about nutrition had certified that the meals for Betty, Margaret, Lito, and Jack were all up to the mark, and in fact sounded rather delectable. In the process the records that certified nutrition grew conceptually into more than reflections about diets. They labeled the food, ensured that it was controlled by those in authority, and thus removed the power of evaluation from those who ate it, those who served it, and those who cooked it.

At some time during the afternoon, residents whose

names came up on the bath schedule were informed it was their time for cleaning. It was not a bath, it was a shower; conflict arose occasionally and residents sometimes expressed fear. The temperature of the water varied. It was not bound to be cold, but it might be cold, and if it was, both parties knew that this would not stop the procedure. It was not that the showers were cold any more than that the food was disliked. It was that though it could have been the case, the records would show it to be otherwise, and those feeling the cold water or eating the food had no power to alter or even publicly name the situation.

Because germs are the enemy of modern medicine, in this institutional order cleanliness ruled with a seemingly moral force. No one took precedence over the cleaning man while he constantly ran his buffing machine up and down the halls, making them slippery and smelly but squeaky clean. Clean prevailed over warm, for example, in the case of the undeviating shower schedule. Clean took a formal priority, though it was an externally scheduled and documented clean. That is, to participate in this particular social production of cleanliness was not necessarily to be clean. It was impossible for a staff of three or four nursing assistants to look after the sanitary needs of forty to fifty people, so an intermittent smell of urine hung over the day room and hallways, only to be replaced several times during the day by the smell of cleaning chemicals.

Given the staff–resident ratio, it was deemed most efficient to have diapers put on many of the residents, so that their bodily cleaning could be attended to after the fact. By the time we reached some residents to change diapers, it might have been several hours after they had first called us. Residents had to learn to sit or lie in bed after an accident, waiting for clean to be restored.

Often during the day, Marjorie McCabe, sitting in the

nonporous plastic straight chair, diagnosed her situation while wiggling her back into a new position. "I don't have bedsores, I have chairsores." Still, this life of sitting was not in the control of the sitters, nor was what they sat in. In the record-keeping, in fact, what they sat in was not noted. Bedsores had a medical category, "chairsores" was a coinage casually tossed off.

What these situations have in common is that the residents were expressing specific desires while encased within a system of control that precluded them from satisfying their own needs. Under these conditions of distant control, power from within the local setting became almost nonexistent. Flora Dobbins could not buy a tiny refrigerator for her room because Board of Health regulations forbade it. David Forsythe was unable to obtain a nose inhaler for his cold or Rose Carpenter an aspirin for her headache, because neither was prescribed by the absent doctor. Nor could Sharon Drake and Mary Reynold have a Bloody Mary. Sara Wostein could not get anyone to stay with her. Margaret Casey, as she lay in bed, had no control over her own pain medication, nor did Charlotte Walsh over her itch. Amid intense and elaborate external control, for those who lived and worked there much of everyday life was out of control. Residents became estranged from authority over their own food, cleaning, and medications, as needs, how they were to be met and which ones would remain unmet, became externally defined.[4]

It made a certain kind of sense that these needs would be externally controlled. The sense was typified, for example, in the logic that diapers went on before the toileting for people classified as incontinents, like Juan Loperez, for whom an early morning trip to the toilet was presumed inconsequential. Dirty diapers were a part of nursing assistants' constant cleaning tasks and residents' discomfort.

Within this mode of caretaking dirty diapers had to happen. They were intrinsically connected to too few toilet-tending laborers. Personal spontaneous needs were made to fit into an organizational schedule. This schedule allowed management to trim the labor force. Strapping Juan into a diaper was labor-saving, cost-effective, time-and-motion efficient, profit-accountable, and documentable. The only thing left out of this managed equation was Juan's desire to go to the toilet when he first woke up.[5]

This line of analysis is not intended to generalize that diapers are overutilized in all homes, any more than to assert beyond these incidents that the meat loaf is really potato goulash or the water in the showers is frequently cold. Surely the quality of these materials is better in some nursing homes than in others, and various state and federal regulations are regularly promulgated in an effort to guard against their abuse.[6] However, these incidents do illustrate a process that is generalizable beyond these particular settings.

The process is a power over knowledge, by means of power over documents, created by and open only to professionals and managers. Their concepts and categories define how everyday life in the homes will be made to operate. The ways cleanliness and nutrition are measured render comfort, taste, and texture accidental properties, irrelevant to the essential quantitative index. The leap from the everyday situations to their formal records involves a transformation into abstract measures. As a result of the leap, the diapers, ground beef, and bath water emerge through the filter of their documentation as positive, productive indicators of good health care business. The driving force that makes them positive indicators comes from the creation of the concepts, scales, measures and consequent work practices contained within the documents, products of professionals and managers outside the context of their actual experience.

Within this kind of health care there was no longer any need for a physician actually to be present, night or day; there was need only for the monthly consultation, the time when the charts needed to be signed. When this person of authority came along in the mid-afternoon once a month, the data were already organized in the documents ready for him to check: Fern's weight, Juan's incontinence, Mary's nutrition, Lorraine's blood pressure, Margaret's pain medication, Charlotte's salve for her itch.

Helen Donahue's response to the visiting doctor came to make more sense. Day in, day out, she had a lot to say about her care to those around her, but to him she said nothing.

"Is there anything I can do for you, Helen?" he asked, as he stood behind her with his hand on her shoulder.

"No, Doctor," came her cold response.

By the time the doctor stood behind her, one hand on her shoulder, one holding her chart, anything he could do for her, any way that he might patch up the conditions of her life would be of little consequence, as Helen seemed to acknowledge. He was an integral part of the system of authority that set those conditions in motion. Notwithstanding his kind motivation on that pass-through visit, by the time he gave her shoulder its unsolicited touch, he was too late. He had already recertified her into patienthood, signing her vitals as the signs of her life.

Doctor is a word drawn from the Latin, meaning "teacher." But for Helen this doctor had become a mere physician and one of a radical sort. He had, through his power to document her life, made radical claims on it, certifying it as a physical phenomenon, a body, making claims that her life could be put into the terms and numbers of the charts and then evaluated through them by his fleeting, essentially absent authority. There was, by the time he stood behind her, little he could do to change the conditions which she complained about to others, for he was part of their ongoing construction. Helen's evaluated response, "No, Doctor," was brief and matter-of-fact.

"That's So They Don't Have to Hire Any More of You"

Mary Ryan, like many others, spent all day in the day room, secured to her chair with a restraint vest. "How y' doin' today, Mary?" I once asked in passing.

She answered the question with a question. "Why do I have to sit here with this thing on?"

I responded automatically with the trained answer, "That's so you won't fall. You know that."

"Oh, get away from me," she reacted with disgust. "I don't trust anybody in white anymore."

Stunned by her rejection, and not completely confident of my own answer, I passed the question on to Beulah Fedders, the LPN in charge. "Beulah, why does she have to wear that thing all the time?"

Beulah accompanied her quick comeback with a chuckle. "That's so they don't have to hire any more of you."

We snickered together at the humor of her explanation, but an explanation it was, and more penetrating than mine to Mary. It posed a relationship between technology and labor, and in that connection Beulah explained that the use of one could mitigate the need for the other. A different kind of answer to the same question was given during our orientation. "The restraint vests save on incidents." This rationale echoed Mr. Store's admonition in the training course: "Never forget that the Incident Report is the most important document in the place."

Beulah's answer was more accurate than "so you won't fall" and "vests save on incidents," because she connected them both to a common denominator—available labor. If no nursing assistant was there to be with Mary, to walk with her or anticipate her dizziness, and if she sat in the chair without a restraint and without anyone to keep an eye on her, she might have fallen, thus generating an incident. Her restraint vest saved on incidents while it saved on labor costs.

The record indicated that it was the obviously appropriate procedure. As a nursing assistant I was part of the process that made it that way. On Mary's sheet, the nursing assistants regularly and dutifully marked every two hours that Mary was "up with restraints." The sheets spanned a one-month period. On this monthly visit, the doctor signed a whole series of such sheets. It was doubtful that the physician was familiar with the experience of sitting strapped in a chair all day, every day, nor was he present to deal with Mary's rebellion against her treatment. However, his power was surely present all day and all night—there at the bottom of the restraint and position sheet, quelling Mary's question with his authorizing signature, transforming her complaint, and Beulah's analysis of it, into proper health care.

The women and the relatively few men who have done caretaking work in earlier times have done so as family members or as nurses, servants, or nuns. As caretaking gets continually molded into a capitalist industry there emerges a change in the definition of its labor. Earlier, as now in families, more hands meant lighter work and therefore were intrinsically valuable. When workers come under the business logic they are defined as labor costs to the owners and managers, to be cut back wherever possible.[7] However discordant with caregiving as a responsive mode, the industrial mandate is for more work to be done by fewer workers, as a consequence of the drive toward managed productivity. On the wards as the days went along, moving through historical as well as daily time, the press was on to speed up the work. "Damn you, you've made a mess again today," from a nursing assistant was regularly echoed by residents' "Damn you, can't you just take a little time for me?" Tensions mounted under this pressure of time and motion, as caretaking was jammed into this streamlined labor form.

The change of shift approached at 2:45, and the talk of getting out bubbled among the staff. One day the head nurse gathered the nursing assistants to report a change in procedure. "From now on there's only going to be a five-minute change of shift report, and some of you are going to be cut from eight hours to seven and a half." Turning toward part-time workers was also a strategy for cutting labor costs, one that had enormous impact on the income and benefits, especially health care, for the part-time staff.

Toward the end of the day shift, there were last-minute duties for nursing assistants, including turning those confined to their beds and giving most a quick massage with lotion to moisturize their dry skin. This task could not begin before 2:30 because to do so earlier would have disrupted the schedule of the two-hour turning, which technically was to occur at 3:00. So the cream had to be applied somewhat hurriedly during that last half hour of the shift. "Don't worry about giving a back rub," one nursing assistant told of being instructed on her orientation to this schedule. "The point is to put the lotion on." Back rubs became a luxury within this worker–resident ratio and were eliminated.

From within the logic of the administrative calculations it had been determined that the schedule for turning and the moisturizing task could be achieved together during that last half hour. It was work nearly impossible to manage upstairs with anything but the briefest sweep of the lotion, while downstairs it became a rational distribution of labor time. Resident Lorraine Sokolof pinpointed this dynamic of caregiving as industry with a seasoned observation. Sitting all day in the day room, watching the hustle at the close of shifts, she once noted, "You know, I've been here for three years. Seems like it gets faster and faster in here all the time."

These observations by Beulah Fedders, Mary Ryan and Lorraine Sokolof helped clarify the status of nursing assistants within this framework of caretaking as business. They put into perspective some of the basic themes of the training course and the wage structure under which we worked.

In the formal schooling of nursing assistants the theory part of the course emphasized biology, measurements, and medical procedures. The taking and recording of the vital signs—blood pressures, temperatures, respirations, and pulses—were constantly drilled and tested. Yet within the formal training there was no language of caregiving beyond the biological. There were no concepts taught or debated relating to caregiving as a social and emotional encounter. Mrs. Bonderoid's notion of mother's wit crystallized this contradiction. She referred to it only by way of an aside, apart from the texts and tests. The formal knowledge became privatized, to be purchased for tuition, while conceived and judged by medical, corporate, and state administrators. In this sense the training curriculum was not separate from the overall commercialization of nursing home care, but was an integral part of it; what was only part of the work, the science and measurements, was taught and sold to the students as its whole.

This extraction was a starting point in the process of making gray gold. The potential caretakers could be monitored and tested with multiple-choice questions by outside authorities who had no experience of actual nursing home life and the face-to-face human encounters of the work. The social organization of this knowledge was such that it could be taught in school and on the job by professionals who did not themselves do the work. The military metaphor with which the school's owner greeted us took on increasing appropriateness: the training of foot soldiers to go to the firing line of health care armed with the manageable, mechanical, medical model of what went on inside.

These foot soldiers are, overwhelmingly, women of color. As the industry grows, it builds off labor that has a distinct gender, class, and racial foundation. In the everyday settings these social distinctions did not disappear from the encounters, even if blanketed by the conceptual transformations of care into biophysical tasks. They were mentioned continually by the workers and the residents. Student Vivienne Barnes wondered whether they were "teaching us to be nurses' aides or black women." With her irony, Vivienne captured the contradictory processes of learning skills and unlearning them that this form of training involved.[8]

Though policy planners through the 1980s called for formal training for nursing assistants as a way to improve nursing home care, most policies and reports conspicuously avoided the issue of wages.[9] Yet the persistent wage structure of less than five dollars an hour created a class process that was the opposite of the professionalization promised in the schooling. Searching for extra work, double shifts, or two jobs, was not an idiosyncrasy of eager workers. It was a systemic feature of this new profession. The learning, or enskilling, that was the promise of the professionalization was confronted by the reality of the wages, which placed these women, mostly women of color, at the margins of subsistence income, recreating them into the status of poor women. The administrator where I first applied for work understood the conflation of these gender, race, and class dynamics, summarizing them with his suspicious question, "Now why would a white guy want to work for these kinds of wages?"

The status of nursing assistant, then, has emerged with job specifications and a wage structure based in a particular conceptualization of the work. What the job entails and the staff–resident ratios considered adequate for its performance—these are not intrinsic to health care, nor are they dictated by its needs as expressed by the people who live or work in this setting. Rather, these ratios and concepts have been shaped to conform to industrial forms of production. In their wake they have created a constant turnover of workers, who move in search of a quarter or half dollar more in pay. The structure of labor creates a revolving door of workers, as though they were replaceable parts, while the inter-personal nature of caregiving gets systematically ignored.

A related element evident in almost all nursing homes in the United States is that the labor foundation of this developing institution is made up of workers drawn not just from within the society. The Filipino nursing labor force, as the primary example, has become central to the infrastructure of health services. The United States depends on the Philippines not just for military bases in the Pacific but for its health care personnel as well.

Almost every afternoon Bessie Miranda engaged in a pitched battle with Anna Ervin, pressed into carrying out the externally-timed bowel and bladder regimen. Bessie embodied nursing homes' dependency on imported labor.

This geopolitical linkage brought Bessie and Anna into conflict. When Anna was still practicing as an LPN twenty-five years before they first met, Bessie was just being born in Manila. She would become part of a training corps and then a labor force that would serve the health care needs of the United States at a cost cheaper than native workers. Bessie and Anna, both women, both nurses, both devout Catholics, the religious medals around their necks hanging only inches from each other as they struggled on those afternoons, were locked in a battle not of their own doing, organized by relations of ownership far beyond their control.

These multinational dimensions were often recognized and spoken about in the local encounters of what Flora Dobbins called "the United Nations around here." Frank Sagan, whom Mrs. Carmona called a rough one, was rough in part because he insulted her culture when she had to enforce rules he did not like, such as forbidding him to smoke at certain times and in certain places. Having fought in the Philippines in World War II and having smoked all his life, he frequently lashed out: "I liberated them people and look where it got me!"

The nurses from the Philippines were well trained and highly qualified, but they were from another country and language, and this generated some communication gaps. Sometimes they did not understand American colloquial slang and customs. Art Jacobs, seventy-nine, sang in his room "You Are My Sunshine" and "Clementine" with full voice, but almost no teeth. To someone not familiar with the tunes, his singing was only a jumble. Charge nurse Carla Alvarez, in the States less than two years, took him for demented, made a comment to that effect, and infuriated him to a frenzy. When she realized her mistake she apologized. Yet that a nurse could be in charge by virtue of medical training and exhibit such cultural misunderstanding was not even recognized as an incongruity of nursing by the time it was translated into the multinational corporate logic within which foreign nurses became cheaper labor costs.

When these nurses talked informally about their situations it became apparent that working in the United States meant living under a tight system of rules. After Laina Martinez and I became friendly I asked where she lived. She told me, then quickly added, "But don't mention that to them [the supervisors], and don't ever send me anything there. There's only three people registered for that apartment." She and another friend also lived there, both still paying for their plane tickets and saving money to send home. They worked under contracts signed before they left Manila. It was not clear what the consequences would be if they were fired and their contracts broken, but they did use the word "scared" many times. With Florence scared to have to do an Incident Report and scared to punch in with her coat on, with Laina scared to be late, and Bessie scared to go on break too long, the word was spoken often enough to seem to be less a casual term than a necessary attribute of their work status. Their stories and their fears suggested that the corporate arrangements under which they worked supplied the ownership hierarchy with more than just cheaper labor; they provided a mechanism of social control as well. Their position sounded less like purely professional employment than a cross between paid work and bonded labor.

As the charts were pulled out and constantly checked for accuracy by the business, state, and medical authorities who appeared on those afternoons, none of these race, class, gender, wage, or multinational dimensions of the work appeared there. They remained, however, intrinsic to the organization, and they left lingering questions in their wake. "How do you make it on just one job?" turned out to be a rationally calculated question from the standpoint of someone who had to live on this wage, just as "How are your revolutions doing today?" was asked by a foreign-trained nurse who could see out from her basement cafeteria to the operations of a world labor system.[10]

"I Guess the Board of Health Stopped In"

One persistent question about nursing homes is what role the government plays in their development. An entrée to this issue loomed one afternoon when I was working an evening shift in a home populated mostly by people on the rolls of public aid. I was particularly eager to get to work because earlier on this day the home had been scheduled for a Board of Health inspection. The rumor was that the officials would be especially interested in nutrition on this visit.

In this home residents and staff often commented negatively on the food. For example, one lunch on the repetitious menu consisted of tomato soup, a toasted cheese sandwich, and pears. "Ah," said Dorothy Tomason regarding the first item, "water soup again, I see." The sandwich was one slice of American cheese between white bread that had been toasted in the ovens downstairs earlier and placed on a steam table, so it was occasionally a bit soggy, less than warm, and commonly left half-eaten. The cards on the trays moved along regularly, recording proper nutrition and delivery.

On inspection day, after asking some of the nursing assistants, I was surprised to learn that most who had worked during the day did not know whether or not the inspection had occurred. As it turned out, it had, though none of the officials had come to our floor. After I pursued the matter, the charge nurse finally said, "I guess the Board of Health stopped in. Someone said we passed."

What had occurred was that the inspectors came to the offices downstairs, where they inspected the records. The rumor was true: they had been especially interested in nutrition. Since all of the meal cards had been carefully collected, alphabetized, coded, and entered into the computer, the officials' job was made easier. After a glance through the kitchen and a fleeting exchange with a few residents, they simply had to look at the records to see that proper nutrition had been delivered. On the basis of the records, the home passed the inspection.

Food became units of food, separately countable, scientifically consistent, and programmed as data, with the results printed on a computer sheet. In the process the tomato soup and cheese sandwich became something other than what they were when mocked and left half-eaten upstairs. Downstairs they became units of nutrition, coded sustenance for the administrators and state officials to agree in their shared language that food service was adequate and certifiable.

The word *inspection* is drawn directly from the Latin, meaning "to look at." Through the new technologies and codes of this emerging industry, "look at" came to mean inspect the records and rendered superfluous the need to look at the food or the people who ate it. A leap occurred here from quality to quantity that represented not just a recording of the events and the food, but a transformation of them, and an appropriation of the judgment of what was eaten beyond the eaters and servers. It involved a leap of logic and power.

In this instance, as with training nursing assistants or licensing imported labor, the government was not separate from the business of health care, but enmeshed in it. Like the physicians and other professionals, the state officials were rarely present in the local setting, but they, too, exercised a documentary power of presence, certifying the proprietary power of the organization over those who lived there.[11]

All along the bureaucratic hierarchy, beginning with inspection, state officials define reports as the reality they will recognize. Reports are what they pay for and get paid for, the entities they recognize for money exchanges. There in the homes authorities saw the records; they saw what they needed to see. The inspectors, like the owners and doctors, had no need to be present most of the time, for the categories that provided the currency they exchanged among themselves had already been extracted from its base in lived experience and delivered over to them. A set of procedures had been set in motion that did more than count the events of everyday life. It made the events of everyday life countable.[12]

Yet this stance gave rise to contradictions. These standards, abstracted into quantitative terms, turned inside out what they claimed to be about. Inspectors claimed to have inspected the food, but what they looked at were socially constructed measures of it. While food was a constant source of conversation and evaluation by the eaters, servers, and cooks, these abstractions ignored legitimate speech by those who lived and worked in the setting, while certifying the industry mode of production and authority. This procedure established not just a particular form of caretaking but also a form of external control. Outsiders came to judge the inside through methods and criteria that remained outside, while those inside remained outside any evaluation. Those inside were placed outside the boundaries of the privileged communication about them, locked out by the documents that turned the key.

Control by absent authorities permeated everyday life. One late afternoon in a private-pay home, Margaret Casey's nephew came to visit her. When Miss Casey had entered the home she brought with her a bottle of Black Velvet whiskey. Permission for an occasional cocktail was an amenity that this $120 per day home was proud to advertise as one of its liberal policies. Having a cocktail before dinner was a custom she had occasionally practiced while living alone for nearly sixty years. The liquor was kept under lock at the nurses' station. The drink, under doctor's orders, was to be dispensed by the charge nurse in the prescribed amount—one ounce of liquor to three ounces of water. The nurse could not dispense it before dinner since she was busy elsewhere and had to squeeze Margaret's requests amid many more pressing demands, often not having the time to attend to it.

On the occasion of her nephew's visit, Margaret tried to offer him a drink. "How about a cocktail?" she solicited in a rare burst of enthusiasm.

The nurse informed them that it was not possible for both to have a drink. Under doctor's orders she could dispense the drink only to specified patients, not to guests, for which she said she would need a liquor license.

For a few seconds all three looked at each other speechless and dumbfounded. Then the nurse left the room, and Margaret and her nephew changed the subject. Margaret's gesture had been rejected by the distant authorities; in the local situation all would-be participants in the convivial sharing—Margaret, nephew, and nurse—had no control over it. After that incident I never heard Miss Casey ask for a cocktail again, and the bottle remained locked and untouched in the nurses' cabinet. The liberal rhetoric remained, that patients could have an occasional cocktail.

Periodically, residents' council meetings were called in

the late afternoons or early evenings. "You are all welcome to participate in the democratic process," came the announcement over the public address system. The notion of democratic process was surely overstated in this context, for these settings in no sense lent themselves to government by the people. The agenda, largely organized by the activities director, consisted of announcements of events and birthdays, and discussion about internal problems with the rules of the institution: spats between residents, requests for room changes, proper procedures for requesting second helpings of food and for using call buttons.

The rules themselves were not open to question. It was a democratic process of a highly specific sort, limited to issues within patienthood. Margaret Casey may have had ideas about the liquor privilege, Jack Connolly may have had strong opinions about hunger on the ward, but these were not issues to be brought to the residents' council as though it were a forum for legitimate recourse. Food, room arrangements, drug therapies, communication channels with the outside world—these were subjects that could be brought up, but only to be grumbled about, then clarified in terms of the rules, which were not seriously challenged. This form of democracy was severely restricted; it did not correspond to the participatory rights of members of the larger society. It operated not beyond but strictly within the limits of patienthood and medical authority and within the enveloping parameters of ownership.

One evening about 7:30, Mary Karney motioned to two nursing assistants to join her in a remote corner of the day room. She beckoned secretively, with a "psst" and a wave of her finger, to a quiet corner. She had ten gumdrops rolled into a paper towel for both of us. We ate them immediately, giggling among ourselves. But all the while we kept our eyes on the nurses' station and the elevator, for there were at least three rules being broken here. Residents were not supposed to have unauthorized food, they were not supposed to give gifts to members of the staff, and staff were not supposed to accept them.

Mary's caution was like that of Mrs. Herman's, the woman who furtively turned her hand palm down when trying to slip a tip, aware that another rule was being broken. Rules of gift giving are always tied to issues of who owns what and who can give what to whom; they are enmeshed within systems of ownership.[13]

Correspondingly, a particular kind of health care prevailed, a kind that could be owned. While the charge nurse dispensed medications about 8:00 P.M., the nursing assistants gathered residents into a line and chatted with them.

"How are you, Rose?"

"Fine. You got a quarter?"

"No. How are you, Fred?"

"Not bad. Can we watch TV late tonight?"

"Maybe. What's up, Mary?"

"Not much. What's for snack tonight?"

"Same. Cookies and juice."

"Are you going to help me make a phone call later?"

"Sure, Mickey, when I get time. How are you, Grace?"

"Fine. How's your mother?"

"Better, thanks, but I haven't got time to talk about it right now."

After receiving meds, most residents drifted back into the day room to join the others in the place where the day had begun at 7:30 A.M. As a consequence of forty or more people sitting in the room all day, the air became dense and foul-smelling, from the breathing and coughing, the food that had passed through, the bodily smells that had collected, and the cleaning chemicals used to combat them.

Visitors frequently got pale and weak when first confronted by the odors.

It was easy to see how trivial conversations like "How are you?" "What's for snack?" and "Can we watch TV?" might be left off any system of record keeping. Less easy to understand was how a health care system operated in which medications were scrupulously monitored and recorded, but there was no account taken of the stench of the air, the longing for food, the overworked staff bordering on sickness. Food, good air to breathe, relaxed living and working conditions—these have long been recognized as the cornerstones of modern health.[14] Yet they were not part of the monitoring or measurement systems. What took their place were countable indicators of individual bodies, like vital signs, and the pills dispensed. In this setting health care conformed to the process of commodity production, in making patients and itemized goods and services rendered to each of them. This was not just "health care" but health care in a commercialized form.

"They All Smell the Same to Me"

During evening hours, among others sitting and walking around the floor, were Georgia, her shoes on the table and mumbling to herself, under the watchful eye of Rose; Claudia, secretly wanting to sneak upstairs to cuddle with her mother; Sharon reading; Mickey counting money for his phone call; some watching television, some chatting— most of them helping to make the place a social milieu, not just passively produced by it.[15] Lorraine sat and spoke with Rose, Violet, and Bernice, and on occasion one of the nursing assistants had a chance to sit in the day room and talk, while combing hair, giving a shave, or cutting fingernails.

One topic that came up frequently was other homes, a topic shared by both residents and nursing assistants.

Outsiders, those who have been neither, often assume that there are important differences among homes—that there are good ones and bad ones and that the main issue for public policy and personal decisions is to find the good ones and sanction or avoid the bad ones. Of course the distinction is valid, and the decisions difficult when choosing among homes. There is a class hierarchy among them, to be expected in an institution enmeshed in a marketplace. Most homes in the United States are owned by corporations, three-fourths of which are run for profit, with increasing control in the hands of investor-owned chains.[16] Some depend on direct payment from clients, and some glean more income from the public aid programs. Many have a mixed private-pay and public clientele. Listening to the talk of residents and staff, however, reveals a certain connectedness, an overall system, that links the rich and poor homes.

A debate arose frequently in conversation when it came to comparing other homes. Some contended there were better homes and worse, while others argued that there were no real differences, that the commonalities among nursing homes overshadowed differences. Lorraine Sokolof was a passionate supporter of the first position, since she missed the home she first lived in, one close to her former church and owned by her religious affiliation. "That was better," she said. "We had a bus and they took us to church, and I still belonged to my parish, sort of." Anna Ervin took Lorraine's side: "Where I was before they had glee clubs and lots more activities, and the food was better." They had both been in private-pay, nonprofit institutions. Both had been asked to leave them some time after their private resources ran out.

The other side of the debate was that differences were overshadowed by similarities. "You seen one, you seen 'em all, as far as I'm concerned," was Rose Carpenter's opinion, "and I've been in three."

Nursing assistant Caroline Burns agreed with Rose. "I've worked in quite a few; they all smell the same to me."

The discussion surfaced frequently and encompassed experiences in private-pay homes, both profit and nonprofit, as well as the public aid settings, and the range in between. Before hearing this talk, I had thought of nonprofit homes as somehow different from those run for profit, but similarities overshadowed differences. Once when visiting a nonprofit home I asked the head nurse whether this was a church-supported facility. She chuckled, "Well, yes, either that or a facility-supported church."

Her analysis was incisive, since private and some public monies flowed into the organization, the surplus for which was not profit in the strict sense, because it went into the nonprofit church, which was tax-sheltered. As became evident, nonprofit homes operate with the same administrative mandates to produce balance sheets and bottom lines, demonstrating productivity and efficiency. They provide services with similar staff ratios and wage rates, within the same medical model, utilizing the same documentary processes, producing the same regimented, administratively controlled daily life. Both operate, in other words, within the larger societal context of caretaking as a business.

The consumers were removed from participation in any bargaining over costs for their residency, as were their family members. That did not mean they were passive about prices. Those who had moved along to the public aid phase spoke bitterly of their journey through the industry. The paupers often had more years of experience and brought to the conversations a broader view than those still in their private-pay phase. They talked of turbulence, social insecurity, and the roller-coaster movement along the road to the rolls of public aid. The poor had something to teach the rich.

Issues of paying and costs and charges were a continual source of day-to-day conversation in the homes. Cost was not taken as a given; talk of it was alive and active among these former mothers, homemakers, nurses, and teachers, and those who came to visit them, most of whom knew something about managing caretaking in other spheres. To be in these homes for any length of time was to hear constant urgings to reclaim control of assets, to enjoy once more some financial independence. Though they were unable to challenge in any formal way how these funds were calculated or by what systems of transfer they were circulated, residents and family questioned them daily.

The development of caregiving as a business has involved not just the circulation of money, but of ideas as well; and certain ideas have dominated.[17] One is that the people on public aid transfers are recipients of state beneficence. The prevailing ideology is that if they were at all a part of the circulation of money, they were a cost drain. This notion made Helen View, despite her fine wool suits and elegant posture, shy away from the administrators, having heard the rumor that "they don't care much for welfare bums."

Miss Black usually stayed in the day room as late into the evening as she was allowed, making conversation that often had a political content. It was she who had asked repeatedly, "Where's my Social Security?" only to have her outbursts recorded as "acting out." Apart from the business logic of the administrators and state officials and the medical logic of the charts, there were also historical changes in the transfer of these funds that her outbursts embodied.

When Miss Black started her teaching career fifty years earlier, Social Security was just being instituted. During her working years she willingly participated in this trust fund, and apportioned a percentage of her pay for the federal insurance program. Years later she sat in the day room claiming that the government had not kept its promise. Her Social Security amounted to just under four hundred dollars per month. She was told that this payment had to be taken prior to any public aid support for what it cost to keep her there. Late into the evenings, she offered an analysis of this situation. "They've been making money off me since I got here."

She might have been told in answer to her question that there was no Social Security for her, that long-term nursing home residence had come to mean pauperization, and that these public monies went to the corporation that housed her. Thus Miss Black's lifelong participation in this retirement security system was not over, but the transfer of her funds was helping to fuel the growth of an industry. Though she was the necessary link in the transfer of funds, she was removed from any agency in it.

These residents were members of a cohort that has never before existed: their life-expectancy projects into their eighties and nineties. These women and men were living through a specific history as well as a specific phase of their own life course.[18] In early years most worked, built savings, produced estates either as paid workers or as homemakers, paid federal and state taxes, and helped build the Social Security system. These sources of money now provide the base upon which the nursing home industry is founded, a base produced partly by the people who live in the setting, whether their bills are paid through public or private sources. This generation was the first to live full working lives under a Social Security system. All through their working lives they offered a portion of their paycheck to this system in the hope that it would protect them in old age.

Through the 1980s and early nineties, however, health care became increasingly privatized. Rather than incorporating health care into its social welfare programs, the government sponsored the expansion of private corporations. In the emerging relations of ownership, care has been continually reinvented as a premium, a privilege for those who can pay the price, rather than a right of citizenship.[19] The position of the government was that it could not afford to support health care for its citizens. It insisted that the citizenry bear much of the cost of health care, while it did little to govern prices.

Federal and state agencies set limits of time and category on what they pay the corporations and physicians through the Medicare and Medicaid programs. These public programs have evolved as part of the ongoing creation of nursing home care as corporate industry. They do not operate as a national health care system, but in effect as policies that serve to promote privatization.

Although the programs are said to be for older persons and the poor, a recipient does not receive benefits from either one directly. These public monies are transferred to corporations and physicians. The Medicare program puts a strict limit on the time care is paid for in a nursing home, after which residents or spouses, or both, have to exhaust their resources, the process called spend down. *Spend* is a term used by governments but drawn from the language of the marketplace, as though one freely and rationally engaged in this depletion. In fact, residents and their families are completely removed from decision making on the issue of prices, except to cancel residency altogether. "Spend" is therefore a totally inaccurate label.[20]

The Medicaid programs vary from state to state, but all, in effect, insist on poverty as a criterion for eligibility. They do so in two ways. First, one can possess no more than a certain amount of money in order to qualify, typically the cost of burial. Then, with the pittance of a monthly personal allowance, one is engaged in the progressive dispossession even of a material base—of glasses, then teeth, clothing, slippers, smokes, cokes, phone calls. Over the course of time that Miss Black, Ralph Sagrello, and June Popper learned to live without these specific items, fifteen to twenty thousand dollars passed each year from state to industry in the name of their health care costs. Public funds are such a large part of the income of these businesses that nursing homes constitute an industry subsidized by the state.

As inspector, the state functions to endorse nursing homes as a private industry. It inspects for cleanliness and exact records with appropriate numbers, all the while validating and encouraging the process of pauperization for staff and residents. In inspection, the state implicitly certifies poverty wages and spend down. State policies are thus in collusion with corporations in the creation of caregiving as a commodity. The state acts to guarantee profits—not for each home, for some lose money, but for the sector as a whole.[21] In these ways, the state's role is not distinct from but part of the ownership and business processes.

In the nursing homes, poverty, or the threat of it, was excluded from the record keeping, which made this way of life over into an exclusively medical or charity event. That erasure did not end the continual drain of resources, either as a social fact or as a topic of conversation. Ralph Sagrello grumbled about it during his late night tour of the ashtrays in search of the longest cigarette butts. In the public discourse he was a recipient; in ongoing daily life he spoke of himself as a practitioner, foraging within a specific economic mode. For those who lived in nursing homes under this momentum, their sicknesses and their pauperized conditions were collapsed together and called sickness. Reduced ideologically to the status of receivers of aid, they were dispossessed not only of the basic means to secure their own amenities but also of a narrative through which they and those who read about them might see them as silenced and pauperized contributors to the production of nursing homes as capitalist industry.

Miss Black's analysis, it turns out, was accurate in one sense. She and her neighbors had spent their earlier years contributing to all the various funds that underwrote the organization. Care was not something the industry or the state gave to them. It was made into a commodity through which money was exchanged between state and industry. As sources of income for the industry, whether through private or public funds, all residents participated in the production of care. The math teacher was right. They were making money off her.

Nursing assistant Solange Ferier tended to Miss Black on some of those evening shifts and they conversed. They might have had a lot to talk about; their predicaments and evaluations mirrored each other's.[22] It was Solange who summarized the labor-management exchange with, "Yeah, we do the work, they make the money." Both women were kept poor under this system of ownership and the public policies that supported it. Together they produced the actual caretaking encounters, while being named as the produced and the managed. Reduced to different but similar dependency on the organization and the state, they constituted the raw materials for the extraction process. "They've been making money off me since I got here" could have been said not just by the women and men who lived there, but by any of the nursing assistants who took care of them.

"Now, Sharon, You Know We Don't Have Any Food"

By 1:00 A.M. some people were usually up and about, and some requests were forthcoming from the bedridden. Sharon Drake often showed up at the desk, complaining about not being able to sleep. "I'm hungry. Got anything to eat?"

"Now, Sharon," we urged, "you know we don't have any food. Why don't you try to go back to sleep?"

This former waitress was hungry in the middle of the night, and nursing assistants were practicing health care by urging her to sleep it off. The corporation and the state had established a specific regimen for the distribution of food, following the regulation of no more than fourteen hours between meals. This particular definition of nursing meant trying to assuage her into forgetting her hunger, again trying to mediate the gulf between an administrative directive and everyday life.

Encounters with Sharon brought increasingly to light the importance of the charts for making nursing home care into a commodity and the residents into manageable units. The encounters highlighted not so much what went into the documentation as what was left out. It was not easy to convince Sharon to return to bed. The exchange took some skills, finding a line of reasoning to convince her. Sometimes it worked and sometimes it failed. For both parties it always took some psychic effort. Yet, at the instant Sharon returned to bed and we clicked off her light, both her hunger and the work it took to talk her out of it disappeared. Neither was recorded anywhere on any form. Formally, they never happened. Both Sharon's hunger and the nursing acts it required were systematically eliminated, night work lost in the shadows.

By contrast, according to the records, Sharon was well fed. Her knowledge of the situation, and that of the nursing staff, was silenced. The record of her being well fed depended on that silence.[23] As she rolled over in search of sleep, her daily work of patienthood was not yet over. She had more conscious effort yet to expend. She had to practice fasting in the middle of the night until the designated time when food would be delivered to her so that she could finally break fast.

"Oh, there's Arthur's moans again." Dorothy Tomason recognized them, though they remained inaudible to me. She had developed a sensitivity to his utterances and a repertoire of ways to deal with him that she passed on to others in her daily instructions. In this emotionally charged environment, some personal relations were good, some not so good. After a while, as Erma Douglas observed, "If you like 'em, it's like your baby." So much advice centered around the relationships created that I began to understand more about Mrs. Bonderoid's term for "what this work is going to take." Mother's wit was more than an attribute of the work; it was its constituent element. While the tasks formally named the job—vitals, weights, showers, beds, feeding, toileting—the subtle, human interaction provided the matrix within which those tasks got accomplished.[24] Most of the work, therefore, went unrecorded.

Tending, conceived as responsiveness, building relations, and "a kind of just being there" did not fit the industrialized model of productivity.[25] The capitalist construction of caretaking, by contrast, erased whatever could not be counted, coded, externally controlled, inspected, and sold—that is, made into a commodity. Much of what could not be named in these terms was made invisible, as caretaking was made over into a process mediated by documents. The work was made menial in its documentary construction by the elimination of all the productive sequences of the work that preceded the execution of tasks.

The work behind the scenes was accomplished almost entirely by women, and it involved caregiving knowledge that they brought from other realms of their experience. Both the prior work and the gender of the worker were eliminated in the formal definitions of the job. For the nursing assistants the job was constructed into a set of menial tasks, extracted out from the gender-based skills intrinsic to their life's work. The position was named as though it was only a coincidence that it was filled by women, but the connections between the work and the fact that it was women who did it were more complex. The documentary process degendered the work by eliminating the mother's wit that lay behind it. Still, these skills remained, even if passed on only in an oral tradition, practiced by the women who did the invisible work.

Late into the night, with the charts taking up the light at the nurses' station, much was being pushed into the shadows. The documents eliminated a great deal from the realm of visibility. Here it was certifiably not possible that there might have been hunger in the night, or that stale, urine-drenched air might have accumulated all through the day, or that tomorrow the showers might be cold or the pancakes soggy. Here there could be no talk of being trapped in a restraint vest, no puzzle about why this barren care cost so much. Each of these problems was transformed into its own measure of health care: hunger into nutrition, air into chemical sanitation, showers into a schedule of cleaning, restraints into day room coverage, while questions of cost were outside the authority of the menial workers and those acted upon. The questions about these matters went on all day and night, but the voices that raised them carried only up to the documents, not into or beyond them.

The maintenance director knew how they should look. But the residents themselves were not supposed to do much looking, at least not at administrative operations. By 5:00 A.M., some morning duties were beginning for the night shift, so we were all away from the nurses' station for several moments at a time. Joanne Macon was often up and around at this hour—and curious. She would sneak a peek at her chart. Technically, residents were allowed to read their charts, but informally our job was keep them away from inside the nurses' station. On catching her, I had to speak sternly: "Joanne, what do you think you're doing? You know you're not supposed to be looking at that stuff." When she did not move away immediately, I began to worry, for if I were caught by a higher authority letting this happen, I too would have been in trouble. "Please leave now, Joanne!" I insisted. Joanne did not have much time to learn anything from this private knowledge about her before she was driven away.

As 6:00 A.M. crept near, the nursing staff began fighting the enemy of any night worker—sleep. Should a person in authority catch someone dozing, serious trouble would follow. It would have mattered little if Dorothy Tomason, at the end of her double-shift, nodded off at the desk after her thirteenth hour of work. Nor, unless they had been with her for those hours, would they have much idea of what had tired her out, so little of it had been recorded. They would have seen someone failing to provide coverage, and Dorothy would have automatically received some

days of suspension or been fired outright. We forced ourselves and each other up—to move around, to go check on
someone.

So Dorothy got up and moving, even if her blood pressure made her feel "hot all over." In this industry the
health of the health care workers has been placed in jeopardy. The jobs, being cordoned off into a set of designated
tasks for an industry—specified number of workers, generated continual complaints of low–back pain, headaches,
and dizziness. The designated jobs—nursing assistant,
cleaning person, laundry person—made their incumbents
ill from their jobs in health care. "This job's got me sick,"
was Vera Norris's observation. The answer that came back
to her was that "someone's got to do it." Yet this expedient
retort did not dismiss the critical edge of Vera's complaint,
for the "it" was a social construction of caretaking—a
particular definition of the work and how many should do
it under what working conditions. Vera complained about
her job, not about caretaking in and of itself. The job's
occupational hazards were a product of this specific form
of business, replete with these industrial by-products. Vera
made many suggestions as to how she would like to have
seen her work organized. None included abandoning her
chosen profession; all included changes in the organizational form in which it had become embedded.

Coverage, vigilantly monitored and recorded, was
stressed heavily. It did not matter if at night two nursing
assistants and one floating LPN were running around
tending ten to twenty awake and needy residents—"putting out brushfires," as nurse Pearl DeLorio called it—and
Sara Wostein's request to stay with her had to go unanswered while other calls pressed more urgently. From
the distant standpoint of the corporate, medical, and state
administrators who conceived and measured the abstract

concept of coverage, all was fine during those nights. Proper health care had been achieved with appropriate labor ratios and the lowest possible costs of production, including wage costs. The empty hall at night was translated through its documentary procedures into good productivity. Absence became coverage.

The record keeping, therefore, was not so much a reflection of what actually happened as an extraction from it. Named and managed by the owners and inspectors of the industry, caretaking became something that the organization delivered, not the nurses. An extraction process occurred here, like gold brought to the surface of the earth by one group, then taken, counted, measured, and owned by another. A specific work process was involved in this documentation, culling neatly sanitized units and measures and check marks. Caretaking was reduced to the quantities that filled the chart pages that made health care into an enterprise of industrial production, in the ongoing project of trimming labor costs to produce patients and tasks—and surplus profits.

After the actual work was turned into tasks that could be numbered, scaled, and checked, it could be controlled by people higher in the hierarchy, whether or not they had ever done the work or knew how it got accomplished. Once the leap was made that the work could be named in the quantitative terms of the charts and its units counted up, it could be claimed, managed, and owned. Human needs for caretaking then could become defined as the demand from these consumers for something the organization could own and parcel out in its own terms. To the extent that everyday needs and tending to them could be turned into a countable, accountable logic, a bottom line was made possible.

This procedure had the consequence of molding the for-

mal records of residents' lives into a history of progres-
sively separate, isolated individuals: reduced to the status
of those acted upon, from social relations to individuals,
from individuals to patients, to sickness, to units of health
service, and ultimately to objects. All these components
went together to make up the bed. The leap from person
to bed was thus not direct. It followed an ideological pathway: from socially contextualized person to isolated individual, on to patient and disease categories, to bodies and
behaviors and tasks done to them, then to the records to
code them. "Beds" came into the logic at the end of this
conceptual conveyor belt, fully accomplishing the fusion
of person and bed, resident and commodity. "Today you
have beds 201 to 216" was more than a figure of speech.

The means of production was sitting under the light at
the desk. Here the patient was created and the work that
went on prior to, during, after, and around these measures
got erased. Out beyond the light, in the shadows, the distinction between consumer and product became blurred.
Like "beds," "If It's Not Charted, It Didn't Happen" was
more than a bold way of making the workers keep accurate records. It captured precisely caretaking as business.

Both living and working there, then, involved being broken down into bits and pieces. It involved being calibrated
as task doers and task receivers by administrative categories. In the formal documentation of their lives and
work, both residents and those who tended directly to
them became broken down into units and measures about
them.

After gold is chipped from the mines it undergoes
changes. The work it took to produce it is erased. Then, if
it is to be bought and sold as a priced commodity, gold has
to be broken down into units and measures. Even gray
gold.

The three chapters that comprised the first part of this book concerned the relations of production involved in making nursing home care into a capitalist industry. The women and men living long-term in the setting and those tending directly to them both spoke of teetering on the brink of poverty. They were kept in a state of, or threat of, pauperism. In this way they were broken down into raw materials, dependent on the organization even as it was dependent on them, made ready to be socially constructed into patients and task performers.

Chapters Four, Five and Six have addressed the means by which this was accomplished, wherein patients, tasks, and beds were brought into being. The documentary processes provided the essential leaps from quality to quantity so that residents and workers could be transformed into these entities. Once the leap was made, once it was granted that residence and the work of caretaking could be named in chart talk of the documentary processes and counted in its units, life inside could be externally managed, inspected, priced, and owned. Gold could be made from gray.

These relations and means of production provided a base from which caregiving as business could be developed. Ownership did not emerge merely as an abstract force that descended on everyday life. Rather, it drew its existence from that life, extracting and transforming the actual production of care brought about within its face-to-face labor context into a discourse compatible with its own quantitative conceptual schemes. Bureaucratic control continually expanded into the everyday setting as the various professionals, managers, and certifiers went about their work practices naming the everyday life in terms of their categories.[26]

Nursing home care in general is not synonymous with

the particular mode of production that has developed under industrial capitalism. Nor is this mode—private ownership underwritten by profit-promoting state policies—necessarily the only organizational form possible for the future. The findings in this study suggest that although nursing homes in the United States at the close of the twentieth century are being developed as businesses, they are being built on a series of inherent contradictions.[27]

Making gray gold is not the same thing as making real gold. But the relation is more than metaphorical, for the processes share similarities in the larger mode of production that guide both enterprises. Both involve extracting commodities that can be measured, bought, and sold. In both cases, that which is measured is controlled by people who do not do the work but who own the means to exploit those who do. Both systems involve a dominance of class, race, gender, and world labor. A sequence of work prior to its measurement has to occur, whether in the mines in South Africa or in tending to a nagging hunger at 1:00 A.M., without which the commodities could not be created. In both examples the prior production sequences are erased as part of the ownership process, while the enterprise is documented as being produced from the top down, as though management made it all happen. Those who bring forth the elements of gray gold, like the miners of real gold, are named as menial workers, listed as costs in its production.

Yet in the local realities where caretaking was occurring, things did not go smoothly. People do not passively get made into objects, like beds and labor costs; there was restiveness on the floors. Not just old and frail patients, not just robot workers, they were living a socially constructed set of circumstances. Their comments and situations pointed to contradictions between their experiences and the language used to control it.

Being fed, toileted, and walked is being done to, not self-directed activities. Sickness and frailty do not equal patient, nor does caregiving necessarily imply the job specifications and tasks it has been named as, any more than mother's wit is the same as medical science. The cheese sandwiches were not necessarily edible food, even after they were turned into measures of nutrition. A vest is not a vest when it ties one to a chair, and a shower in cold water is not the same as one in hot, even if the bath record displayed no difference.

Five to ten residents huddled around the nursing station at change of shift to beg for quarters is not the same as "Did anything happen today?" "No, just a few cuts and bruises." Pauperization is not the same as sickness, nor poverty wages the same as professionalization. Tending to the signs of life is not the same thing as taking vital signs, nor is inspection the same thing as looking at, any more than being tied down to a chair is the same thing as being "up."

In each of these instances the former terms were lived and spoken about by residents and nursing assistants, but they speedily became the latter when transformed into the bureaucratic narrative of care. With care made into a commodity, responsiveness could be written off altogether, slow could be made fast, putting the lotion on could replace the backrub, the halls could be emptied of caretakers at night, and all of these could emerge as the consequence of good productive management. All former terms were changed into the latter as everyday life was made into its documentation. The former became the latter with strokes of the pen.

Nonetheless, bureaucratic control, however dominant and expansive, remained incomplete. It could not fully suppress the actual situations or reactions offered by those who lived and worked under its rule. The halls remained empty of caregivers at night, even if justified by the measures of coverage. Even if the cheese sandwich and what Dorothy Tomason called the "water soup" were both conceptually reconstituted into units of nutrition, they remained on the trays half-eaten. They remained there as such and were known and spoken about and refused. Though turned into quantities, their qualities remained. The hunger that followed them in the middle of the night remained as well. And though Fern Parillo regularly got on and off the scales and had her weight recorded by their numbers, Dorothy Tomason, her blood pressure rising, knew that nothing was wrong with the scale. It was the building that was tipped.

The people living out these conditions recognized them among themselves and other workers and visitors and family members. Talk erupted about rest, food, pain, loneliness, communication, cost, and lack of control over any of these. That those living there and those tending to them did not have control over these basic elements conformed to the logic of management that dominated the settings, but it did not conform well with the everyday experience of it.

In their everyday speech, many of the people inside these settings resisted the language and rules that made them into products of an industry. Their voices may have been eliminated in the records, but they were still analysts of the organization. They were the ones who lived and worked under its conditions, and they did something beds and labor costs cannot do. They spoke.

7

Now for "A Little Rest Around Here"

As the women and men who lived and worked in these homes continued to speak about their situations, they often expressed resistance to the system of rules and ownership that dominated their lives. They talked about how they would have liked their settings to have been organized differently. Their voices remained submerged under the language of bureaucratic management and medicine, but in their ongoing talk and ordinary struggles they raised points of departure for alternative ways of thinking and speaking about nursing homes. There were two kinds of narratives on caregiving: one formal, written, and shared by the professionals and administrators; another submerged, unwritten, and shared by the people who lived and worked on the floors.[1]

The purpose of this chapter is to continue exploring these two narratives for points of disjunction and contradiction. These disjunctions are like cracks in the edifice of a building that is tipped. Their internal logic needs to be analyzed to see whether patchwork will be enough to reform the situation or whether deconstruction and reconstruction of the whole building is in order. The gaps provide spaces where action can be and needs to be taken, in this case of a social and political sort.

What follows is a review of some of the comments and situations reported earlier, now considered as to how they might form a base for a different kind of everyday life in nursing homes. I suggest a set of possibilities based on the words and actions that appeared earlier. Now I mix them with some sociological imagination and cast them into an alternative context of power.

Nursing assistants, nurses, residents, some family members and friends who visited—all expressed specific objections to the system of care they encountered. They expressed these reactions within a political economy of nursing homes that is neither natural nor inevitable. It is a social construction, a product of certain kinds of human labor, authority, and ownership. Since it is an ongoing human production, it can be transformed. From the words that were spoken in the situations reported here, it is possible to imagine change, not just the kind directed by outside authorities, but also that which begins from inside.[2]

Welcome to the Mother's Wit of Health Care

In the schooling there were several points of contradiction. Mrs. Bonderoid, the first teacher, was fired from her post halfway through the course. Students never did find out exactly why, but some surmised that it was because she did not agree with the philosophy of caretaking that was being fostered. As an aside from the formal curriculum, she professed mother's wit to be the core of the work, a notion that seriously disrupts the science and measurement-based lessons that formed the texts and tests and that undermines the way the state, through its multiple-choice examinations, claims to be able to judge who is qualified to do the work. So in a sense it is logical that Mrs. Bonderoid was fired. Her ideas, based on a submerged narrative of what nursing was all about, were too radical for making menial task performers in a medical industry.

In stressing mother's wit, she was teaching through a narrative of relations: "Keep looking in their eyes," "Remember that hearing is the last to go," "Even if they die, they're still your patient." By contrast, the school's state-approved curriculum took on an intellectual expertise only by reducing the complex emotional and interactive work to a set of biomedical, measurable tasks.

The training does not have to be so. It could be taught on the job by the people who actually do the work, the nursing assistants themselves. Trainees could learn while they worked and earn while they learned. Indeed, nursing assistants taught most of the lessons that student trainees needed to know. Diana from Ghana urged the teacher who replaced Mrs. Bonderoid, "We don't need to learn all these Latin terms, we need to learn how to clean someone." The lesson we struggled most to comprehend during the training was how to overcome the fears, embarrassment, and nausea through building the work into a relational context, which Erma Douglas and other on-the-job veterans taught best.

The classes would be better taught if they were supervised by veteran nursing assistants and residents. The workers themselves know how the work needs to be done, as well as how many are required to do it. The residents know when it is done well. Such reintegration could help break down the we-give-to-them approach and redirect the objective toward discovering a language of caretaking based in mutual social exchange, as it actually happens in caretaking encounters.[3]

Student Beverly Miller understood the conflict in these alternative approaches. When Mr. Store was looking for an additional task to assign to students in clinical training, he suggested, "Umm . . . why don't you go back and do some psychosocial stuff." Beverly had to ask [twice] whether that meant "talk," and when he acknowledged that it did, she inquired, "What do you think we've been doing all day?" If Beverly were to contribute to an alternative curriculum, she would urge that talk be given a central place in learning the work, not tacked on to the end of a set of procedures or separated as a quasi-scientific task that staff performed on residents.

With a reorientation away from the dichotomy that staff were the givers, residents the receivers, the caregiving knowledge of the latter could be brought to the foreground at the outset of training. Mrs. Herman, in nursing homes for four years, had a crucial lesson to teach about speech volume. She monitored the newcomers until they learned how to speak slowly and distinctly and most of all not too loud. "I'm blind, you fool, not deaf!" she snapped. Those to come after Elizabeth Stern, who missed her husband more than ever, would want to put an understanding of grief uppermost in the training, to recognize its expressions even among people diagnosed with Alzheimer's disease. Grace DeLong knew more about the experience of arthritic hands than most of the teachers could imagine. "Don't go near the babies," she instructed. Those who follow Mary Karney would point out that to take someone's vital signs when they were smiling and when they were crying ought not be construed as the same caregiving act.

New nursing assistants were frequently quizzed on the question, "What is the most important thing to do for a bedridden patient?" The required answer was "to turn them every two hours and record it in the restraint and position sheet." Charlotte Walsh disagreed. Dying of cancer and besieged with constant itching, she had much to teach about the experience of spending all day and night in a bed for months and about knowing when moisturizing lotion was needed. Those who follow her and who live through similar agony could help students and new nursing assistants unlearn the language and thinking that proceeded from industrialized tasks and mechanized records.

Students can learn one dimension of the work from the authorities but quite another from the people in the beds and the chairs with whom they share the caretaking exchanges. Staff and residents' common interests are obscured by organizational divisions that dichotomize them into actors and those acted upon.[4]

Issues of race belong as part of any curriculum as well, for most nursing homes are racially stratified organizations. The formal curriculum stripped the context of the black, brown, and yellow skins that were under the white uniforms. If race continues to be suppressed in the formal training, as though it were not a factor in it, women of color who follow Vivienne Barnes will continue to ask, "Are they teaching us to be nurses' aides or black women?" Future students and residents might well be more concerned with how to function in a multicultural environment. Instead of learning, as the assistant school director made clear, that nursing assistants should never criticize the places where they worked or question what they were told to do, future students like Vivienne will want to unlearn a training based in a language of submission.

Speaking from their own experiences, women from Third World countries, especially from the Philippines, could offer training sessions on nursing's increasing embeddedness in a world system of labor. Those who follow Juanita Carmona and Frank Sagan may not have to repeat the racial conflicts of an earlier time. Frank "liberated them people," he said, "and look where it got me." In open discussion of their mutual oppressions under these multinational corporate arrangements, residents and Filipino nurses of the future may act locally but think globally and they may decide that there are struggles of liberation they can still work on together.

The owner of the vocational school said he wanted to be able to bounce quarters on the beds we made. As it turned out, tens of thousands of dollars were bouncing on those beds. The owner was making money even as he was helping the state draft the law demanding the training he had to sell.

Yet out on the firing line of health care, Debra Moffit expressed shell shock at the brutality of the wage. The lofty talk of professionalization in an industry founded on caring was harshly contradicted by the stark reality of a wage that hardly met the cost of survival. To hear the talk of the everyday struggles it entails and the rage it spawns is to imagine how organized revolt could burst out from such a fissure. Workers and residents alike could correct the wider misconception that minimum wage provides subsistence.

Carol Davis was eager to be a spokeswoman on the issue. She wanted to be a union steward but was afraid of losing her job. She spoke of pressures being put on workers to avoid union activity, but she seemed to sense it might be the only way to halt this form of industrial production until minimum wage is transformed into a living wage.[5] Residents and their families, rather than being hurt by worker solidarity and activism, such as work stoppages or strikes, might well support them. It was they who had to endure the consequences of dealing with a physically and emotionally exhausted work force and a revolving-door structure of labor.

Carol made another proposal she wanted to put on the union agenda that would change daily life for nursing staff and residents alike. She was upset because she lost pay when her daughter got sick. She was caught in the industrial-capitalist split between caretaking for wages and caretaking for one's own children. She thought how nice it would be if she could bring her daughter to the nursing home during her convalescence. Mother and daughter could be in the wards together, the daughter partially cared for by those who lived where her mother worked. Maggie Kuhn, leader of the Gray Panthers, has argued that every nursing home should be a day-care center.[6] Both Maggie Kuhn and Carol Davis suggested that having children around could alter everyone's mood: resident's, mother's, and child's.

The industry and state have developed systems of accountability that prescribe how many workers are required to complete its defined tasks. But on the wards many staff suggested that more workers were required to give proper attention to residents' needs, and to their own as well.[7] They also implied that the tasks need to be differently distributed so that, for example, the cleaning women and laundry workers are less constantly exposed to the nauseating chemicals and the bed makers to back pain. Comments like Vera Norris's "This job's got me sick" need to become more than unrecorded side comments of those workers and recognized as direct results of the way these jobs are being organized and parceled out into segmented labor. Teamwork might also be reintegrated to the physically demanding efforts of lifting people.

Such goals, again, would directly confront the aims of the business managers, whose efforts centered on cutting rather than expanding labor costs. The administrator who announced his new plan to cut the work force summarized it with "You used to work together, now you're on your own." Under his plan, three and a half workers were to do the work that four could not.

LPN Pearl DeLorio, among others, urged that more men be hired to do this work. While the physical strength that nursing assistants displayed was often awesome, years of

222 Melting the Gold Bricks Down

lifting and bending generated lots of body pain. Paradoxically, those women became less able to fulfill the job descriptions even as their seasoned experience and their advancing age helped them better to empathize with those they cared for. Men could help with the physical chores and in some cases make it easier for men residents to cope as well. At least Lito Esparza thought so, as he scratched his face and commented that women did not know how to shave a man.

More pay, more workers, more children, more men—these recommendations provide only springboards. They are listed here more because of their source than their content; they are drawn not from the official experts on nursing home management but from the expert practitioners of its everyday life. On many of these issues their views are not just different, but opposed. For management, the lowest possible wage and the fewest workers signify good productivity, while for workers and residents they are counterproductive. Caretaking involves a good deal of cooperation, but when run as a business, it also involves conflict and division. Information about the conflict is not available in official documents. On the wards it is hard to miss.

Where's Our Social Security?

Miss Black sat in her wheelchair insisting on moving beyond the logic of costs that the administrators had presented to her. She seemed to suggest that the economic web in which she was trapped was only one possible logic, one with which her sense of things was in stark contrast. She had lived through the social plague of spend down that descended on her from forces far beyond the administrators. There may be many like Miss Black for whom losing all assets becomes a radicalizing experience, leading them to question the system itself. Shrouded in the public discourse of Medicaid as benefits, they are silenced not just by tranquilizers but by an ideology of public policy as well. Perhaps those who follow Miss Black will take up her cause and resist the systems of control that prompted her comments. Her anger was medicalized, tranquilized, and called "acting out." The time may not be far off when these gestures of control wear thin as a means of dealing with the deeper politics of her complaint.

With their powerful prefixes of "medi" and their seductive suffixes of "care" and "aid," Medicare and Medicaid have slid uncritically into public discourse as "benefits for the elderly." In fact, they are payments to medical corporations and physicians. For decades the only question on the political landscape has been whether the "benefits" should be increased or decreased. Another approach would be to abandon these programs altogether. A fresh start on health care as a social right would help the United States catch up with the industrialized world on the issue. To judge from inside these homes, these programs have not delivered the kind of care or aid implied in bureaucratic discourse. Many residents felt that these programs were doing themselves and their neighbors very little good. Both programs fed the inflation of prices in a profit-promoting policy while they fostered for those who lived them ongoing dependency and disempowerment.

Transformation to a publicly supported system of health care does not loom large on the political horizon of the United States, but dissatisfaction with the present system is almost universal. The Social Security program itself was brought about during the Great Depression, in no small part due to the active agitation of a vocal working class, some of whom will be spending the final years of the century in nursing homes. Members of this cohort have memories of radical critique of the system, as do their children of the sixties.

The social movements for health and welfare of the 1930s and 1960s were subdued through the 1980s. Meanwhile, the government committed massive funding to military contracts and operations. The defense budget ballooned to $300 billion every year for over a decade. Simultaneously, the government claimed not to be able to afford for its citizens a nationally supported system of medical care, opting instead for a mix of private pay and corporate subsidy approach. Unlike most industrial countries, which assumed medical care to be a mark of a modern civilized society, the United States has made medical services a privilege for those who could afford them, directly or through insurance, rather than a right of citizenship.[8]

The annual cost of nursing-home care for the nation is estimated to reach $40 to $60 billion by the end of the century, assuming that no controls are placed on the market prices, as has been the ongoing policy. Maggie Kuhn of the Gray Panthers once noted that the entire nursing home bill could be assumed for less than the Star Wars military budget. By way of similar comparison, the annual budget for the Central Intelligence Agency was over $30 billion. Sustaining the costs of a publicly supported system of health care was impossible only in the context of putting the country's resources into building a military apparatus.

The state's position is to support nursing home care not as a right of citizenship but as an instrument of capital transfer to corporations. The nursing home industry survives on subsidy from public monies. It is already a nationally subsidized industry, in which prices are left to the corporate managers, and citizens are required to contribute their savings. This policy is justified in the name of cost.

Nationalizing health care would be too expensive, it is said, even as evidence shows that a nationalized program is less expensive elsewhere than the system practiced in the United States.[9]

Private insurance policies are only a small part of nursing home payments, though they will no doubt grow in the absence of a socialized system. They will do for long-term hospital stays what they did for short-term ones for the last half of the century—inflate prices and perpetuate the practice of basing care on class, wherein those who can afford to pay will receive some relief. Privatization of caretaking will itself eventually have to be called into question if residents, families, and caretakers are to live under a broader form of social insurance, one based on social security, not insecurity, to insure against their mutual processes of pauperization.

Workers, residents, and their families, those who produce the raw materials for making gray gold, have something in common with those who work in the mines to bring out the precious gems of South Africa. By 1990 only two industrialized societies did not have a national health insurance plan for its citizens, the United States and South Africa. Exploitation of South African labor was not going smoothly; revolution was simmering. In the other society with privatized medical care, the United States, social and political ferment was also bubbling inside institutions of long-term care. Residents, spouses, and children who had to pay the bankrupting prices were agreeing with Miss Black's conclusion that "They've been making money off me since I got here." Meanwhile, workers nodded at Solange Ferier's comment, "We do the work, they make the money," while they huddled and muttered together and the elevator carried them up the long dark shaft to the mines upstairs.

All nursing homes are linked in that all are part of society's health care policy. Many residents understood the interconnectedness among homes from having lived in more than one. Some wanted to break down the isolation between homes and open channels of communication beyond their own walls. Grace DeLong wanted to exert some influence in this regard. She carried an expired membership card for the American Association of Retired Persons and wanted to rejoin. Some who maintain their membership in the future could form chapters of nursing home residents. One thing they will want to address is the financial journey that awaits almost all nursing home residents. If these residents had more contact with one another, spanning the class divisions that separate them at a given moment, some of the more articulate and angry would point to the pauperization process that is a consequence of commercializing their care, even if it was made to seem a natural course of events that followed from their frailties. Their various experiences would confirm that profits and pauperization are dialectically related in this system, one coming from the other.

Those who lived out the full economic course of long-term care seemed to understand these connections better than those who still had financial means. Maybe the public aid residents will want to instigate some radical changes of their own. With little left to lose, maybe they will rebel through one of the many small but seditious strategies that are at their disposal, following upon the hints offered by their predecessors.[10]

Sharon Drake and Mary Reynold often joked about wanting a Bloody Mary before meals. Margaret Casey might have enjoyed sharing her private stock of whiskey with them. All three wanted to reintegrate the custom of a cocktail into their daily lives to relax and enliven the spirit. It seemed like a simple request. What if they did sneak a cocktail once in a while? It would be severely frowned upon by medical and administrative authorities, not least because it would interfere with dispensing sedatives and other drugs. Outside their walls people are frowned on for taking sedatives, not for drinking; inside the hospital the reverse is true. Beyond the medical reasons, sneaking and sharing a cocktail could pose significant challenges to this system of social control because they involve a switch of agency from those acted upon to actors. Cocktails are too radical a gesture, too risky. People could get thrown out.

Perhaps some mid-evening a few will decide to pool part of their paltry allowance and refuse the evening snack of juice and cookies, preferring instead to have a pizza delivered. This action, too, would break the rules. Residents were strongly discouraged from sharing anything with one another. When Paul Labrietto tried to give Elaine Morrow a television set, he was forbidden, on the grounds that "we try to treat everyone alike here." This rule clearly demarcated who did the treating and who were the treated. For residents to share resources like a pizza, much less a cocktail, would be to challenge this demarcation of social control, and it would not be dealt with kindly. Indeed, sharing money and ordering food would break an even stronger taboo: it would transform the acts of isolated individuals into the action of a collective.

It had been difficult to generate collective collaboration or agitation in the iron cage of dependency in which so many were locked.[11] But bureaucratic control, however pervasive, was not total. It maintained only a gyrating, unsteady lid because complaints kept bubbling up. Collective refusals seemed not out of the question. So many refused specific meals that it seemed a short leap to the organized gesture of a collective no, especially if there were alternative sources of food.

Flora Dobbins wanted to provide that alternative. The rules about germs and ownership of food kept her from buying a small refrigerator to supplement her own and others' sustenance. For her and her neighbors to whom she wanted to offer snacks, the rules may have had less to do with sanitation than with the perpetuation of dependency. Those who follow Mrs. Dobbins may take up her idea of a small refrigerator and may fight for the right to have one. Again, however, danger would be involved, for such a demand challenges a basic operating assumption. It implies that residents themselves can care for their own and each other's needs.

Miss Black's comments in the 1980s were radical claims for the time. Lack of control over one's Social Security payments is not likely to be accepted readily by future groups of pensioners gone broke, nor is the argument that their funds are helping to build an industry. Some night over one of those shared snacks, maybe a collective voice will ask what Miss Black in her isolation could only scream. Groups of residents will echo her question, change the singular to the plural, and demand "Where's *our* Social Security?"

I'm Down, Not Up

No doubt these ideas about collective activity from residents are fanciful and romantic.[12] Many residents are incapable of social interaction of any kind, much less political. It is unrealistic to pose them as agents of change in and of themselves, without coalitions of family and staff support. The rest of the chapter moves in that direction. Still, before leaving off the notion of latent power among residents, I cling to a basic finding of this research: that residents, even if intermittently confused, had a lot to say about their care and how they would like it to be different.

Even the heavy silences that seemed to hang over the day rooms turned out not to be silences after all, at least not of an empty sort. Around the day rooms there were many different kinds of silence: some stemming from drowsiness and dementia, some from hurt and estrangement, boredom and anger. For others it seemed a form of social relation, the only way to deal with complex and inexpressible emotions. Some curled into themselves in the absence of anyone who could stay with them long enough to understand their specific kinds of confusion. Silence did not necessarily mean that order prevailed; sometimes it seemed like chaos quieted, a logical option in living out the passivity endemic to patienthood.

Amid the silences there were conversations and conflicts; many residents helped create the social life of the places where they lived. They worked on their own health care, complied with their prescribed health regimens, or rejected them, and helped staff and other residents along the way. Most struggled to make sense of their lives, mediating their experiences and desires through the grid of medical and administrative policies and regulations imposed on them.[13]

Charlotte Walsh, for example, remained bedridden, but far from passive. She had to deal literally with an iron grid. In frequent need of medication for her pain and itching, and not adequately helped by the prescribed, timed doses, she took to banging her call button against the two-foot rails that rose along her bed. Hers was a desperate attempt to communicate, heard helplessly by those who lived and worked around her. It was a form of interaction among people who were almost completely without power to respond to her needs.

Charlotte's moans can be heard as an expression not just of physical pain but of bureaucratic contradiction as well. The prescribed regimen, which means rule, had been ordered by a physician, a word that has the dictionary meaning of "one exerting a remedial or salutary influence." He was almost never there. Control had been so removed from the local situation that Charlotte's pain and itch were not given remedial or salutary influence, while those around her were trapped into listening to her screams, and nurses themselves were powerless to act beyond the prescriptions.

Within this circumstance there are seeds of something that could sprout into a growing collective agitation.[14] Most of the people who heard the moans were women, most of whom had been caregivers for some or all of their lives. The rules forbade residents from giving each other much help in the form of treatment or therapy. In future years someone's moans may be just too much for a few residents to bear, and they may go ahead and salve her itch with moisturizing lotion. Residents would feel less bound by the organization of power that insured only staff could give services, trying instead to figure out, while sharing the lotion and massage, how to reclaim opportunities to act on their own and others' behalf.

Mary Ryan and Buelah Fedders spoke for those in restraint vests all day long. Mary finally lost trust in anyone in white who tied her up and left her alone. On the restraint and position sheet she was "up with restraints." To be around her was to hear her complain that she was down, not up.

By 1990, federal regulations were instituted that restricted restraints and sedatives, strengthened inspection procedures, and made staff qualifications stricter.[15] It remains highly questionable whether such outside administrative reform as represented by these OBRA regulations can address the underlying issues that make nursing homes arenas of internal contradiction. The regulations do not tamper with the staff shortage that Buelah explained as the root of the problem of restraints—"so they don't have to hire any more of you." The new rules ignore the wage structure, spend down, pauperization, and prices. In ignoring these fundamental problems, the state perpetuates them. In that sense, OBRA regulations are deregulation as much as regulation. They leave untouched these structural incongruities while proposing solutions of more training and stricter rules for the people who have the very least to do with the source of the problems in the first place.

Meanwhile, those acted upon have their own agenda.[16] Marjorie McCabe once snapped at a staff member in reaction to a shower in lukewarm water, "Just you get in here and try it!" This challenge was echoed by others regarding the food, the straps, and the experience of lying in bed for weeks and months. So many spoke to the staff in this vein that it seemed like a theme, a strategy for pointing out that something was there to be learned from the bottom up.[17] Future residents will probably continue to urge staff, managers, owners, and inspectors to experience directly some of the conditions they helped create in their caretaking industry: a few days and nights alone in a bed, a few cold showers, some potato goulash, an extra cookie for being good. It would be an interesting research study, or a curious videotape, to record reactions of those who set such procedures in motion but had no idea how they tasted or felt.

Again, these speculations are not to lay out a model of nursing home life, but to open some windows from the

inside, from the residents and staff who provided the base
of the specific content suggested. Other recommendations,
perhaps more accurate and feasible, are on the tips of the
tongues of many staff and residents. Some literature is also
available that adopts an insider's view. There is a growing
body of autobiography of nursing home residents.[18] In addition, there is a rich tradition of ethnographic social science of institutions, which will interest residents, students,
staff, and families.[19] More residents, with help from all
four of these groups, may want to write and tape biogra-
phies of their own. Oral histories could provide projects
for gerontology and nursing students interested in recording stories of these pioneers.[20] All of these methods offer
alternatives for developing the narrative of caretaking
while circumventing the hegemonic grip of industry logic.

Inside homes, residents' councils could become more robust and adversarial, especially with outside help from
families, attorneys, and ombudspeople.[21] John Kelley was
one resident who had monetary and educational resources
he might have contributed to such an effort. Proud that he
had his own power of attorney, he was acutely aware of
the fragility of democratic rights in this setting. In later
years some with John's independent means might want to
hire attorneys to come inside and consult on what consti-
tutional rights are in jeopardy under this form of ownership.

Some patient rights' cases are being brought into courts
of law. Karen Thompson was forbidden to visit her lesbian
lover who resided in a home. She brought a suit defended
by the Minnesota Civil Liberties Union, which warned
that the case raises "fundamental questions concerning
nursing home residents' and visitors' rights to free speech
and association as guaranteed by the First Amendment."[22]

The case calls up issues of family rights. Families have

been remarkably powerless in the face of rules and prices. Primarily the spouses and daughters tend to their relatives and to some of their relatives' neighbors, sometimes making a request or a complaint to the charge nurse. Often they are frustrated on a one-to-one basis since they are relatively without resources themselves. By forming and joining associations they could become less so, as parents who have worked through parent-teacher associations have discovered. Residents' councils, aligned with state and national coalitions for nursing home reform, in conjunction with legal action, could help spouses and children voice their resistance to the medical-industrial model of caretaking, in which they have been reduced to silent consumers in the marketplace. Family members share a common posture with residents and frontline caretakers in having little authority over day-to-day operations or the shape of social policy.[23] All three groups are up against a medical model of a hospital, with professionalized job descriptions and state regulations, a business with prices and profits, a model of rationality and cost-effectiveness, and a discourse ideologically loaded with words like *care*.

Yet the very rationality they confront is itself mired in contradiction, forcing disjunctions between everyday life and administrative reality. Because the managerial drive is toward corporate balance sheets and government regulatory procedures, it distorts the central rituals of everyday life. Medical and corporate rationality negate residents' emotional expressions, like anger and grief, and redefine them as part of diagnostic categories, in effect denying their existence.

A core example of this conflict concerns mourning for the dead. Residents and staff had to deal with death continually. Under the dominance of the medical model, death takes on a particular social form. It is whisked away, cov-

ered, unspoken, treated in hushed tones as if the subject
were taboo. "The Spanish man must have died last night,"
whispered Mrs. Dobbins. "That's the only time they close
the doors around here."

Many residents had spent much of their earlier years at
wakes and funerals. They were spending the last years of
their lives in an environment with no public forum to
mourn together. Praying permeated the homes as a private
act, but, except for an occasional mass when a priest
stopped in, not as a public ritual expression of mourning.
Mrs. Dobbins asked others to pray with her on occasion;
she never organized a public ritual, though it seemed reasonable that she might have.

However, against the strong ideological force that created the isolated individuals of patienthood, reclaiming the
desire and need to mourn collectively might also prove to
be a revolutionary demand. Any attempts at changing the
social organization of death and mourning, as with food,
rest, communication, and restraint, may also have to start
with small, secretive gestures. Perhaps some who follow
Mrs. Dobbins will gather around with two or three of her
neighbors, and some members of the family and the nursing staff to interrupt the medical-industrial day and make
collective rituals of prayer and hymns a part of it.[24]

How Has Monica Been Eating Lately?

Eventually some of the more radical residents, their sons
and daughters, and their nursing assistants may find the
need to trespass across the boundary line to the other side
of the nurses' station, to the secret, sacred codes where the
secular gods who rule their lives reside. They may storm
the charts. Joanne Macon wandered the halls frequently at
night and tried to sneak a peek at hers. Being told to "get
away from those charts" did not satisfy her appetite for

learning about how her life was recorded. Future residents may be more eager to break the bonds of this managerial barrier and insist on access to these documents. Their words, opinions, desires, and analyses were silenced in the records. Still, residents had much to say that could have enlightened written and recorded material. Family members, as well, spoke of this possibility, often wanting their requests written down. With increasing recognition of the fundamental fulcrum of power that these documents have become, residents and families might work, legitimately and illegitimately, for more involvement in record-making procedures.[25]

They could hardly proceed on this path without the co-conspiracy of certain staff members. But staff, too, might be interested in a revolutionary approach to the documents that defined and drove their work. Many of their words and interpretations became silenced under the ruling practices implied by "If It's Not Charted, It Didn't Happen." Staff could work together with residents on expanding and redefining the contours of the charts or contriving an alternative set of records that reflected their everyday lives. Anna Ervin, former LPN, wanted to design an alternative toileting regimen. She rejected the language that made this schedule seem like streamlined and efficient productivity. What if Bessie and Anna had scribbled a few words of their own on the chart? The pages would look different if next to the check marks there suddenly appeared Anna's words, "Leave me alone. What do you expect, miracles?"

What if Joanne Macon jotted above the sheet that listed her as on public aid what she had called out on the streets, "Hey, mister, you got a quarter?" or if Ralph Sagrello had amended his financial record with "Public aid? I'd rather call it poverty aid"? If comments like these were regularly documented, future generations could better disentangle the fusion of long-term frailty and poverty that had so dominated Joanne's life and Ralph's.

What if Rose Carpenter scribbled, "I want aspirin, not sleeping pills," or Lorraine Sokolof wrote her prescription for a sprained ankle—an elastic bandage and a glass of water instead of an ambulance and a hospital stay? Suppose Claudia Moroni, with the help of a nursing assistant, scratched over her behavior profile, "I want to go cuddle with my mother and not have it written about as lesbian behavior." What would happen if David Forsythe and nurse Terry Arcana noted his desire for a nasal spray, and their mutual plea that such common remedies should be at a nurse's disposal? What if Vera Norris had vented her frustration at not being available for Sara Wostein by scrawling across the coverage sheet Sara's simple request, to "Stay with me"?

The more the charts became supplemented, replaced, or simply played with, the less sanctity and mystery they would hold. They are carefully written, checked, and guarded, with an aura of the inviolable, like magic icons only the anointed can touch. Yet they conceal as much as they reveal.[26] Records dominate and distort reality. Unable to capture the quality of life within their quantities, they create and mystify one set of ideas while suppressing another.

No one need tamper with the existing contents on medical matters or challenge that expertise. What needs to be deconstructed is the broad reach over areas of their lives that this medicalized authority has come to control. [27] Restive residents, staff, and families might not want to tamper with the practice of medicine, but they will no doubt, like those in the past, have a lot to say about nursing and how it could be practiced differently. With more mutual collaboration, some reading and writing in the records, they can study how the charts have served to mute their common interests and perpetuate parallel exploitations. Florence Castenada had to encode an answer to "How has Monica been eating lately?" She knew more than the check mark for "requires assistance" allowed her to reveal, among other things that we wanted to feed Monica, who we knew was hungry. What if Florence's frustration at those cross-purposes spilled over onto the page, and she wrote of her disgust at being overwhelmed with paperwork? Or what if Dorothy Tomason wrote what she often said, that she should be able to give her people food when they needed it?

Had Vera, Florence, or Dorothy written anything like this, they would have jumped from one narrative to another, crossing over into forbidden terrain, putting words to what is meant to remain silent. They would be identifying that complex work of trying to close the gap between everyday needs and administrative imperatives, activities that are not named but that mediate between the two, filling in the gaps and endlessly attempting to resolve its oppositions. They would be writing from the practices of mother's wit.

Mother's wit requires a host of unwritten emotional, physical, and interpersonal skills. But it also involves working with residents under a specific set of rules and regulations and trying to make sense of them and make them livable, trying to bridge everyday needs and external control. Take away mother's wit and the industry is left without the women and the work that hold the building up, mediating between its base in everyday caretaking and the superstructure of ownership that has been built over it.[28]

The state and industry have worked together in devising

a bureaucratic discourse that provides the means of their external control and undergirds market-based commodity production. In so doing they have undermined caretaking. In their rush to control the jobs, they have ignored what goes into the work and suppressed the narrative that is based in its actual experience. Making people into commodities and labor costs has meant extracting everyday expressions of need and desire, and silencing them. Under the weight of these contradictions, the medical-industrial complex sags.

Patchwork will not hold these buildings for long. The disjunctions are too deep for quick-fix plaster, like regulations that restrict restraints. Solutions can no longer come merely by asking managers to ease the rules or conform to reformist government policies and regulations. Marjorie McCabe did not have bedsores, for which there were categories and therapies; she had "chairsores," for which there were not. If those who follow her are to prevent them, it will take more than asking the management to buy new chairs or make a new category; it will take more than asking the state to make a new regulation. The whole capitalist industrial order that underwrites this life of sitting has to be brought continually into question, as it was implicitly on those floors. Those in the future may not wait for corporate or state beneficence, skeptical after all these years that they can be relied upon as a source of support for their reclamations, preferring instead to confront their oppression at its execution point, searching for ways to name and satisfy their own needs.

The search for the tools to do this naming can begin and end with the speech that is already there. It is in the caretaking narrative of those who gave and received it. They knew what they wanted and needed even if they were within an administrative apparatus that denied them access to expressing it. The fantasy of residents or nursing assistants seizing the charts and scribbling over them stems from the idea that language enters into, shapes, and sustains power relations and that their words based in actual caretaking have been taken away.

Bringing forth the relational narrative of mother's wit means working forward from the common interests of the women in the white uniforms and those between the white sheets, needing local control, for instance, over such basics as food and pain relief. It might mean seizing the secret codes and splashing some of their messy lives over the pages, rejecting the medical and administrative language that sanitized the documents. The narrative of mother's wit orients the work of caring, a word drawn from sorrow,[29] away from a set of mechanical tasks toward the social, emotional, political, and practical skills that undergird the present organization of nursing homes and contain the power to bring about transformation within them.

The domain of mother's wit does not rule or regulate; it is not paid and for the most part not named. It is written out of the language of the owners, administrators, doctors, and inspectors. It must remain invisible if the organization is to appear produced from the top down. Yet the work is so fundamental to the very existence of the organization that the standpoint of those who engage in its exchanges provides a submerged narrative from which a range of radical revisions can be imagined.

Proceeding from the speech of the residents and nursing assistants, two related jumping-off points can be identified: that there is considerable conflict within the organization, and that the conflicts point precisely to the disjunctions where changes need to be made to reconstitute nursing homes.

Most of the requests that have peppered these pages were neither grandiose nor impractical. Taken separately, each seems simple. But taken together they constitute pockets of pressure, strain, agitation—gaps between their needs for caretaking and the structure in which they arise. These rumblings at the base of the building, these pockets of agitation, show no signs of diminishing and every sign of deepening, even as administrative language continues to spread its thin layer of conceptual plaster over them. The root causes deepen. Down at this level the trembling is audible and visible.

The former waitress wanted a snack at night, the nurse wanted to give her one, the working mother wanted to make it on just one job, some wanted someone to stay with them, others wanted to mourn, some asked to be cleaned, almost everyone asked for more people to do the cleaning.

Somebody wanted to talk about race, somebody else about revolutions in her country, a third was livid about the wages, a fourth about Social Security. Somebody wanted to bring her daughter in, somebody wanted to bring back rubs back, some wanted more of their own autonomy back.

All this rumbling undercurrent of agitation needs to be dealt with every day and every night. The people who bring them up, and the people they bring them to, have to somehow make sense out of this shaky structure that was creating or at least not meeting the causes of these complaints. The issues circulate among the nursing assistants, nurses, residents, their wives, daughters, husbands, and sons—those who put caretaking together day in and day out and who participate in its narrative.

Those who practice the wit and wiles have to make the connections between everyday life and its external control, right at the disjunctions, mediating the contradictions—

explaining and working with the materials at hand, stretching scarce resources, trying to live out the administrative, regulatory, and economic imperatives of the industry. It is they who do the necessary internal repair work, urging a hungry resident to go back to sleep or a frightened one to learn to live alone. They are there at the gaps at the base of the building. As best they can, they move the most crucial bricks around, plugging them into the most critical intersections, working feverishly to preserve this fragile structure. They occupy the physical and social space where the internal needs and the external forces, the narratives of administration and caretaking come together and where they need to be mediated.

This vantage point also gives them enormous knowledge and potential power. Since they are required to fill in the gaps, they see and hear them. They hear both narratives, and they operate in the shaky area where the foundation and superstructure split off from one another. They struggle to cement the cracks.

The knowledge available from this standpoint can also be the source of change. Since the nursing assistants, nurses, residents, their wives, and their daughters put together the actual caretaking foundation, there is much they can do to deconstruct the way it is controlled. Their standpoint gives them insight into what changes need to be made and how to make them. Mother's wit is not an abstract concept or a set of ideas; it is the wide range of practices that hold the organization together. Mother's wit is required precisely in the gaps where action occurs and where action needs to be taken, and it therefore, provides the matrix for an agenda of change. Since they have to move around the strategic bricks to hold base and superstructure together, they know which ones would, if removed, make the edifice collapse.[30]

Mother's wit and its narrative based in caretaking provides not a priority list of changes that need to be made but the illumination of a base of knowledge from which they can be made. It is a constant and widespread set of practices. It is more than an attitude, more than a set of invisible skills, and more than coordinating the internal and external forces. Since it is all of these, it can be a base for a revolutionary set of practices.

In this sense it matters little which of these bubbling requests congeal into coalitions of collective agitation and take the form of demands. There are many points of departure from which to proceed for those who live and work within the narrative of caregiving. One gesture of resistance is related to all the others, as a part of the rumbling under the narrative of control. It does not matter which groups of bricks are taken out to begin the deconstruction, save for those needed to fortify the base. Rebellion can erupt from the pressure in the pockets wherever mother's wit has to mediate. Change can proceed, building on the foundation that is already there, from the critiques expressed at the points where the two narratives conflict.

Looking out from this foundation gives a language and content with which to think about change and an actual base from which it can proceed. It is, in some ways, already proceeding. A nursing assistant or mobile resident might brazenly bring in a cocktail or a pizza or a refrigerator. Nursing assistants, residents, spouses might sneak food in and out it for each other. Someone might give a massage or loosen a restraint or hold a memorial service. Some group might seize the records and insist on declaring that they were all going broke. They might juggle with the numbers to reject being made into them. Some beds might be left unmade. Maybe no one would care but the managers and inspectors.

The point is not just to deconstruct the already unstable superstructure but to build a stronger foundation for the caretaking base. Mothers, and those who practice mother's wit, usually start with the basics, like those that were out of reach for so many of the people in these stories. Change that proceeds from mother's wit will probably have to do with activity relating to feeding, cleaning, teaching, laughing, comforting, holding, scolding—stopping to take the time to do any of them. It might include expanding and playing with the skills that have been made invisible and unnamed, nurturing, comforting, assuaging fears, counseling confusions, dressing, combing, cleaning, conversing, building relations, waiting, joking, touching, refraining from touching. It does not matter from what points it takes momentum. The daily struggles occur at many points within the matrix. It amounts to making into a home that which has been made into a hospital.

Every day and night, in other words, the caretakers try to build a rest home. But each day the factorylike schedule starts up the production of patients and tasks and timed and measured units of service at the crack of dawn. The 7:00 A.M. start-up burdens the lives of those bound to its schedule, and it interferes with the original purpose of the place. Perhaps those who labor under its rule will decide that their mutual interests can be better served by facing each other as rested people. If the miners of gray gold refused to move at that hour, the making of beds could not proceed.

Retrieving control over that hour might be just the revolt it will take to remake a rest home. They may have to shorten the shifts and make more of them, and devise ways to divide up the work and double the workers. Then the necessity for Dorothy Tomason to work double shifts, even if dizzy and hot all over, can be more seriously challenged by residents and staff who recognize its hazards to both.

It might mean they will decide that 9:00 A.M. is a better time for the caretaking co-participants to start their day. At least that would give the nursing assistants who follow Ina Williams and Aileen Crawford time to tend to their children, and then to make a relaxing stop at some nearby café.

And those who follow Helen Donahue might be just waking up at that time. When 7:00 A.M. dawned they might have awakened, but only slightly. If those early morning regimens on the firing line of health care are dissolved, many like Helen will wish to deal with this time of day by sleeping through it. Having lived for almost a century, Helen had to spend much time under a blanket of authority that made her think she was "going to smother in here." When those who follow her refuse any longer to live under the contradictions of being made into gray gold, they will be able to pull up a blanket on those mornings, smile, and doze off again. They will be reclaiming power over all Helen asked for in the first place. They will be on their way to getting "a little rest around here."

Notes

Introduction

1. All names are pseudonyms. When first introducing each person I use a full name. Thereafter I use the first or full name, depending on how that person was addressed in the nursing home.

2. Eric P. Bucy, "Health Care Field Continues to Boom" *Los Angeles Herald Examiner*, 18 Nov. 1988, sec. 2, p. 1, indicates a growth rate for nursing assistants' jobs of 22 percent in the 1980s; Natalie Waraday, "Nursing Assistants Have Big Role in World of Need," *Chicago Tribune*, 23 Oct. 1988, sec. 19, p. 15, citing Bureau of Labor Statistics, notes that "the most promising growth in available jobs lies in the nursing assistant positions, for which a 33 percent growth rate is expected nationwide by the year 2000." Charles P. Alexander, "The New Economy," *Time*, 30 May 1983, 64, reports that there were 1,175,000 nursing assistant jobs, estimated to grow to 1,682,000 by 1990, an increase of 507,000. Nursing assistants were second only to secretaries in the size of the labor force and its rate of growth.

3. Among the few references in social science literature discussing nursing assistants' work, three that influenced this study are Jaber F. Gubrium, *Living and Dying at Murray Manor* (New York: Martin's Press, 1975); Charles Stannard, "Old Folks and Dirty Work: The Social Conditions for Patient Abuse in a Nursing Home," *Social Problems* 20 (1973): 329–42; and Jeanie Kayser-Jones, *Old, Alone and Neglected: Care of the Aged in Scotland and the United States* (Berkeley and Los Angeles, Calif.: University of California, 1981).

4. Michael J. Weiss, "Oldsters: The Now Generation," *American Way*, July 1982, 96.

5. In 1989 there were approximately 15,000 nursing homes in the United States, according to Mary Elizabeth O'Brien, *Anatomy of a Nursing Home* (Owings Mills, Md.: National Health Publishing, 1989), xiii.

6. Jeff Blyskal, "Gray Gold," *Forbes*, (23 Nov. 1981), 80–84.

7. Among the participant-observation studies most influential for this research are Michael Burawoy, *Manufacturing Consent: Changes in the Labor Process under Monopoly Capitalism* (Chicago: University of

Chicago Press, 1979) and Judith A. DiIorio, "Sex, Glorious Sex: The
Social Construction of Masculine Sexuality in a Youth Group," in *Feminist Frontiers*, ed.
Laurel Richardson and Verta Taylor (New York:
Random House, 1989), 261–69,—studies that place everyday observations within a wider political context; Erving Goffman, *Asylums*
(Garden City, N.Y.: Doubleday, Anchor Books, 1961) and Jaber F.
Gubrium, *Living and Dying at Murray Manor*—studies that supply a
wealth of details about everyday life in institutions. This research is also
indebted to the ethnographic tradition of sociology known as the Chicago school. See, for example, Everett C. Hughes, *The Sociological Eye*
(Chicago: Aldine, 1971) and William F. Whyte, *Street Corner Society:
The Social Structure of an Italian Slum*, 3d ed. (Chicago: University of
Chicago Press, 1981).

8. The primary methodological and theoretical source for the research comes from the writings of Dorothy E. Smith. This work is an
attempt to carry out the method of institutional ethnography. As Smith
explains it, institutional ethnography makes the everyday world its
problematic, working with a kind of sociology that "like Marx and
Engels's conception of the materialist method, begins not within the
discourse but in the actual daily social relations between individuals.
The problematic explicates, as the basis of inquiry, an actual socially
organized relation between the everyday world of experience and the
social relations of capitalism." See Smith, *The Everyday World as Problematic: A Feminist Sociology*, (Boston: Northeastern University Press,
1987), 98; *The Conceptual Practices of Power: A Feminist Sociology of
Knowledge* (Boston: Northeastern University Press, 1990); and *Texts,
Facts, and Femininity: Exploring the Relations of Ruling* (Boston:
Routledge, Chapman and Hall, 1991).

9. On issues of how to construct the narratives I have drawn from
Laurel Richardson's work, especially "The Collective Story: Postmodernism and the Writing of Sociology," *Sociological Focus* 21 (1988):
199–208 and *Writing Strategies: Reaching Diverse Audiences* (Newbury Park, Calif.: Sage, 1990); also from Carol A. B. Warren, *Gender
Issues in Field Research and Field Work* (Newbury Park, Calif.: Sage,
1988); and from Susan Krieger, *The Mirror Dance: Identity in a Women's Community* (Philadelphia: Temple University Press, 1983).

1. "Welcome to the Firing Line of Health Care"

1. Rose Schniedman, Susan Lambert, and Barbara Wander, *Being a
Nursing Assistant.* (Bowie, Md.: Robert J. Brady, 1982), xiii.

2. Some literature explores the skills and knowledge that arise from
the practice of mothering. See, for example, Sara Ruddick, *Maternal
Thinking: Toward a Politics of Peace* (New York: Ballantine, 1990).

3. Schniedman, Lambert, and Wander, *Being a Nursing Assistant*, 66.

4. The jolting transition for nurses from school to actual medical settings has been studied by Virginia Olesen and Elvi W. Whittaker, *The Silent Dialogue: The Social Psychology of Professional Socialization* (San Francisco: Jossey-Bass, 1968); and for student physicians by Howard S. Becker et al., *Boys in White: Student Culture in Medical School* (Chicago: University of Chicago Press, 1961).

5. For discussions of ethics of disclosure in fieldwork, see Barrie Thorne, "You Still Takin' Notes?': Fieldwork and Problems of Informed Consent," *Social Problems* 27 (1980): 284–97; Severyn T. Bruyn, *The Human Perspective: The Methodology of Participant Observation* (Englewood Cliffs, N.J.: Prentice-Hall, 1966); and Joan E. Sieber, ed., *The Ethics of Social Research: Fieldwork, Regulation and Publication* (New York: Springer-Verlag, 1982). I found it impossible to plan disclosure prior to the research, and though I had not intended to be secretive, the situations left me no choice. When I said I wanted to do research no one hired me. For other references on the issue see chap. 2, n. 6.

6. Elizabeth Elliott, in her insightful study, concurs that many home health care workers demarcate their professional boundary at the same dividing line that Vivienne Barnes identified: cleaning floors. See "I Don't Do Floors," "Private Duty Nurses Aides and the Commercialization of Sickness Care in the Home," (Ph.D. diss., Northwestern University, 1991), chap. 3.

7. For an excellent overview of research on women's invisible work, see Arlene Kaplan Daniels, "Invisible Work," *Social Problems,* 34 (1987): 403–15.

8. What the work actually involves, as compared with how it is written and spoken about in administrative discourse, is a theme of this research, as it is generally of Dorothy Smith's approach. See especially *The Everyday World as Problematic,* chap. 3.

9. For discussions of the medical model, see Andrew C. Twaddle and Richard M. Hessler, *A Sociology of Health* (St. Louis: C. V. Mosby, 1987); Howard Waitzkin, *The Second Sickness: Contradictions of Capitalist Health Care* (New York: The Free Press, 1983); and Caroline Currer and Meg Stacey, eds., *Concepts of Health, Illness and Disease: A Comparative Perspective* (New York: Berg, 1986).

2. "How Do You Make Do on Just One Job?"

1. On the international labor market, see especially Adele Mueller, "The Bureaucratization of Feminist Knowledge: The Case of Women in Development," *Resources for Feminist Research* 15 (1986):36–38. Mueller, who works with Smith's method, writes perceptively concern-

ing the "production of professional knowledge" about women in developing societies. See *In and Against Development: Feminists Confront Development on Its Own Ground.* (East Lansing, Mich.: Michigan State University, 1991); and "The 'Discovery' of Women in Development: The Case of Women in Peru," paper presented at the annual meeting of the Comparative and International Education Society, Washington, D.C., March 1987. See also *Crossroads of Class and Gender: Industrial Homework, Subcontracting and Household Dynamics,* ed. Lourdes Beneria and Martha Roddan (Chicago: University of Chicago Press, 1987). Jeannine Grenier, "Nurses from Manila," *Union* (Oct.–Nov. 1988), 26, estimates that ten thousand foreign nurses are practicing in the United States under temporary work permits; see also Tomoji Ishi, "Politics of Labor Market: Immigrant Nurses in the United States," paper presented at the annual meeting of the American Sociological Association, Atlanta, 1988; and Michael Pressor, "Foreign Nurse Graduates: Exploitation and Harassment," *Health Activists Digest,* 3 (1982): 37–39.

2. This proportion of nursing assistants is generalizable throughout the United States. See, for example, Committee on Nursing Home Regulation, Institute of Medicine, *Improving the Quality of Care in Nursing Homes* (Wash., D.C.: National Academy Press, 1986), 52.; and O'Brien, *Anatomy of a Nursing Home,* 110–13.

3. Rebecca Donovan, "'We Care for the Most Important People in Your Life': Home Care Workers in New York City,'" *Women's Studies Quarterly* 1 and 2 (1989): 56–65, reports on similar wages for nursing assistants who do home health care.

4. In 1986 the poverty line was $8,570 for a family with two children. William Hines, "Kids and Poverty Mix for City's Teen Moms," *Chicago Sun-Times,* 14 April 1986, p. 16.

5. The union was the Service Employees International Union, to which almost all nursing assistant staff belonged, often against some pressure. In 1990 the National Labor Relations Board found Beverly Enterprises, the nation's largest nursing home chain, guilty of harassment against union activity in thirty-five facilities in thirteen states. See Bob Baker, "Nursing Home Chain Guilty of Unfair Labor Practices, *Los Angeles Times* 17 Nov. 1990, p. 28.

6. On the occasional necessity of clandestine methods, see Murray L. Wax, "Paradoxes of 'Consent' to the Practice of Fieldwork." *Social Problems* 27 (1980): 272–83; and, in the same issue, John F. Galliher, "Social Scientists' Ethical Responsibility to Superordinates: Looking Up Meekly," 298–308; Judith A. DiIorio, "Being and Becoming Coupled: The Emergence of Female Subordination in Heterosexual Re-

lationships," in *Gender in Intimate Relationships,* ed. Barbara J. Risman and Pepper Schwartz (Belmont, Calif.: Wadsworth, 1989): 94–107. I was especially encouraged by DiIorio's work and that of Judith Rollins, *Between Women: Domestics and Their Employers* (Philadelphia: Temple University Press, 1985). See "The Ethical Issue" in Rollins, 11–17.

7. Paul Willis, *Learning To Labor: How Working Class Kids Get Working Class Jobs* (New York: Columbia University Press, 1977), was instructive on what to look for in learning the labor, and Judith Wittner was personally helpful in learning ways to write about it. See Michal M. McCall and Judith Wittner, "The Good News about Life History," in *Symbolic Interaction and Cultural Studies,* ed. Howard S. Becker and Michal M. McCall, 46–89 (Chicago: University of Chicago Press, 1990). On experimentation with textual presentation, see especially George E. Marcus and Michael M. J. Fischer, *Anthropology as Cultural Critique: An Experimental Moment in the Social Sciences* (Chicago: University of Chicago Press, 1986), chaps. 2 and 3; also Kath Weston, *Families We Choose: Lesbians, Gays, Kinship* (New York, Columbia University Press, 1991).

3. "Where's My Social Security?"

1. The price of nursing home residency rises rapidly. Estimates cited in "Who Can Afford a Nursing Home?" *Consumer Reports,* 53 (May 1988), 300, gives an average price of $22,000 in 1988 and predict that by the year 2018 "it will cost about $55,000 if inflation stays at recent moderate rates."

2. Jon D. Hull, "Insurance for the Twilight Years," *Time,* 6 April 1987, 53, reports that by 1986 there were 700 life-care communities providing for about 200,000 people, with the number expected to double in the next decade. Julie Amparano, "Marriott Sees Green in a Graying Nation," *Wall Street Journal,* (11 Feb. 1988), p. 28, reports that average entrance fees range from $80,000 to $200,000, with monthly maintenance fees of $800 to $1500.

3. For general outlines of these policies, see Elizabeth Ann Kutza, *The Benefits of Old Age: Social Welfare Policy for the Elderly* (Chicago: University of Chicago Press, 1981); Bernice L. Neugarten, ed., *Age or Need?* (Beverly Hills: Sage, 1982); E. Richard Brown, "Medicare and Medicaid: Band Aids for the Old and Poor," in *Reforming Medicine: Lessons of the Last Quarter Century,* ed., Victor W. Sidel and Ruth Sidel, 50–78 (New York: Pantheon Books, 1984); Robert M. Ball with Thomas N. Bethell, *Because We're All in This Together* (Wash., D.C.: Families U.S.A., 1989). A comprehensive review of these policies is of-

fered by William G. Staples, *Castles of Our Conscience: Social Control and the American State, 1800–1985* (New Brunswick, N.J.: Rutgers University Press, 1990), chap. 6.

4. Jean Grover, "Caring and Coping," *Women's Review of Books,* 4, no. 9 (1989): 25–26; Allan L. Otten, "States, Alarmed by Outlays on Long-Term Care, Seek Ways to Encourage More Private Coverage," *Wall Street Journal,* 11 Feb. 1988 p. 48. These articles report that of the total nursing home bill of $38.1 billion in 1986, less than 1 percent was paid by private insurance, while 51 percent was paid by patients and their relatives, 41 percent by Medicaid, and 2 percent by Medicare (6 percent "other"). See also Charlene Harrington, "Public Policy and the Nursing Home Industry," *International Journal of Health Services* 14 (1984): 481–90.

5. The Committee on Nursing Home Regulation, *Improving the Quality of Care in Nursing Homes,* 371, reports that slightly over 1.5 million persons resided in nursing homes in 1980, with that number projected to increase to over 2.5 million by 2000. Peter Kemper and Christopher M. Murtaugh, "Lifetime Use of Nursing Home Care," *New England Journal of Medicine* 324 (28 Feb. 1991): 595–600, project from their survey that of the 2.2 million persons who turned 65 in 1990, more than 900,000, or 43 percent, are expected to enter a nursing home at least once before they die.

6. The time limit on coverage relates to Medicare Part A. See *Consumer Reports,* "Who Can Afford a Nursing Home?" See also Annette Winter, "Long-Term Care Options," *Modern Maturity,* (June-July 1986): 70–71; Elizabeth Arledge, "Who Pays for Mom and Dad?" "Frontline" (Public Broadcasting System, aired 30 April 1991); M. Garey Eakes and Ron M. Landsman, "Medicaid Money—and You," *Modern Maturity,* (Feb.–March 1990): 85–90.

7. Miss Black insisted on being called Miss Black. Again, I assign surnames to all persons when first introducing them, following the advice of Weston, *Families We Choose,* 9; "Introducing strangers by given names alone paradoxically conveys a sense of intimacy while subtly withholding individuality, respect and full adult status from research participants." But because first names were often used on the wards, I use them in subsequent naming except for the actual people who indicated a desire to be addressed more formally.

8. Daniel J. Schulder, "At Last, A Promise of Nursing Home Reform," *Public Policy Report,* 17 (Jan.–Feb., 1988): 30–31. OBRA regulations increased the personal needs allowance for residents in Medicaid nursing beds from $25 to $40. Schulder reports that this was the first increase in personal allowance in fifteen years.

9. Barney J. Feder, "What Ails a Nursing Home Empire," *New York*

Times, 11 Dec. 1988, sec. 3, p. 1, reports that the average daily payment for Medicaid was $52 in 1985. Multiplied by 365 days, this comes to an average annual payment of $18,980.

10. On hospitals discharging patients "sicker and quicker" as a result of the Diagnostic Related Groups system (DRG), see Carroll L. Estes and Elizabeth A. Binney, "Toward a Transformation of Health and Aging Policy," *International Journal of Health Services* 18 (1988): 69–82. For a discussion of the impact of the Prospective Payment System, instituted in 1983, which has encouraged growth of lower-paid workers, staff cuts, and workload increases, see Karen Brodkin Sacks, "Does It Pay to Care?" in *Circles of Care: Work and Identity in Women's Lives,* ed. Emily K. Abel and Margaret K. Nelson (Albany, N.Y.: State University of New York Press, 1990), 188–206.

11. Nora K. Bell, in "What Setting Limits May Mean," *Hypatia* 4 (1989): 177, reports that "a disproportionate number (74.6 percent) of nursing home patients are very old, white, female, and without spouse." See also Charlene Harrington, "Public Policy and the Nursing Home Industry."

12. Thanks to Bari Watkins for pointing out this particular gender process. For historical accounts of the development of public policies about nursing homes, see Staples, *Castles of Our Conscience,* chap. 6; Michael Harrington, *The New American Poverty,* (New York: Viking, Penguin Books, 1984), chap. 5; and an especially provocative paper by Barbara G. Brents, "Policy Intellectuals, Class Struggle and the Construction of Old Age: The Creation of the Social Security Act of 1935," *Social Science and Medicine,* 23 (1986): 1251–60.

13. On the process of deinstitutionalization, which often meant transinstitutionalization, see Robert M. Emerson and Carol A. B. Warren, "Trouble and the Politics of Contemporary Social Control Institutions," *Urban Life,* 12 (1983): 243–47, and the other readings in this issue, all devoted to the same theme; also Robert W. Habenstein and Phyllis B. Kultgen, *Power, Pelf, Patients* (Columbia, Mo.: Missouri Gerontology Institute, 1981); and Carroll L. Estes and Charlene A. Harrington, "Fiscal Crisis, Deinstitutionalization, and the Elderly," *American Behavioral Scientist* 15 (1981): 811–26.

14. On family as a process involving different relationships rather than a singular monolithic institution, see Barrie Throne with Marilyn Yalom, eds., *Rethinking the Family: Some Feminist Questions,* (New York, Longman, 1982). All of the essays in this collection deconstruct the notion of "the" family; see especially Barrie Thorne, "Feminist Rethinking of the Family: An Overview," 1–24; and Rayna Rapp, "Family and Class in Contemporary America: Notes Toward an Understanding of Ideology," 168–87. See also Weston, *Families We Choose.*

15. The term *determined survivors* is borrowed from Janice A. Smithers, *Determined Survivors: Community Life Among the Urban Elderly* (New Brunswick, N.J.: Rutgers University Press, 1985).

4. "Why Can't I Get a Little Rest Around Here?"

1. For additional discussion of the gender composition of nursing homes, see Sally Bould, Beverly Sanborn, and Laura Reif, *Eighty-five Plus: The Oldest Old* (Belmont, Calif.: Wadsworth Publishing, 1989), 35–42.

2. Maggie Kuhn, "The Future of Aging," University of Illinois, Chicago, 24 Nov. 1984.

3. In 1990, a set of federal regulations went into effect. Called OBRA, as part of the Omnibus Budget Reconciliation Act, one provision restricted use of restraints. Claire Spiegel, "Restraints, Drugging Rife in Nursing Homes," *Los Angeles Times,* 25 March 1991, p. 1, reports from California's Little Hoover Commission that between 68 percent and 80 percent of California nursing home residents are put in restraints and that the National Senior Citizens Law Center estimates that the OBRA regulations reduce the use of restraints across the country by 25 percent. It remains questionable how much impact external regulations can have. I take up this issue more fully in chaps. 6 and 7.

4. Trying to make sense of a social order created and controlled elsewhere is a major theme of Smith's analysis; the "problematic" of everyday life, while "the logic of its transformation is elsewhere." See *The Everyday World as Problematic,* 94.

5. Arlene K. Daniels's research opens up the domain of volunteer activity as a work form. See *Invisible Careers: Women Civic Leaders from the Volunteer World* (Chicago: University of Chicago Press, 1988).

6. Ellen Newton, in her fascinating autobiography of life in a series of Australian nursing homes, writes of being admitted on the same diagnoses. Neither Helen Donahue nor Ellen Newton ever expected to stay in this setting for the rest of her life. See Ellen Newton, *This Bed My Centre* (London: Virago, 1979). Some research suggests that only "short-stayers" ever leave once they enter; see Joan Retsinas and Patricia Garrity, "Going Home: Analysis of Nursing Home Discharges," *The Gerontologist* 26 (1986): 431–36.

7. Paul C. Luken, "Social Identity in Later Life: A Situational Approach to Understanding Old Age Stigma," *International Journal of Aging and Human Development* 25 (1987): 177–93, shows how social identities like "out of it" emerge in specific social situations.

8. She was, as Dorothy Smith would say, ordering their lives into textually mediated processes. See Smith, *The Conceptual Practices of*

Power, 5: "Through the work of those who reconstruct the patient's life as a case history, it is obliterated as it was experienced and lived." See also Mueller, "The Bureaucratization of Feminist Knowledge."

9. Alexander Solzhenitsyn, *One Day in the Life of Ivan Denisovitch* (New York: Viking, Penguin Books, 1963) offers one explanation for silence during meals: "No one talked during food. These moments were holy." I hesitate to analogize nursing homes to prison camps, or to any other kind of inmate institution for that matter. Thus I shy away from Erving Goffman's notion of "total institution," as described in *Asylums* (Garden City, N.Y.: Doubleday, Anchor Books, 1961). While this book was significant in my studying sociology in the first place, I've also spent time in seminaries, the military, hospitals, and nursing homes, and they seem to contain more essential differences than any overarching concept can convey. This research, again following Dorothy Smith, does not seek to find or generate abstract concepts.

10. The issue of sedatives is a complex one. Outsiders often asked me "Were they drugged?" They were, for sure. Yet, I decided that the use of tranquilizers was not something I was qualified to analyze. Don Riesenberg reports on recent studies that do indicate excessive use of psychotropic drugs. See "Drugs in the Institutionalized Elderly: Time to Get It Right?" *Journal of the American Medical Association* 260 (1988): 3054.

OBRA regulations have attempted to restrict excessive use of tranquilizers. Again, their impact is questionable since they leave physicians with unchallenged autonomy. As Eliot Freidson has clearly demonstrated, regulation that leaves this domain autonomous only augments a physician's authority; see *Doctoring Together: A Study of Professional Control* (Chicago: University of Chicago Press, 1980).

11. This situation seemed like one of many examples of residents simply getting "worn down" from trying to compete with rules everywhere they turned. On residents and families getting "worn down," see Carolyn L. Wiener and Jeanie Kayser-Jones, "The Uneasy Fate of Nursing Home Residents: An Organizational-Interaction Perspective," *Sociology of Health and Illness* 12 (1990): 84–104.

12. Jaber F. Gubrium has written a detailed account of the dynamics of death in nursing homes in *Living and Dying at Murray Manor,* chap. 6; see also Elizabeth Gustafson, "Dying: The Career of the Nursing Home Patient," *Journal of Health and Social Behavior* 13 (1972): 226–35.

13. For the "survival strategies" and "work" of residents, see Anselm S. Strauss, et al., "The Work of Hospitalized Patients," *Social Science and Medicine* 16 (1982): 977–86; also Margaret Stacey, "Who Are the Health Care Workers? Patients and Other Unpaid Workers in Health

Care," paper presented at the International Sociological Association Conference, Mexico City, 1982.

14. On the issue of social control institutions creating as well as responding to "problems" and "caseloads" I draw especially from the work of Robert Emerson. See, for example, Robert M. Emerson, "Holistic Effects in Social Control Decision-Making," *Law and Society Review* 17 (1983): 427–55; Robert M. Emerson, E. Burke Rochford, Jr., and Linda L. Shaw, "The Micropolitics of Trouble in a Psychiatric Board and Care Facility," *Urban Life* 12 (1983): 349–67; Robert M. Emerson and Melvin Pollner, "Dirty Work Designations: Their Features and Consequences in a Psychiatric Setting," *Social Problems* 23 (1976): 243–55.

15. At least in the United States the corporate incentive for establishing separate units for those diagnosed with Alzheimer's disease serves a dual purpose. Alix M. Freedman, "Nursing Homes Try New Approach in Caring for Alzheimer's Victims," *Wall Street Journal*, 26 Sept. 1986, p. 21, explains it: "Above all, more nursing homes recognize that caring for such patients ensures the good will of their burned-out families— and good profit. Indeed, the special units, which are primarily geared to private-pay patients, cost an estimated $5 to $15 a day more than standard nursing home care, which averages roughly $45 to $65 a day."

16. On the subject of documents erasing needs, Marie L. Campbell, who also works with Smith's methods, is particularly insightful. See "Management as Ruling: A Class Phenomenon in Nursing," *Studies in Political Economy* 27 (1988): 29–51; also "The Structure of Stress in Nurses' Work" in *Sociology of Health Care in Canada*, ed. B. Singh Bolaria and Harley D. Dickenson (Toronto: Harcourt Brace Jovanovich, 1988), 393–405.

17. Adrienne Rich, "Integrity," in *A Wild Patience Has Taken Me This Far: Poems 1978–81* (New York: W. W. Norton, 1981), 8; I am indebted to Catharine R. Stimpson for noting the phrase "wild patience" and using it with characteristic elegance in her address for the Tenth Anniversary Celebration, Wellesley College Center for Research on Women, 23 May 1985.

5. "If It's Not Charted, It Didn't Happen"

1. Regarding the skills of monitoring and anticipating needs, I draw from Alison Griffith and Dorothy E. Smith, "Mother's Work and School," paper delivered at the conference on "Women in the Invisible Economy," Simone de Beauvoir Institute, University of Concordia, 1985; also Mary E. Hawkinson, "Women's Studies Office Workers." *Sojourner* 13 (1986): 4–8.

2. "Family members" in caretaking work are predominantly women, hence the naming of these gendered roles. For discussion and various

applications of this issue, see Abel and Nelson, eds., *Circles of Care*; and Janet Finch and Dulcie Groves, eds., *A Labour of Love: Women, Work, and Caring* (Boston: Routledge and Kegan Paul, 1983).

3. A theme elaborated in Daniels, *Invisible Careers*.

4. The schedule of tasks that eliminates the mental and emotional aspects of the work exemplifies "the organization of power in texts and the relations of ruling mediated by texts." Smith, *The Everyday World as Problematic*, 212.

5. On the fluid and contingent nature of tending work, see Marjorie L. DeVault, *Feeding the Family: The Social Organization of "Caring" as Gendered Work* (Chicago: University of Chicago Press, 1991).

6. On the passage of time in medical settings, see David R. Maines, "Time and Biography in Diabetic Experience," *Mid-American Review of Sociology* 8 (1983): 103–17; Evitar Zarubel, *Patterns of Time in Hospital Life* (Chicago: University of Chicago Press, 1979).

7. Herbert Marcuse, in his *Negations: Essays in Critical Theory*, may have captured the confusion we felt: "In the unfolding of capitalist rationality, irrationality becomes reason . . . [and] higher productivity becomes a destructive force." Quoted in Sondra Farganis, *The Social Construction of the Feminine Character* (Totawa, N.J.: Rowman and Littlefield, 1986), 195.

8. On caretaking as a complex set of skills as well as emotions, see Hilary Graham, "Caring: A Labor of Love," in *A Labour of Love*, ed. Finch and Groves, chap. 1; and Clare Ungerson, "Why Do Women Care?" in *A Labour of Love*, chap. 2. See also Emily K. Abel and Margaret K. Nelson, "Circles of Care: An Introductory Essay," in *Circles of Care*, ed. Abel and Nelson, chap. 1; and Berenice Fisher and Joan Tronto, "Toward a Feminist Theory of Caring," chap. 2.

6. "There's Nothing Wrong with the Scale . . ."

1. The theme owes much to the writings of Michel Foucault. I draw indirectly on his work from Kathy E. Ferguson, *The Feminist Case against Bureaucracy* (Philadelphia: Temple University Press, 1984); Smith, *The Conceptual Practices of Power*; Jaber F. Gubrium and David Silverman, eds. *The Politics of Field Research: Sociology beyond Enlightenment* (Newbury Park, Calif.: Sage, 1989); and Hubert L. Dreyfus and Paul Rabinow, *Michel Foucault: Beyond Structuralism and Hermeneutics* (Chicago: University of Chicago Press, 1982).

2. On commodity creation and production, see T. R. Young, *Red Feather Dictionary of Socialist Sociology* 2d ed., (Red Feather, Colo.: Red Feather Institute, 1978), 25: "Commodity: the transformation of a good or service from its meaning as a support for social relationships to a meaning of private profit"; also Claus Offe, *Contradictions of the*

Welfare State, ed. John Keane (Cambridge, Mass.: MIT Press, 1984), 262–65. On the practice of treating health care as a commodity, see Howard Waitzkin, *The Second Sickness: Contradictions of Capitalist Health Care* (New York: The Free Press, 1983).

3. On deskilling of labor, see Harry Braverman, *Labor and Monopoly Capital* (New York: Monthly Review Press, 1974); Michael Burawoy, *Manufacturing Consent.* On deskilling specific to nursing, see Susan M. Reverby, *Ordered to Care: The Dilemma of American Nursing, 1850–1945* (New York: Cambridge University Press, 1987).

4. The notion of estrangement is drawn from Isidor Walliman, *Estrangement: Marx's Conception of Human Nature and the Division of Labor* (Westport, Conn.: Greenwood Press, 1981).

Allan Schnaiberg discusses efficiency as the cornerstone of the industrial mode in *The Environment: From Surplus to Scarcity* (New York: Oxford University Press, 1980), 139: "Efficiency is the standard of accountability, the ideological basis, for the industrial system and individual corporations. Other goals must be *forced* politically into the calculus of the firm, directly or indirectly, by governments and organized political forces." Compare with Marie Campbell, "The Structure of Stress in Nurses' Work," 401: "The administrative capability to assess 'needs' at the point of service production finally comes down to applying 'efficiency.' In the 'efficiently' organized hospital, there is in fact more work to do than is provided in purchased hours of labour. This excess must somehow be accommodated through nurses' efforts."

5. Like the separate Alzheimer's units, the use of diapers is considered efficient and cannot be separated from capitalist interests. Jean Dietz, "Incontinence in the Elderly Has an Estimated $8 Billion Annual Price Tag," *Chicago Tribune,* 14 July 1989, sec. 5, p. 8, notes that this $8 billion "exceeds the amount spent annually in this country for dialysis and coronary-artery bypass surgery combined." She goes on to point out that diapers save on labor costs.

6. I refer especially to OBRA regulations, although there is considerable doubt about their potential efficacy. Robert L. Kane, "A Nursing Home in Your Future?" *New England Journal of Medicine* 324 (1991): 628, notes that "in fact the average resident receives less than three hours of care in all per day." In such a context, "regulations to protect frail elderly people now restrict their options and raise costs for the very people we want to serve."

7. See especially Sacks, "Does It Pay to Care?" *Circles of Care,* 189–90, 201–2; Celia Davies offers a comparative analysis for Britain in "The Regulation of Nursing Work: An Historical Comparison of Britain and the U.S.A." in *Research in the Sociology of Health Care,* ed. Julius A. Roth (Greenwich, Conn.: JAI Press, 1982), 2: 121–60.

8. On the interlocking nature of race, gender, and class oppression,

see Patricia Hill Collins, "Learning from the Outsider Within: The Sociological Significance of Black Feminist Thought," in *Beyond Methodology: Feminist Scholarship as Lived Research,* ed. Mary Margaret Fonow and Judith A. Cook, 35–59 (Bloomington and Indianapolis: Indiana University Press, 1991).

9. The 415-page report by the Committee on Nursing Home Regulation, *Improving the Quality of Care in Nursing Homes,* gives the issue of wages one sentence (101). Jill Frawley, in her two-page article, is more informative: "We're always short-staffed. We know it's to save money. One tired aide does a double shift, straining to do a job it takes two people to do correctly. I guess when you're making four dollars and something an hour, it takes working double shifts (that's sixteen hours) to make enough to live on." "Inside the Home," *Mother Jones,* (March-April, 1991), 31.

10. On knowledge available from the standpoint of women I draw especially from Smith, *The Everyday World as Problematic,* chap. 2; Alison M. Jaggar, *Feminist Politics and Human Nature* (Totowa, N.J.: Rowman and Allenheld, 1983), 385–89.

11. In certifying the proprietary power of corporate ownership, the state is involved in a contradictory position. As John Keane explains Claus Offe's thesis, "The likelihood of permanent fiscal deficits also grows because there is a contradiction between the ever-expanding costs associated with the welfare state's 'socialization' of production and the continuing private control over investment and the appropriation of its profits." Offe, *Contradictions of the Welfare State,* 19.

12. See Lynn M. Olson, "Bureaucratic Control in Health Care: The Technology of Records," Ph.D. diss., Northwestern University, 1986. Olson expands on the earlier work of Nancy Cockran, Andrew C. Gordon, and Merton C. Krause, "Proactive Records," *Knowledge: Creation, Diffusion, Utilization* 2 (1980): 5–18; and on that of Kai Erikson and Daniel E. Gibertson, "Case Records in the Mental Hospital," in *On Record,* ed. Stanton Wheeler (New Brunswick, N.J.: Transaction, 1976), 389–412.

13. On gift giving tied to power and ownership, see Richard M. Titmus, *The Gift Relationship: From Human Blood to Social Policy* (London: George Allen and Unwin, 1970), chap. 7.

14. See, for example, Thomas McKeown, *The Role of Medicine: Dream, Mirage, or Nemesis?* (Princeton: Princeton University Press, 1979).

15. A richly detailed account of residents producing the social milieu is offered by Linda L. Shaw, "Board and Care: The Everyday Lives of Ex-Mental Patients Living in the Community," Ph.D. diss., University of California, Los Angeles, 1988.

16. Staples, in *Castles of Our Conscience,* 125, notes that "more than

70 percent of all nursing beds are in for-profit homes and the private
sector stands poised to capture this expansive market." Increasingly, as
Carolyn Wiener and Jeanie Kayser-Jones observe in "The Uneasy Fate
of Nursing Home Residents," 101, they are controlled by investor-
owned chains.

17. Dorothy Smith's conception of ideology, which she draws from
Marx and Engels's *The German Ideology*, refers not to abstract ideas
but to actual practices that can be explored and deconstructed. "The
terrain to be explored and explicated by the institutional ethnography
is one of work processes and other practical activities as these are rendered accountable within the ideological schemata of the institution."
The Everyday World as Problematic, 176; see also *The Concepetual
Practices of Power,* chap. 2.

18. On the intersection of biography and history and on the effect of
living in a particular historical place and time, see C. Wright Mills, *The
Sociological Imagination* (New York: Oxford University Press, 1959),
chap. 8. See also Maggie Kuhn, "Challenge to a New Age," in *Readings
in the Political Economy of Aging,* ed. Meredith Minkler and Carroll
L. Estes (Farmingdale, N.Y.: Baywood, 1984), 7–9.

19. On the distinction between collectivist and individualist oriented
societies, and the latter incorporating health care as a right of citizenship, see Derek G. Gill and Stanley R. Ingman, "Geriatric Care and
Distributive Justice: Problems and Prospects," *Social Science and Medicine* 23 (1986): 1205–15.

20. On patients being removed from decision making in health care,
see Derek G. Gill and Gordon W. Horobin, "Doctors, Patients and the
State: Relationships and Decision-Making," *The Sociological Review*
20 (1972): 505–20; regarding families being removed from medical decision making, see Abel, *Who Cares for the Elderly?* chap. 2.

21. On the state as guarantor of profits for the health care sector, see
J. Warren Salmon, "Organizing Medical Care for Profit," in *Issues in
the Political Economy of Health Care,* ed. John B. McKinlay (New
York: Tavistock, 1984), 143–86.

22. The point here is to step aside from bureaucratic dichotomies that
separate categories of women, to move toward a dialectics of gender.
See Mary O'Brien, "Feminist Theory and Dialectical Logic," *Feminist
Theory: A Critique of Ideology,* ed. Nannerl O. Keohane, Michelle Z.
Rozaldo, and Barbara C. Gelpi (Chicago: University of Chicago Press,
1982), 99–112.

23. On ruling being dependent on a culture of silence, see Paulo
Friere, *Pedagogy of the Oppressed,* trans. Myra Bergman Ramos (New
York: Continuum, 1990), 76.

24. *Matrix* and *mother* are derived from the same root. Judith Witt-

ner, personal communication, noted that analysis of caretaking only as a set of tasks leaves out this interactive matrix. Abel, *Who Cares for the Elderly?* 7, makes a parallel point: "Studies seeking to correlate stress with various aspects of caregiving suffer from the shortcomings common to positivist social science. In order to establish connections between two variables, it is necessary to abstract these variables from the context that gives them meaning. I have noted the importance of examining the complex web of relationships within which caregiving is embedded."

25. In *Feeding the Family*, DeVault shows that feeding a family, like tending to human needs, does not fit into an industrial model.

26. Drawn from Mueller, "The Bureaucratization of Feminist Knowledge," 38, and from Smith, *The Conceptual Practices of Power*, chaps. 3 and 4.

27. On the concept of contradiction, see Offe, *The Contradictions of the Welfare State*, 130–34; also Ferguson, *The Feminist Case Against Bureaucracy*, 21–22 citing a paper by Roslyn Wallach Bologh: "A contradictory situation is one that is based on premises that cannot be simultaneously realized, so that to pursue one it must repress the other, and thus become self-refuting." In nursing homes, I suggest, the dictates of human caretaking and of business constitute just such a contradictory situation. Ferguson points to the incompleteness of bureaucratic domination as a way out of the contradiction: "To seek out and articulate alternative voices it is necessary continuously to recall the two competing dimensions of human experience within bureaucratic society: the dominance and pervasiveness of bureaucratic discourse, the manifold incursions that it makes into daily life, and the incompleteness of bureaucratic discourse, its inability totally to absorb the field of conflicts within which it operates."

7. Now For "A Little Rest Around Here"

1. The term "ordinary struggles" is Judith Wittner's, from "Ordinary Struggles: The Politics and Perspectives of Displaced Factory Women," paper presented at the annual meeting of the Society for the Study of Social Problems, Berkeley, August 1989. The notion of two competing narratives comes from Michel Foucault, especially Ferguson's reading of his work on dominant and submerged discourses, the latter constituting "subjugated knowledges." See Ferguson, *The Feminist Case Against Bureaucracy*, p. 23.

2. My effort here is to grapple, as Smith suggests, with "how to write a sociology that will somehow lay out for women, for people, how our everyday worlds are organized and how they are shaped and determined by relations that extend beyond them." *The Everyday World as*

Problematic, 121. The objective is to hold to the context that residents and workers pointed to in trying to meet daily needs, like food and rest, and to experiment with what Smith calls an "insider's materialism."

On materialist analysis, I draw also from Hartsock, "The Feminist Standpoint," 283–310; and from Jaggar, *Feminist Politics and Human Nature,* 87–88.

The practice of proceeding from the contradictions of everyday life is drawn in part from Joan Acker, Kate Barry, and Joke Esseveld, "Objectivity and Truth: The Problems of Doing Feminist Research," in *Beyond Methodology,* 144: "We saw that the themes of everyday life we were identifying could be understood as manifestations of contradictions or dilemmas inherent in the underlying social relations." See also Mary Margaret Fonow and Judith A. Cook, "Back to the Future: A Look at the Second Wave of Feminist Epistemology and Methodology," *Beyond Methodology,* 1–15.

3. On framing a policy agenda from actual caretaking encounters, see Abel, *Who Cares for the Elderly?* chap. 9. From nursing assistants in particular, see Bobbie J. Hyerstay, "The Political and Economic Implications of Training Nursing Home Aides," *Journal of Nursing Home Administration* 8 (1978), 24: "Since nursing homes are profit-motivated and medically oriented, the implications for training and giving voice to the 'lowly aide' could prove somewhat revolutionary."

4. To break down the dichotomy of givers and receivers is to approach caretaking from an ontology of relations. Jaggar connects radical feminism and traditional Marxism in that both are based on a relational ontology; see *Feminist Politics and Human Nature,* 368.

5. On bringing minimum wage up to a living wage, see Ruth Needleman and Anne Nelson, "Policy Implications: The Worth of Women's Work," in *The Worth of Women's Work: A Qualitative Synthesis,* ed., Anne Statham, Eleanor M. Miller and Hans O. Mauksch (Albany, N.Y.: State University of New York Press, 1988), 293–308. On women's growing union activism, see Ruth Needleman, "Women Workers: A Force for Rebuilding Unionism," *Labor Research Review* 11 (1991): 1–13; also Gail S. Livings, "Discovering the World of Twentieth Century Trade Union Waitresses in the West." *Current Perspectives on Aging and the Life Cycle* 3 (1989): 141–73.

6. Address by Maggie Kuhn, "Dedicated to the Future," presented at the Immanuel Presbyterian Church, Los Angeles, 2 Dec. 1989.

7. Campbell, "The Structure of Stress in Nurses' Work," 402, summarizes the problem: "Abstract documentary information, reported through proper channels, replaces procedures for listening to and relying on experienced professionals. Only nurses at the front line are aware of the disjuncture and what it means. And these nurses are si-

lenced and disempowered by the management information systems and procedures."

8. Vicente Navarro, "Why Some Countries Have National Health Insurance, Others Have National Health Services, and the United States Has Neither," *International Journal of Health Services* 19 (1989): 383–404.

9. Steffie Woolhandler and David U. Himmelstein, "The Deteriorating Administrative Efficiency of the U.S. Health Care System," *New England Journal of Medicine* 324 (1991): 1253–58. The authors calculate that by adopting a Canadian-like nationalized system of health care, the U.S. would save close to $100 billion in administrative costs.

10. Some of the spirit of the following discussion is drawn from Alison Jaggar, "Love and Knowledge: Emotion in Feminist Epistemology," in *Gender/Body/Knowledge,* ed. Alison M. Jaggar and Susan R. Bordo (New Brunswick, N.J.: Rutgers University Press, 1989), 145–71; also, on strategies of resistance, from William D. Darrough, "In the Best Interest of the Child II," *Journal of Contemporary Ethnography* 18 (1989): 72–88. Darrough pointed me to another strategy of resistance that some residents actually did deploy, what Jessica Mitford called "a pee in": "'Next time Mrs. —— rings her bell, I'll count to ten. If a nurse hasn't come by then, let's all wet our beds.' It worked beautifully." Jessica Mitford, *A Fine Old Conflict* (New York: Alfred A. Knopf, 1977), 27.

11. The iron cage is Max Weber's term, from *The Protestant Ethic and the Spirit of Capitalism* (New York: Charles Scribner's Sons, 1958), 181. Weber's pessimism about the power of bureaucracy is not shared by Foucault or by feminist theorists like Smith, Jaggar, Hartsock, and Ferguson. Alvin W. Gouldner, *The Coming Crisis of Western Sociology* (New York: Basic Books, 1970), 40, explains the difference: "Weber's theory of bureaucracy . . . has strongly antisocialist implications, for it implies that change toward socialism will not prevent bureaucratization and alienation." The other writers argue that escape from the iron cage is indeed possible, as suggested in the remaining notes of this chapter. One route to breaking out of the iron cage is possible precisely because bureaucratic control is not totalitarian but, as Ferguson suggests, "a process, a moment in a dialectic of domination and resistance." *The Feminist Case against Bureaucracy,* 19.

12. Lila Abu-Lughod points out that one of the central problematics in the human sciences in recent years has been the relationship of resistance to power, but that there remains a tendency to romanticize the resistance. I am surely doing so here in raising the potential for resident revolt. But I am trying, as she does, to use resistance as a diagnostic of power, to study its methods and historical shifts. See "The Romance of

Resistance: Tracing Transformations of Power through Bedouin Women," *American Ethnologist* 17 (1990): 41–55. Thanks to Suzanne Vaughan for pointing out this theme. She and Paul Luken are applying Dorothy Smith's institutional ethnography to the area of older women and housing. For an initial outline of their work, see Luken and Vaughan, "Elderly Women Living Alone: Theoretical and Methodological Considerations from a Feminist Perspective," *Housing and Society* 18 (1991), 1–12.

13. The grid image is from Adele Mueller, "The Bureaucratization of Feminist Knowledge."

14. John Gaventa shows that quiescence is by no means passivity, in *Power and Powerlessness: Quiescence and Rebellion in an Appalachian Valley* (Oxford: Clarendon Press, 1980). On the notion that everyday, low-profile techniques of resistance are the most significant and effective in the long run, see James C. Scott, *Weapons of the Weak: Everyday Forms of Peasant Resistance* (New Haven: Yale University Press, 1985).

15. Ultimately, the OBRA regulations are patchwork reforms. On patchwork in health care and its contradictions, see Waitzkin, *The Second Sickness*, 230–31.

16. For other research that makes public this agenda, see *Everyday Ethics: Resolving Dilemmas in Nursing Home Life*, ed. Rosalie A. Kane and Arthur L. Kaplan (New York: Springer-Verlag, 1989); also Wiener and Kayser-Jones, "The Uneasy Fate of Nursing Home Residents."

17. This epistemology is pointed out in E. P. Thompson, *The Making of the English Working Class* (London: Victor Gollancz, 1963). My title, *Making Gray Gold*, is derived in part from Thompson, as well as from Michael Burawoy's *Manufacturing Consent*, to convey active agency on the part of residents and workers, those who actually produce the gray gold. In Thompson's words, 9, "The working class did not rise like the sun at an appointed time. It was present at its own making." In nursing homes, of course, the image "from the bottom up" takes on something of a literal significance.

18. See Ellen Newton, *This Bed My Center* (London: Virago, 1979); Joyce Horner, *That Time of Year* (Amherst, Mass.: University of Massachusetts Press, 1982); Carobeth Laird, *Limbo* (Novato, Calif.: Chandler and Sharp, 1979); Sallie Tisdale, *Harvest Moon: Portrait of a Nursing Home* (New York: Henry Holt, 1987).

19. For example, Goffman, *Asylums*; Gubrium, *Living and Dying at Murray Manor*; Renee Rose Shield, *Uneasy Endings* (Ithaca, N.Y.: Cornell University Press, 1988); David L. Rosenhan, "On Being Sane in Insane Places," *Science* 179 (1973): 250–58; Bruce C. Vladeck, *Unloving Care: The Nursing Home Tragedy* (New York: Basic Books, 1980).

20. On the method of oral history, see Debra L. Schultz, "Women

Historians as a Force in History: The Activist Roots of Women Historians," (Master's thesis, City University of New York, 1990); Gail S. Livings, "Discovering the World of Twentieth Century Trade Union Waitresses in the West."

21. On the positive impact of ombudspeople, see Ralph L Cherry, "Agents of Nursing Home Quality of Care: Ombudsmen and Staff Ratios Revisited," *The Gerontologist* 31 (1991): 302–8; on the impact of community organizations, see Constance Williams, "Improving Care in Nursing Homes Using Community Advocacy," *Social Science and Medicine* 23 (1986): 1297–1303.

22. Karen Thompson and Julie Andrezejewski, *Why Can't Sharon Come Home?* (San Francisco: Spinsters/Aunt Lute, 1988); the quotation is taken from Marie Shear's review of the book, *Women's Review of Books* 6 (1989): 23.

23. Alan Walker notes common interests of caretakers and those for whom they care, as well as shared conflicts with the state, in "Care for Elderly People: A Conflict between Women and the State," in *A Labour of Love* ed. Finch and Groves, 106–28.

24. Max Weber wrote about this core example, lamenting the force of rationality and scientific thought that "rejected all signs of religious ceremony . . . in order that no superstition, no trust in the effects of magical and sacramental forces on salvation, should creep in." *The Protestant Ethic and the Spirit of Capitalism,* 105. Foucault shared Weber's concern, as Dreyfus and Rabinow suggest in *Michel Foucault,* 166: "From Weber [Foucault] inherits a concern with rationalization and objectification as the essential trend of our culture and the most important problem of our time." Arlene K. Daniels, personal communication, suggested that feminists raise the possibility of reinserting the "magic" of human emotions into bureaucracy, insofar as they proceed from caring as ethic and epistemology. Her point is corroborated by Jaggar, "Love and Knowledge: Emotion in Feminist Epistemology"; see also Sondra Farganis, "Feminism and the Reconstruction of Social Science," 207–23. Berenice Fisher and Joan Tronto make a similar point in "Toward a Feminist Theory of Caring," ed. Abel and Nelson, 35–62, as does Ferguson in *The Feminist Case against Bureaucracy,* 196–203.

25. All of the writers in the previous note (except Weber) are working within materialist philosophy, rejecting Weber's idealist analysis and with it his pessimism about breaking through the iron cage of bureaucratic rationality. From them, and mostly from Dorothy Smith, I move toward the charts as the concrete repository of "documentary reality," where the submerged narrative of residents and workers gets silenced. See especially Smith, *The Conceptual Practices of Power,* chap. 3.

26. That labels conceal as much as they reveal is a theme I draw from Laurel Richardson. See *The Dynamics of Sex and Gender: A Sociological Perspective*, 3d. ed., (New York: HarperCollins, 1988); and *The New Other Women: Contemporary Single Women in Affairs with Married Men* (New York: The Free Press, 1985).

27. On the medicalization of aging, see Estes and Binney, "Toward a Transformation of Health and Aging Policy,"; and Karen Lyman, "Bringing the Social Back In: A Critique of the Biomedicalization of Dementia," paper presented at the annual meeting of the American Sociological Association, Atlanta, 1988. See also Dale J. Jaffe, "Teaching Health Care and Aging: Toward a Conceptual Integration," *Teaching Sociology* 18 (1990): 313–18.

28. Mueller, "The Bureaucratization of Feminist Knowledge," and personal communication; see also Campbell, "The Structure of Stress in Nurses' Work"; and Celia Davies, "The Regulation of Nursing Work," 154, on the institutional matrices that "shape experience and generate contradictions which provide a focus for forms of group formation and for forms of struggle."

29. Fisher and Tronto, "Toward a Feminist Theory of Caring," 42.

30. Jaggar, in "Love and Knowledge: Emotion in Feminist Epistemology," 165, writes of the acumen women develop in part because of their social responsibility for caretaking, including emotional nurturance: "This emotional acumen can now be recognized as a skill in political analysis and validated as giving women a special advantage in both understanding the mechanisms of domination and envisioning freer ways to live."

References

Abel, Emily K. *Who Cares for the Elderly? Public Policy and the Experience of Adult Daughters.* Philadelphia: Temple University Press, 1991.

Abel, Emily K., and Margaret K. Nelson, eds., *Circles of Care: Work and Identity in Women's Lives.* Albany, N.Y.: State University of New York Press, 1990.

Abu-Lughod, Lila. "The Romance of Resistance: Tracing Transformations of Power through Bedouin Women," *American Ethnologist* 17 (1990): 41–55.

Acker, Joan, Kate Barry, and Joke Esseveld. "Objectivity and Truth: The Problems of Doing Feminist Research." In *Beyond Methodology: Feminist Scholarship as Lived Research,* edited by Mary Margaret Fonow and Judith A. Cook, 133–53. Bloomington and Indianapolis: Indiana University Press, 1991.

Alexander, Charles P. "The New Economy." *Time,* 30 May 1983, 62–70.

Amparano, Julie. "Marriott Sees Green in a Graying Nation." *Wall Street Journal,* 11 February 1988, p. 28.

Arledge, Elizabeth. "Who Pays for Mom and Dad?" "Frontline." Public Broadcasting System, aired 30 April 1991.

Baker, Bob. "Nursing Home Chain Guilty of Unfair Labor Practices." *Los Angeles Times,* 17 November 1990, p. 28.

Ball, Robert M., with Thomas N. Bethell. *Because We're All in This Together.* Washington, D.C.: Families U.S.A., 1989.

Becker, Howard S., Blanche Geer, Everett C. Hughes, and Anselm Strauss. *Boys in White: Student Culture in Medical School.* Chicago: University of Chicago Press, 1961.

Bell, Nora K. "What Setting Limits May Mean." *Hypatia* 4 (1989): 169–77.

Beneria, Lourdes, and Martha Roddan, eds. *Crossroads of Class and Gender: Industrial Homework, Subcontracting and Household Dynamics.* Chicago: University of Chicago Press, 1987.

Blyskal, Jeff. "Gray Gold." *Forbes* 23 November 1981, 80–84.

Bould, Sally, Beverly Sanborn, and Laura Reif. *Eighty-Five Plus: The Oldest Old*. Belmont, Calif.: Wadsworth, 1989.

Braverman, Harry. *Labor and Monopoly Capital*. New York: Monthly Review Press, 1974.

Brents, Barbara G. "Policy Intellectuals, Class Struggle and the Construction of Old Age: The Creation of the Social Security Act of 1935." *Social Science and Medicine* 23 (1986): 1251–60.

Brown, E. Richard. "Medicare and Medicaid: Band Aids for the Old and Poor." In *Reforming Medicine: Lessons of the Last Quarter Century*, edited by Victor W. Sidel and Ruth Sidel, 50–78. New York: Random House, Pantheon Books, 1984.

Bruyn, Severyn T. *The Human Perspective: The Methodology of Participant Observation*. Englewood Cliffs, N.J.: Prentice-Hall, Inc., 1966.

Bucy, Eric P. "Health Care Field Continues to Boom." *Los Angeles Herald Examiner* 18 November 1988, sec. 2, p. 1.

Burawoy, Michael. *Manufacturing Consent: Changes in the Labor Process under Monopoly Capitalism*. Chicago: University of Chicago Press, 1979.

Campbell, Marie L. "Management as Ruling: A Class Phenomenon in Nursing." *Studies in Political Economy* 27 (1988): 29–51.

———. "The Structure of Stress in Nurses' Work." In *The Sociology of Health Care in Canada*, edited by B. Singh Bolaria and Harley D. Dickenson, 393–405. Toronto: Harcourt Brace Jovanovich, 1988.

Cherry, Ralph. "Agents of Nursing Home Quality of Care: Ombudsmen and Staff Ratios Revisited." *The Gerontologist* 31 (1991): 302–8.

Cockran, Nancy, Andrew C. Gordon, and Merton C. Krause. "Proactive Records." *Knowledge: Creation, Diffusion, Utilization* 2 (1980): 5–18.

Collins, Patricia Hill. "Learning from the Outsider Within: The Sociological Significance of Black Feminist Thought." In *Beyond Methodology: Feminist Scholarship as Lived Research*, edited by Mary Margaret Fonow and Judith A. Cook, 35–59. Bloomington and Indianapolis: Indiana University Press, 1991.

Committee on Nursing Home Regulation, Institute of Medicine. *Improving the Quality of Care in Nursing Homes*. Washington, D.C.: National Academy Press, 1986.

Consumer Reports. "Who Can Afford a Nursing Home?" 53 (May 1988): 300–11.

Currer, Caroline, and Meg Stacey, eds. *Concepts of Health, Illness and*

Disease: A Comparative Perspective. New York: Berg Publishers, 1986.

Daniels, Arlene Kaplan. "Invisible Work." *Social Problems* 34 (1987): 403–15.

———. *Invisible Careers: Women Civil Leaders from the Volunteer World.* Chicago: University of Chicago Press, 1988.

Darrough, William D. "In the Best Interest of the Child II." *Journal of Contemporary Ethnography* 18 (1989): 72–88.

Davies, Celia. "The Regulation of Nursing Work: An Historical Comparison of Britain and the U.S.A." In *Research in the Sociology of Health Care,* 2: 121–60, edited by Julius A. Roth, Greenwich, Conn.: JAI Press, 1982.

DeVault, Marjorie L. *Feeding the Family: The Social Organization of "Caring" as Gendered Work.* Chicago: University of Chicago Press, 1991.

Dietz, Jean. "Incontinence in the Elderly Has an Estimated $8 Billion Annual Price Tag." *Chicago Tribune* 14 July 1989, sec. 5, p. 8.

DiIorio, Judith A. "Sex, Glorious Sex: The Social Construction of Masculine Sexuality in a Youth Group." In *Feminist Frontiers,* edited by Laurel Richardson and Verta Taylor, 261–69. New York: Random House, 1989.

———. "Being and Becoming Coupled: The Emergence of Female Subordination in Heterosexual Relationships." In *Gender in Intimate Relationships,* edited by Barbara J. Risman and Pepper Schwartz, 94–107. Belmont, Calif.: Wadsworth, 1989.

Donovan, Rebecca. " 'We Care for the Most Important People in Your Life': Home Care Workers in New York City." *Women's Studies Quarterly* 1 and 2 (1989): 56–65.

Dreyfus, Hubert L., and Paul Rabinow. *Michel Foucault: Beyond Structuralism and Hermeneutics.* Chicago: University of Chicago Press, 1982.

Eakes, M. Garey, and Ron M. Landsman. "Medicaid Money—and You." *Modern Maturity* (February-March 1990): 85–90.

Elliott, Elizabeth. "Private Duty Nurses Aides and the Commercialization of Sickness Care in the Home." Ph.D. diss., Northwestern University, 1991.

Emerson, Robert M. "Holistic Effects in Social Control Decision-Making." *Law and Society Review* 17 (1983): 427–55.

Emerson, Robert M., and Pollner, Melvin. "Dirty Work Designations: Their Features and Consequences in a Psychiatric Setting." *Social Problems* 23 (1976): 243–55.

Emerson, Robert M., and Warren, Carol A. B. "Trouble and the Politics of Contemporary Social Control Institutions." *Urban Life* 12 (1983): 243–47.

Emerson, Robert M., E. Burke Rochford, Jr., and Linda L. Shaw. "The Micropolitics of Trouble in a Psychiatric Board and Care Facility." *Urban Life* 12 (1983): 349–67.

Erikson, Kai, and Daniel E. Gibertson. "Case Records in the Mental Hospital." In *On Record,* edited by Stanton Wheeler, 389–412. New Brunswick, N.J.: Transaction, 1976.

Estes, Carroll L., and Charlene A. Harrington. "Fiscal Crisis, Deinstitutionalization, and the Elderly." *American Behavioral Scientist* 15 (1981): 811–26.

Estes, Carroll L., and Elizabeth A. Binney. "Toward a Transformation of Health and Aging Policy." *International Journal of Health Services* 18 (1988): 69–82.

Farganis, Sondra. "Feminism and the Reconstruction of Social Science." In *Gender/Body/Knowledge: Feminist Reconstructions of Being and Knowing,* edited by Alison M. Jaggar and Susan R. Bordo, 207–23. New Brunswick, N.J.: Rutgers University Press, 1989.

Feder, Barney J. "What Ails a Nursing Home Empire." *New York Times,* 11 December 1988, sec. 3, p. 1.

Ferguson, Kathy E. *The Feminist Case against Bureaucracy.* Philadelphia: Temple University Press, 1984.

Finch, Janet, and Groves, Dulcie, eds., *A Labour of Love: Women, Work, and Caring.* Boston: Routledge and Kegan Paul, 1983.

Fisher, Berenice, and Joan Tronto. "Toward a Feminist Theory of Caring." In *Circles of Care: Work and Identity in Women's Lives,* edited by Emily K. Abel and Margaret K. Nelson, 35–62. Albany, N.Y.: State University of New York Press, 1990.

Fonow, Mary Margaret, and Cook, Judith A. "Back to the Future: A Look at the Second Wave of Feminist Epistemology and Methodology." In *Beyond Methodology: Feminist Scholarship as Lived Research,* edited by Mary Margaret Fonow and Judith A. Cook, 1–15. Bloomington and Indianapolis: Indiana University Press, 1991.

Frawley, Jill. "Inside the Home," *Mother Jones* (March-April 1991): 31.

Freedman, Alix M. "Nursing Homes Try New Approach in Caring for Alzheimer's Victims." *Wall Street Journal,* 26 September 1986, p. 21.

Freidson, Eliot. *Doctoring Together: A Study of Professional Social Control.* Chicago: University of Chicago Press, 1980.

Friere, Paulo. *Pedagogy of the Oppressed,* trans. Myra Bergman Ramos. New York: Continuum, 1990.

Galliher, John F. "Social Scientists' Ethical Responsibility to Superordinates: Looking Up Meekly." *Social Problems* 27 (1980): 298–308.

Gaventa, John. *Power and Powerlessness: Quiescence and Rebellion in an Appalachian Valley.* Oxford: Clarendon Press, 1980.

Gill, Derek G., and Stanley R. Ingman. "Geriatric Care and Distributive Justice: Problems and Prospects." *Social Science and Medicine* 23 (1986): 1205–15.

Gill, Derek G., and Gordon W. Horobin. "Doctors, Patients and the State: Relationships and Decision-Making." *The Sociological Review* 20 (1972): 505–20.

Goffman, Erving. *Asylums.* Garden City, N.Y.: Doubleday: Anchor Books, 1961.

Gouldner, Alvin W. *The Coming Crisis of Western Sociology.* New York: Basic Books, 1970.

Graham, Hilary. "Caring: A Labor of Love." In *A Labour of Love: Women, Work, and Caring,* edited by Janet Finch and Dulcie Groves. Boston: Routledge and Kegan Paul, 1983.

Grenier, Jeannine. "Nurses from Manila." *Union,* October–November 1988, 26.

Griffith, Alison, and Dorothy E. Smith. "Mother's Work and School." Paper presented at the conference "Women in the Invisible Economy." Simone de Beauvoir Institute, University of Concordia, 21–23 February 1985.

Grover, Jean. "Caring and Coping." *Women's Review of Books* 4, no. 9: 25–26.

Gubrium, Jaber F. *Living and Dying at Murray Manor.* New York: St. Martin's Press, 1975.

Gubrium, Jaber F., and David Silverman, eds., *The Politics of Field Research: Sociology beyond Enlightenment* (Newbury Park: Sage, 1989).

Gustafson, Elizabeth. "Dying: The Career of the Nursing Home Patient." *Journal of Health and Social Behavior* 13 (1972): 226–35.

Habenstein, Robert W., and Phyllis B. Kultgen. *Power, Pelf, Patients.* Columbia, Mo.: Missouri Gerontology Institute, 1981.

Harrington, Charlene. "Public Policy and the Nursing Home Industry." *International Journal of Health Services* 14 (1984): 481–90.

Harrington, Linda M. "Long-Term Health Care Plans Faulted." *Chicago Tribune* 17 May 1991, sec. 1, p. 19.

Harrington, Michael. *The New American Poverty.* New York: Viking, Penguin Books, 1984.

Hartsock, Nancy C. M. "The Feminist Standpoint: Developing the

Ground for a Specifically Feminist Historical Materialism." In *Discovering Reality: Feminist Perspectives on Epistemology, Methodology and Philosophy of Science,* edited by Sandra Harding and Merrill B. Hintikka, 283–310. Boston: D. Reidel, 1983.

Hawkinson, Mary E. "Women's Studies Office Workers." *Sojourner* 13 (1986): 4–8.

Hines, William. "Kids and Poverty Mix for City's Teen Moms." *Chicago Sun-Times,* 14 April 1986, p. 16.

Horner, Joyce. *That Time of Year.* Amherst, Mass.: University of Massachusetts Press, 1982.

Hughes, Everett C. *The Sociological Eye.* Chicago: Aldine, 1971.

Hull, Jon D. "Insurance for the Twilight Years." *Time* 6 April 1987, 53.

Hyerstay, Bobbie J. "The Political and Economic Implications of Training Nursing Home Aides." *Journal of Nursing Home Administration* 8 (1978): 22–25.

Ishi, Tomoji. "Politics of Labor Market: Immigrant Nurses in the United States." Paper presented at the annual meeting of the American Sociological Association, Atlanta, 1988.

Jaffe, Dale J. "Teaching Health Care and Aging: Toward a Conceptual Integration." *Teaching Sociology* 18 (1990): 313–18.

Jaggar, Alison M. *Feminist Politics and Human Nature.* Totawa, N.J.: Rowman and Allenheld, 1983.

———. "Love and Knowledge: Emotion in Feminist Epistemology." In *Gender/Body/Knowledge: Feminist Reconstructions of Being and Knowing,* edited by Alison M. Jaggar and Susan R. Bordo, 145–71. New Brunswick, N.J.: Rutgers University Press, 1989.

Kane, Robert L. "A Nursing Home in Your Future?" *New England Journal of Medicine* 324 (1991): 627–29.

Kane, Rosalie A., and Arthur L. Kaplan, eds., *Everyday Ethics: Resolving Dilemmas in Nursing Home Life.* New York: Springer-Verlag, 1989.

Kayser-Jones, Jeanie. *Old, Alone and Neglected: Care of the Aged in Scotland and the United States.* Berkeley and Los Angeles: University of California, 1981.

Kemper, Peter, and Christopher M. Murtaugh. "Lifetime Use of Nursing Home Care." *New England Journal of Medicine* 324 (1991): 595–600.

Krieger, Susan. *The Mirror Dance: Identity in a Women's Community.* Philadelphia: Temple University Press, 1983.

Kuhn, Maggie. "The Future of Aging." Address at the University of Illinois, Chicago, 24 November 1984.

———. "Challenge to a New Age." In *Readings in the Political Econ-*

omy of Aging, edited by Meredith Minkler and Carroll L. Estes, 7–9. Farmingdale, N.Y.: Baywood, 1984.

———. "Dedicated to the Future." Presented at the Immanuel Presbyterian Church, Los Angeles, 2 December 1989.

Kutza, Elizabeth Ann. *The Benefits of Old Age: Social Welfare Policy for the Elderly*. Chicago: University of Chicago, 1981.

Laird, Carobeth. *Limbo*. Novato, Calif.: Chandler and Sharp, 1979.

Livings, Gail S. "Discovering the World of Twentieth Century Trade Union Waitresses in the West." *Current Perspectives on Aging and the Life Cycle* 3 (1989): 141–73.

Luken, Paul C. "Social Identity in Later Life: A Situational Approach to Understanding Old Age Stigma." *International Journal of Aging and Human Development* 25 (1987): 177–93.

Luken, Paul C., and Suzanne Vaughan. "Elderly Women Living Alone: Theoretical and Methodological Considerations from a Feminist Perspective." *Housing and Society* 18 (1991), 1–12.

Lyman, Karen. "Bringing the Social Back In: A Critique of Biomedicalization of Dementia." Paper presented at the annual meeting of the American Sociological Association, Atlanta, 1988.

Maines, David R. "Time and Biography in Diabetic Experience." *Mid-American Review of Sociology* 8 (1983): 103–17.

Marcus, George E., and Michael M. J. Fischer. *Anthropology as Cultural Critique: An Experimental Moment in the Social Sciences*. Chicago: University of Chicago Press, 1986.

McCall, Michal M., and Judith Wittner. "The Good News about Life History." In *Symbolic Interaction and Cultural Studies*, edited by Howard S. Becker and Michal McCall, 46–89. Chicago: University of Chicago Press, 1990.

McKeown, Thomas. *The Role of Medicine: Dream, Mirage, or Nemesis?* Princeton: Princeton University Press, 1979.

Mills, C. Wright. *The Sociological Imagination*. New York: Oxford University Press, 1959.

Mitford, Jessica. *A Fine Old Conflict*. New York: Alfred A. Knopf, 1977.

Mueller, Adele. "The Bureaucratization of Feminist Knowledge: The Case of Women in Development." *Resources for Feminist Research* 15 (1986): 36–38.

———. *In and against Development: Feminists Confront Development on Its Own Ground*. Women and Development Working Papers Series. East Lansing, Mich.: Michigan State University, 1991.

———. "The 'Discovery' of Women in Development: The Case of Women in Peru." Paper presented at the annual meeting of the

Comparative and International Education Society, Washington, D.C., March 1987.

Navarro, Vicente. "Why Some Countries Have National Health Insurance, Others Have National Health Services, and the United States Has Neither." *International Journal of Health Services* 19 (1989): 383–404.

Needleman, Ruth. "Women Workers: A Force for Rebuilding Unionism." *Labor Research Review* 11 (1991): 1–13.

Needleman, Ruth, and Nelson, Anne. "Policy Implications: The Worth of Women's Work." In *The Worth of Women's Work: A Qualitative Synthesis,* edited by Anne Statham, Elinor M. Miller and Hans O. Mauksch, 293–308. Albany, N.Y.: State University of New York Press, 1988.

Neugarten, Bernice L., ed. *Age or Need?* Beverly Hills: Sage, 1982.

Newton, Ellen. *This Bed My Centre.* London: Virago, 1979.

O'Brien, Mary. "Feminist Theory and Dialectical Logic." In *Feminist Theory: A Critique of Ideology,* edited by Nannerl O. Keohane, Michelle Z. Rozaldo, and Barbara C. Gelpi, 99–112. Chicago: University of Chicago Press, 1982.

O'Brien, Mary Elizabeth. *Anatomy of a Nursing Home.* Owings Mills, Md.: National Health Publishing, 1989.

Offe, Claus. *Contradictions of the Welfare State,* edited by John Keane. Cambridge, Mass.: MIT Press, 1984.

Olesen, Virginia, and Elvi W. Whittaker. *The Silent Dialogue: The Social Psychology of Professional Socialization.* San Francisco: Jossey-Bass, 1968.

Olson, Lynn M. "Bureaucratic Control in Health Care: The Technology of Records." Ph.D. diss., Northwestern University, 1986.

Otten, Allan L. "States, Alarmed by Outlays on Long-Term Care, Seek Ways to Encourage More Private Coverage." *Wall Street Journal,* 11 February 1989, p. 48.

Pressor, Michael. "Foreign Nurse Graduates: Exploitation and Harassment." *Health Activists Digest* 3 (1982): 37–39.

Rapp, Rayna. "Family and Class in Contemporary America: Notes Toward an Understanding of Ideology." In *Rethinking the Family: Some Feminist Questions,* edited by Barrie Thorne with Marilyn Yalom, 168–87. New York: Longman, 1982.

Retsinas, Joan, and Patricia Garrity. "Going Home: Analysis of Nursing Home Discharges." *The Gerontologist* 26 (1986): 431–36.

Reverby, Susan. *Ordered to Care: The Dilemma of American Nursing, 1850–1945.* New York: Cambridge University Press, 1987.

———. "The Duty or Right to Care? Nursing and Womanhood in Historical Perspective." In *Circles of Care: Work and Identity in*

Women's Lives, edited by Emily K. Abel and Margaret K. Nelson, 132–49. Albany, N.Y.: State University of New York Press, 1990.

Richardson, Laurel. *The New Other Woman: Contemporary Single Women in Affairs with Married Men.* New York: The Free Press, 1985.

———. *The Dynamics of Sex and Gender: A Sociological Perspective.* 3d ed. New York: HarperCollins, 1988.

———. "The Collective Story: Postmodernism and the Writing of Sociology." *Sociological Focus* 21 (1988): 199–208.

———. *Writing Strategies: Reaching Diverse Audiences.* Newbury Park, Calif.: Sage, 1990.

Riesenberg, Don. "Drugs in the Institutionalized Elderly: Time to Get It Right?" *Journal of the American Medical Association* 260 (1988): 3054.

Rollins, Judith. *Between Women: Domestics and Their Employers.* Philadelphia: Temple University Press, 1985.

Rosenhan, David L. "On Being Sane in Insane Places." *Science* 179 (1973): 250–58.

Ruddick, Sara. *Maternal Thinking: Toward a Politics of Peace.* New York: Ballantine, 1990.

Sacks, Karen Brodkin. "Does It Pay to Care?" In *Circles of Care: Work and Identity in Women's Lives,* edited by Emily K. Abel and Margaret K. Nelson, 188–206. Albany, N.Y.: State University of New York Press, 1990.

Salmon, J. Warren. "Organizing Medical Care for Profit." In *Issues in the Political Economy of Health Care,* edited by John B. McKinlay, 143–86. New York: Tavistock, 1984.

Schnaiberg, Allan. *The Environment: From Surplus to Scarcity.* New York: Oxford University Press, 1980.

Schniedman, Rose, Susan Lambert, and Barbara Wander. *Being a Nursing Assistant.* Bowie, Md.: Robert J. Brady, 1982.

Schulder, Daniel J. "At Last, a Promise of Nursing Home Reform." *Public Policy Report* 17 (January–February 1988): 30–31.

Schultz, Debra L. "Women Historians as a Force in History: The Activist Roots of Women Historians." Master's thesis, City University of New York, 1990.

Scott, James C. *Weapons of the Weak: Everyday Forms of Peasant Resistance.* New Haven: Yale University Press, 1985.

Shaw, Linda. "Board and Care: The Everyday Lives of Ex-Mental Patients Living in the Community," Ph.D. diss., University of California, Los Angeles, 1988.

Shear, Marie. "A Marriage of True Minds," *Women's Review of Books* 6 (May, 1989): 22–3.

Shield, Renee Rose. *Uneasy Endings*. Ithaca, N.Y.: Cornell University Press, 1988.

Sieber, Joan E., ed. *The Ethics of Social Research: Fieldwork, Regulation and Publication*. New York: Springer-Verlag, 1982.

Smith, Dorothy E. *The Everyday World as Problematic: A Feminist Sociology*. Boston: Northeastern Universitiy Press, 1987.

———. *The Conceptual Practices of Power: A Feminist Sociology of Knowledge*. Boston: Northeastern University Press, 1990.

———. *Texts, Facts, and Femininity: Exploring the Relations of Ruling*. Boston: Routledge, Chapman and Hall, 1991.

Solzhenitsyn, Alexander. *One Day in the Life of Ivan Denisovitch*. New York: Viking, Penguin Books, 1963.

Spiegel, Claire. "Restraints, Drugging Rife in Nursing Homes." *Los Angeles Times,* 25 March 1991, p. 1.

Stacey, Margaret. "Who Are The Health Care Workers? Patients and Other Unpaid Workers in Health Care." Paper presented at the International Sociological Associaiton Conference, Mexico City, 1982.

Stannard, Charles. "Old Folks and Dirty Work: The Social Conditions for Patient Abuse in a Nursing Home." *Social Problems* 20 (1973): 329–42.

Staples, William G. *Castles of Our Conscience: Social Control and the American State, 1800–1985*. New Brunswick, N.J.: Rutgers University Press, 1991.

Stimpson, Catharine R. "Our 'Wild Patience': Our Energetic Deeds, Our Energizing Future." Address at Wellesley College Center for Research on Women, Tenth Anniversary Celebration, 23 May 1985.

Strauss, Anselm S., Shizuko Fagerhaugh, Barbara Suczek, and Carolyn L. Wiener. "The Work of Hospitalized Patients." *Social Science and Medicine* 16 (1982): 977–86.

Thompson, E. P. *The Making of the English Working Class*. London: Victor Gollancz, 1963.

Thompson, Karen, and Julie Andrezejewski. *Why Can't Sharon Come Home?* San Francisco: Spinsters/Aunt Lute, 1988.

Thorne, Barrie. " 'You Still Takin' Notes?' Fieldwork and Problems of Informed Consent," *Social Problems* 27 (1980): 284–97.

———. "Feminist Rethinking of the Family: An Overview." In *Rethinking the Family: Some Feminist Questions,* edited by Barrie Thorne with Marilyn Yalom, 1–24. New York: Longman, 1982.

Tisdale, Sallie. *Harvest Moon: Portrait of a Nursing Home*. New York: Henry Holt, 1987.

Titmus, Richard M. *The Gift Relationship: From Human Blood to Social Policy.* London: George Allen and Unwin, 1970.

Twaddle, Andrew C., and Richard M. Hessler. *A Sociology of Health.* St. Louis: C. V. Mosby, 1987.

Ungerson, Clare. "Why Do Women Care?" In *A Labour of Love: Women, Work and Caring,* edited by Janet Finch and Dulcie Groves, 31–49. Boston: Routledge and Kegan Paul, 1983.

Vladeck, Bruce C. *Unloving Care: The Nursing Home Tragedy.* New York: Basic Books, 1980.

Waitzkin, Howard. *The Second Sickness: Contradictions of Capitalist Health Care.* New York: Free Press, 1983.

Walker, Alan. "Care for Elderly People: A Conflict between Women and the State." In *A Labour of Love: Women, Work, and Caring,* edited by Janet Finch and Dulcie Groves, 106–28. Boston: Routledge and Kegan Paul, 1983.

Walliman, Isidor. *Estrangement: Marx's Conception of Human Nature and the Division of Labor.* Westport, Conn.: Greenwood, 1981.

Waraday, Natalie. "Nursing Assistants Have Big Role in World of Need." *Chicago Tribune* 23 October 1988, sec. 19, p. 15.

Warren, Carol A. B. *Gender Issues in Field Research and Field Work.* Newbury Park, Calif.: Sage, 1988.

Wax, Murray L. "Paradoxes of 'Consent' to the Practice of Fieldwork." *Social Problems* 27 (1980): 272–83.

Weber, Max. *The Protestant Ethic and the Spirit of Capitalism.* New York: Charles Scribner's Sons, 1958.

Weiss, Michael J. "Oldsters: The Now Generation." *American Way,* July 1982, 96–101.

Weston, Kath. *Families We Choose: Lesbians, Gays, Kinship.* New York: Columbia University Press, 1991.

Whyte, William F. *Street Corner Society: The Social Structure of an Italian Slum.* 3d ed. Chicago: University of Chicago Press, 1981.

Wiener, Carolyn L., and Jeanie Kayser-Jones. "The Uneasy Fate of Nursing Home Residents: An Organizational-Interaction Perspective." *Sociology of Health and Illness* 12 (1990): 84–104.

Williams, Constance. "Improving Care in Nursing Homes Using Community Advocacy." *Social Science and Medicine* 23 (1986): 1297–1303.

Willis, Paul. *Learning to Labor: How Working Class Kids Get Working Class Jobs.* New York: Columbia University Press, 1977.

Winter, Annette. "Long-Term Care Options." *Modern Maturity* (June–July 1986): 70–71.

Wittner, Judith. "Ordinary Struggles: The Politics and Perspectives of

Displaced Factory Women." Paper presented at the annual meeting of the Society for the Study of Social Problems, Berkeley, August 1989.

Woolhandler, Steffie, and Himmelstein, David U. "The Deteriorating Administrative Efficiency of the U.S. Health Care System." *New England Journal of Medicine* 324 (1991): 1253–58.

Young, T. R. *Red Feather Dictionary of Socialist Sociology.* 2d ed. Red Feather, Colo.: Red Feather Institute, 1978.

Zarubel, Evitar. *Patterns of Time in Hospital Life.* Chicago: University of Chicago Press, 1979.

Index

Abel, Emily K., 254n.2, 255n.8, 258n.20, 258n.24, 260n.3
Abu-Lughod, Lila, 261n.12
Acker, Joan, 259n.2
American Association of Retired Persons, 79, 226

Barry, Kate, 259n.2
Becker, Howard S., 247n.4
Beds: as commodity, 210, 243; as term for people, 77, 172–73
Binney, Elizabeth A., 251n.10, 264n.27
Brents, Barbara G., 251n.12
Burawoy, Michael, 245n.7, 256n.3, 262n.17
Butler, Robert, 2, 6

Campbell, Marie L., 254n.16, 256n.4, 260n.7, 264n.28
Caretaking: administrative definitions of, 28–29, 32–33, 142, 208–10; invisible in charts, 86, 137, 150, 156, 162–63; relational nature of, 20, 30, 78–79, 92–94, 101, 135, 137, 144–45, 163–67, 217–19, 258n.24. See also Narratives: of tasks vs. relations
Charts: as means of production, 180–81, 206–14; changing quality to quantities, 159, 172, 190–92, 206–10, 236; content of, 20, 27, 82–83, 208–10; 84, 88, 121–22; creating patients, 103–4, 110–11, 120–23, 125–29, 166; erasing caretaking, 135, 166, 204–6; 260n.7; erasing gender, class and race dynamics, 189–90, 202–3, 206, 212; forming interactions, 120, 159–61; physi-

cians' authority over, 99–100, 180–83, 230; residents' access to, 177–78, 207, 234–35
Cherry, Ralph L., 263n.21
Collins, Patricia Hill, 256n.8
Conflicts: between residents and staff, 77, 83–84, 102, 113, 138, 141, 155, 187–88, 219; between staff and administrators, 23–24, 48–51, 174, 222, 239
Contradictions of caretaking as business, 63, 212–14, 230, 233, 238, 244, 257n.11, 259n.27, 264n.28
Cook, Judith A., 259n.2

Daniels, Arlene Kaplan, 247n.7, 252n.5, 255n.3, 263n.24
Darrough, William D., 261n.10
Davies, Celia, 256n.7, 264n.28
Death: spoken about and silenced, 2, 15–16, 17–18, 101–2, 118–19; under medical dominance, 119–20, 233–34, 263n.24
DeVault, Marjorie L., 255n.5, 259n.25
DiIorio, Judith A., 245n.7, 248n.6
Disease labels, social consequences of: diagnosis of Alzheimer's, 85, 90–91, 93–94, 125–26, 160–61; "out of it," 101–3, 122, 126
Doctors. See Physicians

Early morning regimens, 1, 77, 80–81, 99, 128, 130, 172, 243–44
Economic journey: gender and class character of, 65–66; for residents, 53–54, 58–60, 64, 73–74; 198–204; spend down, 59, 72, 201–2, 222–23